PRENTICE

WORLD GEOGRAPHY

BUILDING A GLOBAL PERSPECTIVE

Reading and Vocabulary Study Guide

Upper Saddle River, New Jersey
Boston, Massachusetts

ISBN 0-13-133533-2
6 7 8 9 10 10 09

Contents

Student Success Handbook

Success in social studies comes from doing three things well—reading, testing, and writing. The following pages present strategies to help you read for meaning, understand test questions, and write well.

Reading for Meaning

Do you have trouble remembering what you read? Here are some tips from experts that will improve your ability to recall and understand what you read:

★ BEFORE YOU READ

Preview the text to identify important information.

Like watching the coming attractions at a movie theater, previewing the text helps you know what to expect. Study the questions and strategies below to learn how to preview what you read.

Ask yourself these questions:	Use these strategies to find the answers:
• What is the text about?	Read the headings, subheadings, and captions. Study the photos, maps, tables, or graphs.
• What do I already know about the topic?	Read the questions at the end of the text to see if you can answer any of them.
• What is the purpose of the text?	Turn the headings into *who, what, when, where, why,* or *how* questions. This will help you decide if the text compares things, tells a chain of events, or explains causes and effects.

★ AS YOU READ

Organize information in a way that helps you see meaningful connections or relationships.

Taking notes as you read will improve your understanding. Use graphic organizers like the ones below to record the information you read. Study these descriptions and examples to learn how to create each type of organizer.

Sequencing

A **flowchart** helps you see how one event led to another. It can also display the steps in a process.

Use a flowchart if the text—

- tells about a chain of events.
- explains a method of doing something.

TIP▶ List the events or steps in order.

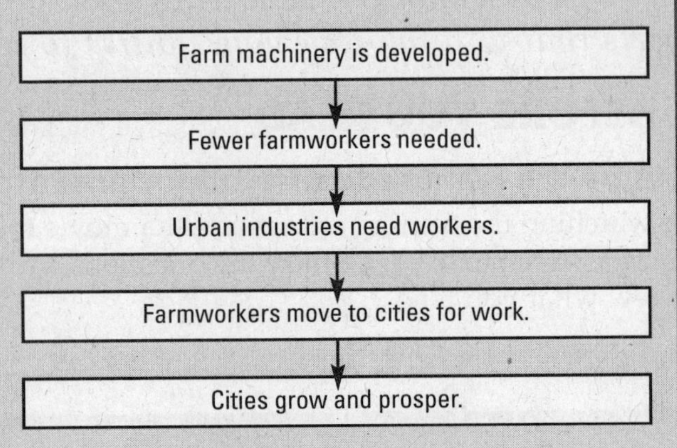

Comparing and Contrasting

A **Venn diagram** displays similarities and differences.

Use a Venn diagram if the text—

- compares and contrasts two individuals, groups, places, things, or events.

TIP▶ Label the outside section of each circle and list differences.
Label the shared section and list similarities.

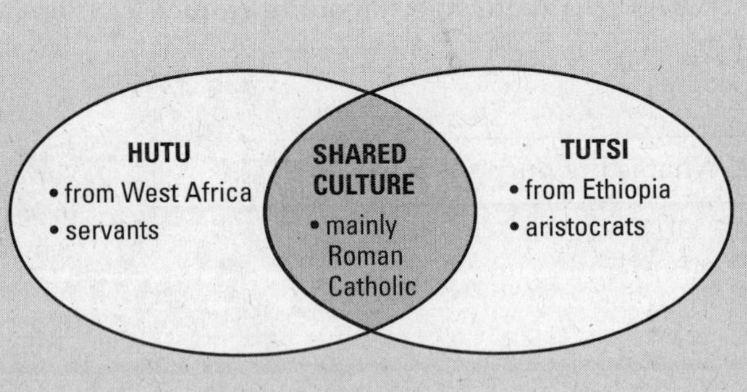

★ AS YOU READ *(continued)*

Categorizing Information

A **chart** organizes information in categories.

Use a chart if the text—
- lists similar facts about several places or things.
- presents characteristics of different groups.

TIP▶ Write an appropriate heading for each column in the chart to identify its category.

COUNTRY	FORM OF GOVERNMENT	ECONOMY
Cuba	communist dictatorship	command economy
Puerto Rico	democracy	free enterprise system

Identifying Main Ideas and Details

A **concept web** helps you understand relationships among ideas.

Use a concept web if the text—
- provides examples to support a main idea.
- links several ideas to a main topic.

TIP▶ Write the main idea in the largest circle. Write details in smaller circles and draw lines to show relationships.

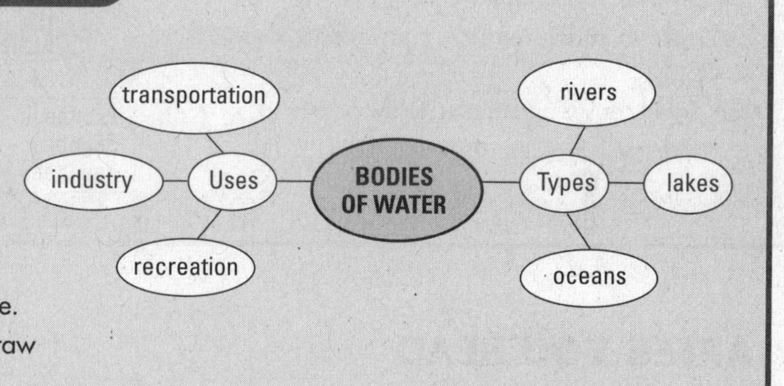

Organizing Information

An **outline** provides an overview, or a kind of blueprint for reading.

Use an outline to organize ideas—
- according to their importance.
- according to the order in which they are presented.

TIP▶ Use Roman numerals for main ideas, capital letters for secondary ideas, and Arabic numerals for supporting details.

I. Differences Between the North and the South
- **A.** Views on slavery
  - **1.** Northern abolitionists
  - **2.** Southern slave owners
- **B.** Economies
  - **1.** Northern manufacturing
  - **2.** Southern agriculture

Identifying Cause and Effect

A **cause-and-effect diagram** shows the relationship between what happened (effect) and the reason why it happened (cause).

Use a cause-and-effect chart if the text—
- lists one or more causes for an event.
- lists one or more results of an event.

TIP▶ Label causes and effects. Draw arrows to indicate how ideas are related.

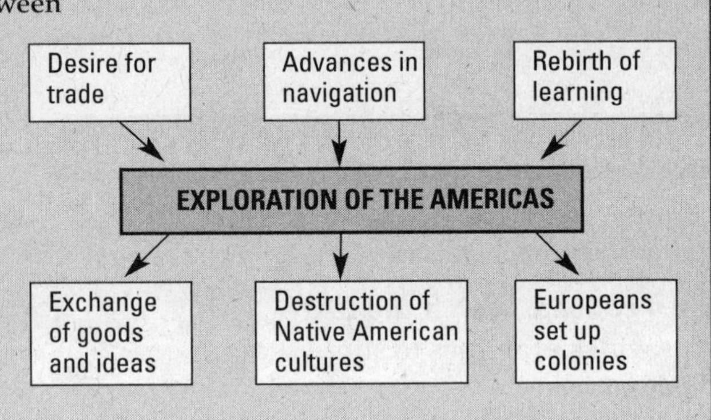

★ AFTER YOU READ

Test yourself to find out what you learned from reading the text.

Go back to the questions you asked yourself before you read the text. You should be able to give more complete answers to these questions:
- What is the text about?
- What is the purpose of the text?

You should also be able to make connections between the new information you learned from the text and what you already knew about the topic.

Study your graphic organizer. Use this information as the *answers*. Make up a meaningful *question* about each piece of information.

Taking Tests

Do you panic at the thought of taking a standardized test? Here are some tips that most test developers recommend to help you achieve good scores.

★ MULTIPLE-CHOICE QUESTIONS

Read each part of a multiple-choice question to make sure you understand what is being asked.

Many tests are made up of multiple-choice questions. Some multiple-choice items are **direct questions.** They are complete sentences followed by possible answers, called distractors.

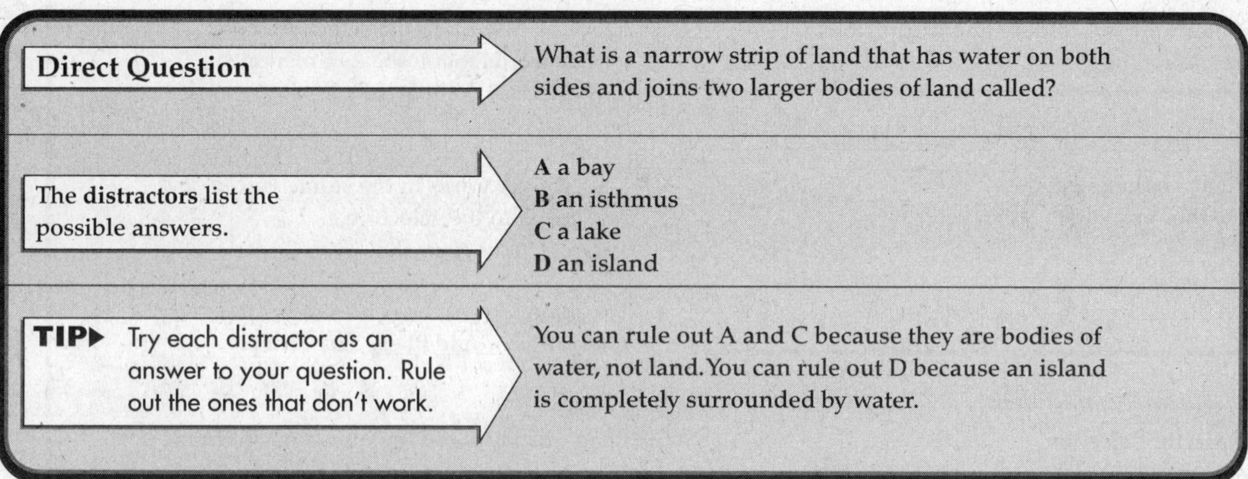

Other multiple-choice questions are **incomplete sentences** that you are to finish. They are followed by possible answers.

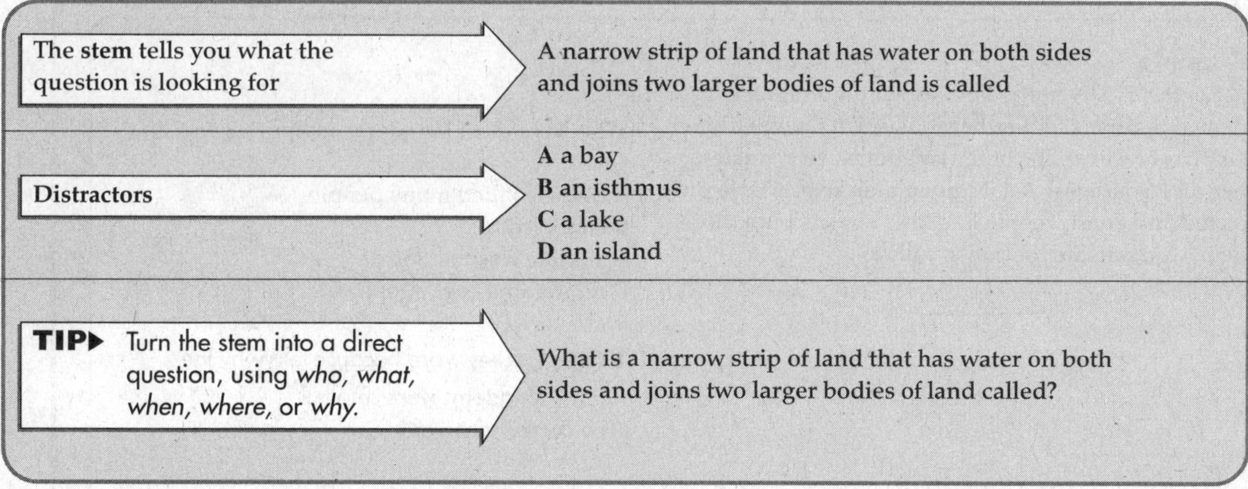

★ WHAT'S BEING TESTED?

Identify the type of question you are being asked.

Social studies tests often ask questions that involve reading comprehension. Other questions may require you to gather or interpret information from a map, graph, or chart. The following strategies will help you answer different kinds of questions.

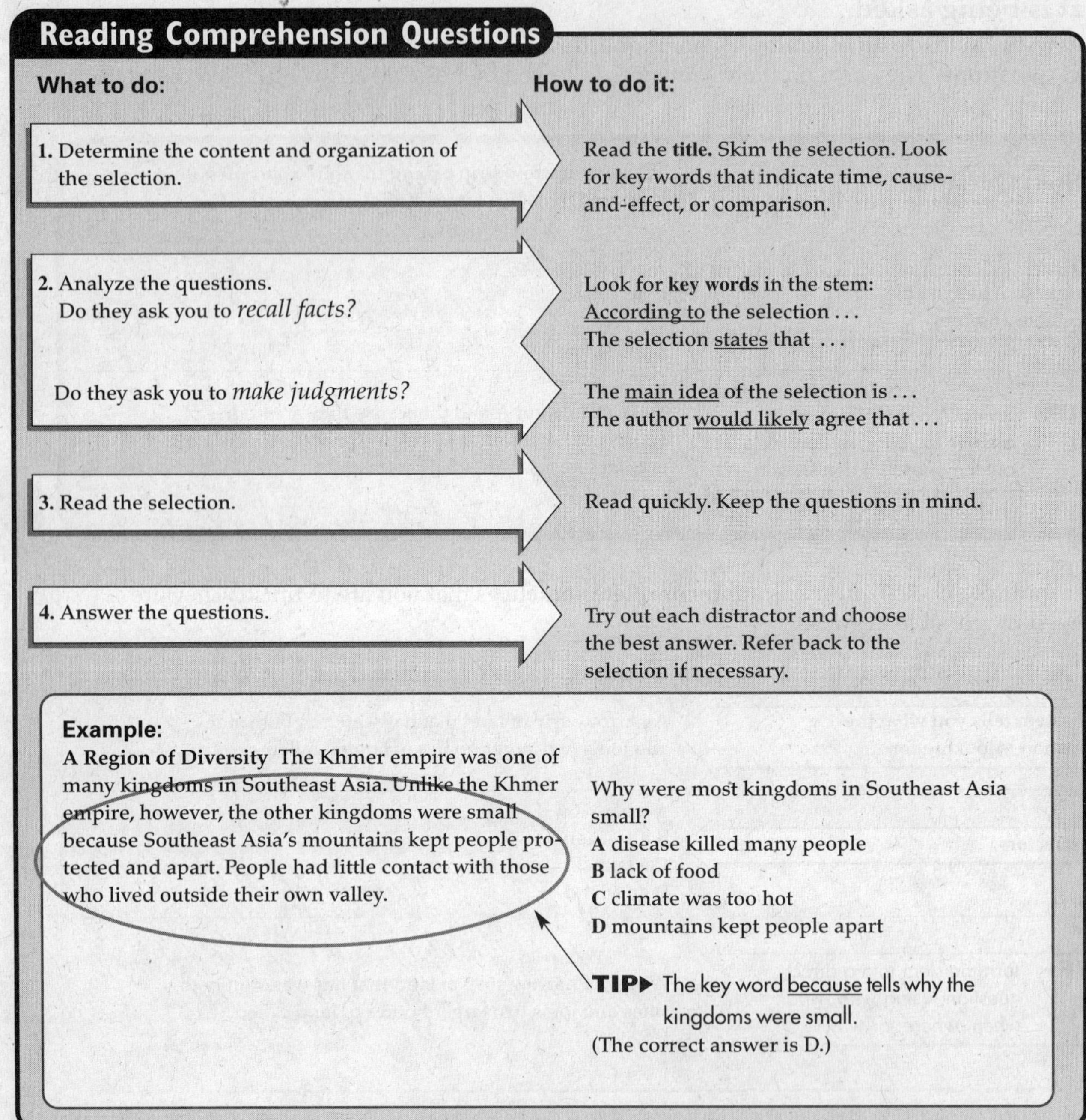

Reading Comprehension Questions

What to do:	How to do it:
1. Determine the content and organization of the selection.	Read the **title.** Skim the selection. Look for key words that indicate time, cause-and-effect, or comparison.
2. Analyze the questions. Do they ask you to *recall facts?*	Look for **key words** in the stem: According to the selection . . . The selection states that . . .
Do they ask you to *make judgments?*	The main idea of the selection is . . . The author would likely agree that . . .
3. Read the selection.	Read quickly. Keep the questions in mind.
4. Answer the questions.	Try out each distractor and choose the best answer. Refer back to the selection if necessary.

Example:

A Region of Diversity The Khmer empire was one of many kingdoms in Southeast Asia. Unlike the Khmer empire, however, the other kingdoms were small because Southeast Asia's mountains kept people protected and apart. People had little contact with those who lived outside their own valley.

Why were most kingdoms in Southeast Asia small?

A disease killed many people
B lack of food
C climate was too hot
D mountains kept people apart

TIP▶ The key word because tells why the kingdoms were small.
(The correct answer is D.)

★ WHAT'S BEING TESTED? *(continued)*

Map Questions

What to do:	How to do it:
1. Determine what kind of information is presented on the map.	Read the map **title.** It will indicate the purpose of the map. Study the **map key.** It will explain the symbols used on the map. Look at the **scale.** It will help you calculate distance between places on the map.
2. Read the question. Determine which component on the map will help you find the answer.	Look for **key words** in the stem. About <u>how far</u> . . . [use the scale] <u>What crops</u> were grown in . . . [use the map key]
3. Look at the map and answer the question in your own words.	Do not read the distractors yet.
4. Choose the best answer.	Decide which distractor agrees with the answer you determined from the map.

Eastern Europe: Language Groups

KEY
- Slavic languages
- Romance languages
- Thraco-Illyrian languages
- Baltic languages
- Non-Indo-European languages

Lambert Azimuthal Equal-Area Projection

In which of these countries are Thraco-Illyrian languages spoken?

A Romania
B Albania
C Hungary
D Lithuania

TIP▸ Read the labels and the key to understand the map.
(The correct answer is B.)

Graph Questions

What to do: | **How to do it:**

1. Determine the purpose of the graph. → Read the graph **title.** It indicates what the graph represents.

2. Determine what information on the graph will help you find the answer. → Read the **labels** on the graph or on the key. They tell the units of measurement used by the graph.

3. Choose the best answer. → Decide which distractor agrees with the answer you determined from the graph.

Example

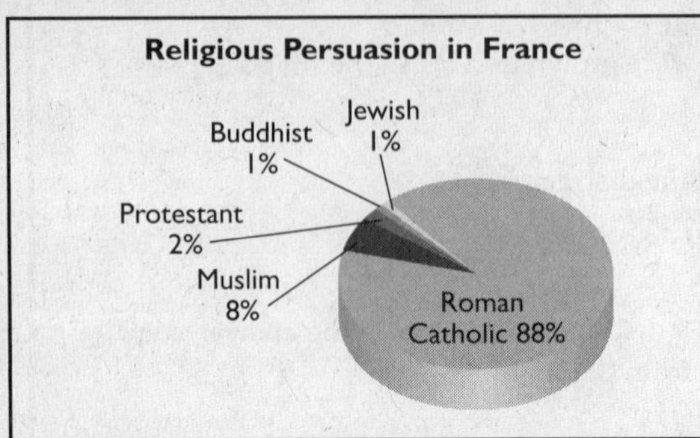

A **circle graph** shows the relationship of parts to the whole in terms of percentages.

After Roman Catholics, the next largest religious population in France is

A Buddhist C Jewish
B Protestant D Muslim

TIP▶ Compare the percentages listed in the labels.
(The correct answer is D.)

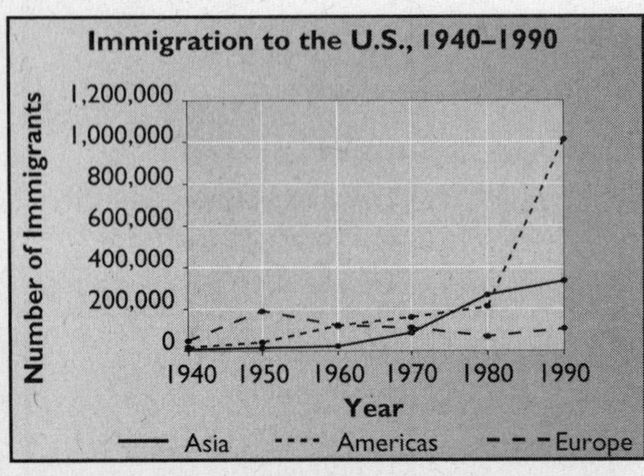

A **line graph** shows a pattern or change over time by the direction of the line.

Between 1980 and 1990, immigration to the U.S. from the Americas

A decreased a little C stayed about the same
B increased greatly D increased a little

TIP▶ Compare the vertical distance between the two correct points on the line graph.
(The correct answer is B.)

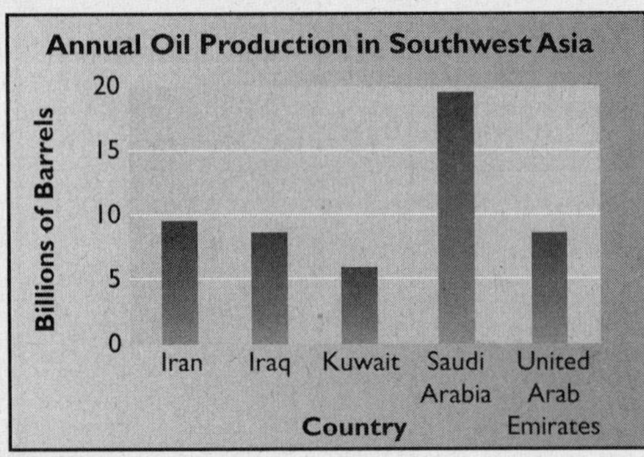

A **bar graph** compares differences in quantity by showing bars of different lengths.

Saudi Arabia produces about how many more billion barrels of oil a year than Iran?

A 5 million C 15 million
B 10 million D 20 million

TIP▶ Compare the heights of the bars to find the difference.
(The correct answer is B.)

Writing for Social Studies

When you face a writing assignment, do you think, "How will I ever get through this?" Here are some tips to guide you through any writing project from start to finish.

★ THE WRITING PROCESS

Follow each step of the writing process to communicate effectively.

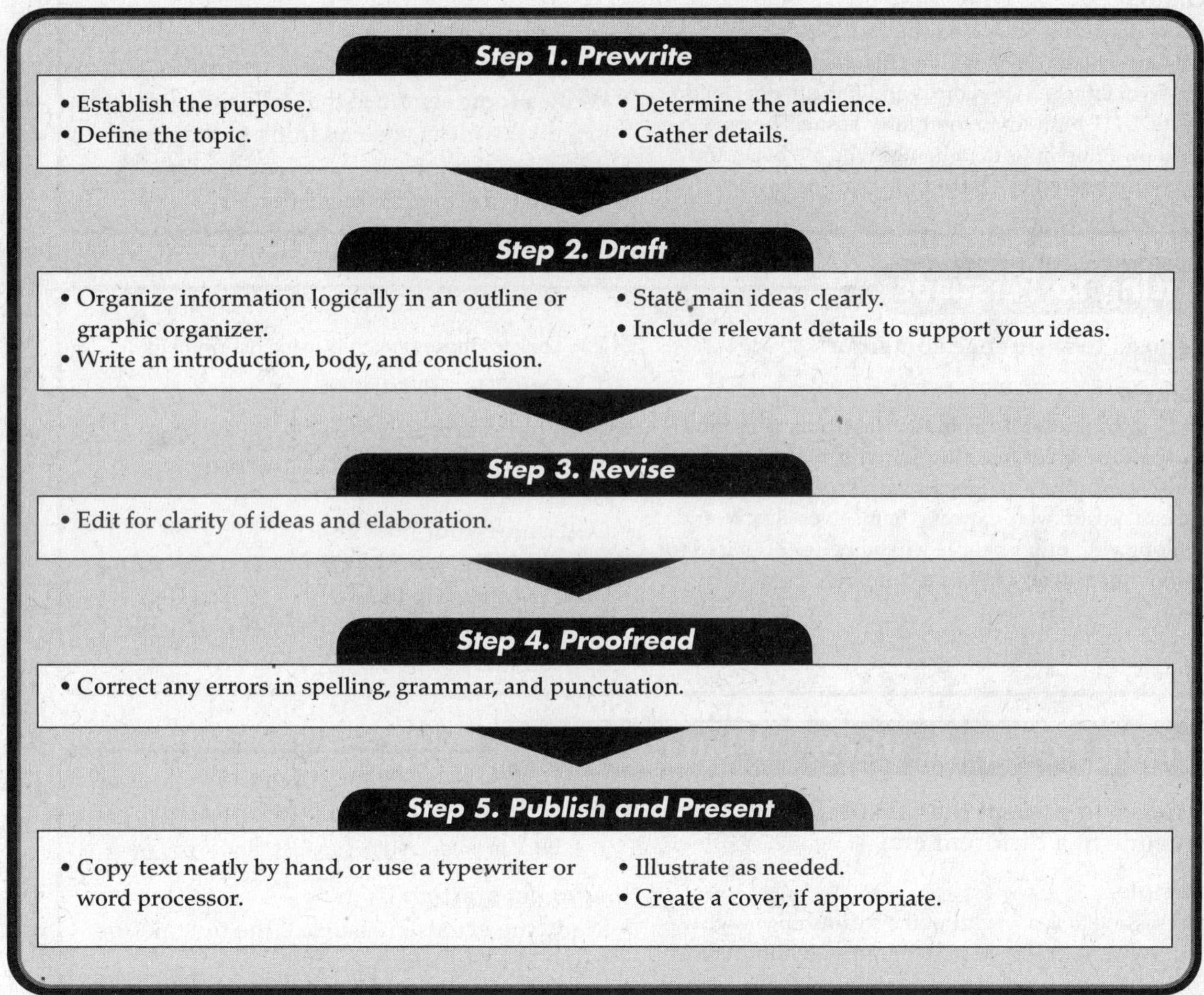

★ TYPES OF WRITING FOR SOCIAL STUDIES

Identify the purpose for your writing.

Each type of writing assignment has a specific purpose, and each purpose needs a different plan for development. The following descriptions and examples will help you identify the three purposes for social studies writing. The lists of steps will help you plan your writing.

Writing to Inform

Purpose: to present facts or ideas

Example

During the 1960s, research indicated the dangers of the insecticide DDT. It killed insects but also had long-term effects. When birds and fish ate poisoned insects, DDT built up in their fatty tissue. The poison also showed up in human beings who ate birds and fish contaminated by DDT.

TIP▸ Look for these *key terms* in the assignment: explain, describe, report, narrate

How to get started:

- Determine the topic you will write about.
- Write a topic sentence that tells the main idea.
- List all the ideas you can think of that are related to the topic.
- Arrange the ideas in logical order.

Writing to Persuade

Purpose: to influence someone

Example

Teaching computer skills in the classroom uses time that could be spent teaching students how to think for themselves or how to interact with others. Students who can reason well, express themselves clearly, and get along with other people will be better prepared for life than those who can use a computer.

TIP▸ Look for these *key terms* in the assignment: convince, argue, request

How to get started:

- Make sure you understand the problem or issue clearly.
- Determine your position.
- List evidence to support your arguments.
- Predict opposing views.
- List evidence you can use to overcome the opposing arguments.

Writing to Provide Historical Interpretations

Purpose: to present the perspective of someone in a different era

Example

The crossing took a week, but the steamship voyage was hard. We were cramped in steerage with hundreds of others. At last we saw the huge statue of the lady with the torch. In the reception center, my mother held my hand while the doctor examined me. Then, my father showed our papers to the official, and we collected our bags. I was scared as we headed off to find a home in our new country.

TIP▸ Look for these *key terms* in the assignment: go back in time, create, suppose that, if you were

How to get started:

- Study the events or issues of the time period you will write about.
- Consider how these events or issues might have affected different people at the time.
- Choose a person whose views you would like to present.
- Identify the thoughts and feelings this person might have experienced.

★ RESEARCH FOR WRITING

Follow each step of the writing process to communicate effectively.

After you have identified the purpose for your writing, you may need to do research. The following steps will help you plan, gather, organize, and present information.

Step 1. Ask Questions

Ask yourself questions to help guide your research.	What do I already know about the topic? What do I want to find out about the topic?

Step 2. Acquire Information

Locate and use appropriate sources of information about the topic.	Library Internet search Interviews
Take notes.	Follow accepted format for listing sources.

Step 3. Analyze Information

Evaluate the information you find.	Is it relevant to the topic? Is it up-to-date? Is it accurate? Is the writer an authority on the topic? Is there any bias?

Step 4. Use Information

Answer your research questions with the information you have found. (You may find that you need to do more research.)	Do I have all the information I need?
Organize your information into the main points you want to make. Identify supporting details.	Arrange ideas in outline form or in a graphic organizer.

Step 5. Communicate What You've Learned

Review the purpose for your writing and choose an appropriate way to present the information.

Purpose	Presentation
inform	formal paper, documentary, multimedia
persuade	essay, letter to the editor, speech
interpret	journal, newspaper account, drama

Draft and revise your writing, and then evaluate it. Use a rubric for self-evaluation.

★ EVALUATING YOUR WRITING

Use the following rubric to help you evaluate your writing.

	Excellent	Good	Acceptable	Unacceptable
Purpose	Achieves purpose—to inform, persuade, or provide historical interpretation—very well	Informs, persuades, or provides historical interpretation reasonably well	Reader cannot easily tell if the purpose is to inform, persuade, or provide historical interpretation	Lacks purpose
Organization	Develops ideas in a very clear and logical way	Presents ideas in a reasonably well-organized way	Reader has difficulty following the organization	Lacks organization
Elaboration	Explains all ideas with facts and details	Explains most ideas with facts and details	Includes some supporting facts and details	Lacks supporting details
Use of Language	Uses excellent vocabulary and sentence structure with no errors in spelling, grammar, or punctuation	Uses good vocabulary and sentence structure with very few errors in spelling, grammar, or punctuation	Includes some errors in grammar, punctuation, and spelling	Includes many errors in grammar, punctuation, and spelling

How To Use This Book

The purpose of the *Reading and Vocabulary Study Guide* is to help you strengthen reading and language skills that you can use both inside and outside the classroom. These skills will help you as you read your textbook, *World Geography: Building a Global Perspective.*

There are four types of worksheets in *Reading and Vocabulary Study Guide.*

Vocabulary Development

Each group of chapter worksheets begins with Vocabulary Development.

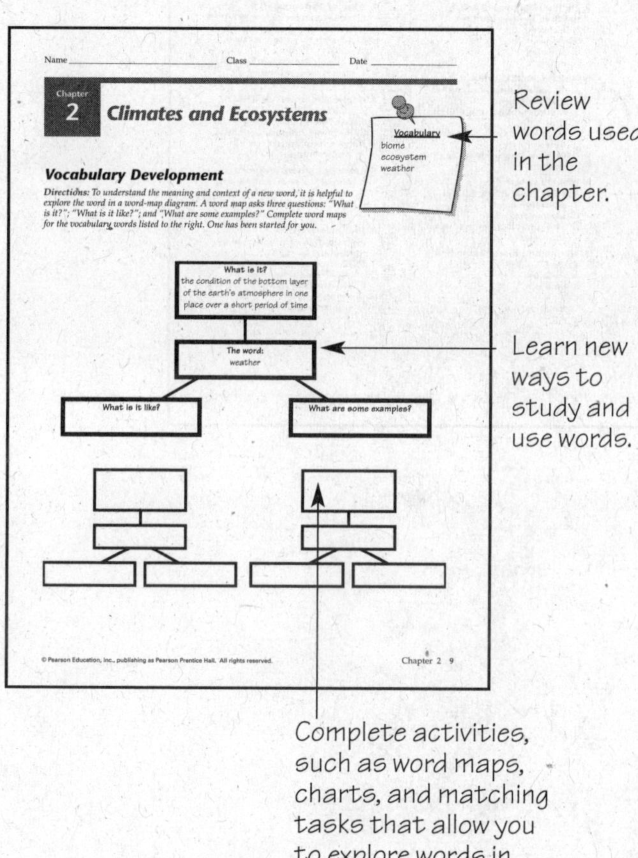

Guide to the Essentials

There is one Guide to the Essentials worksheet for each section in your textbook.

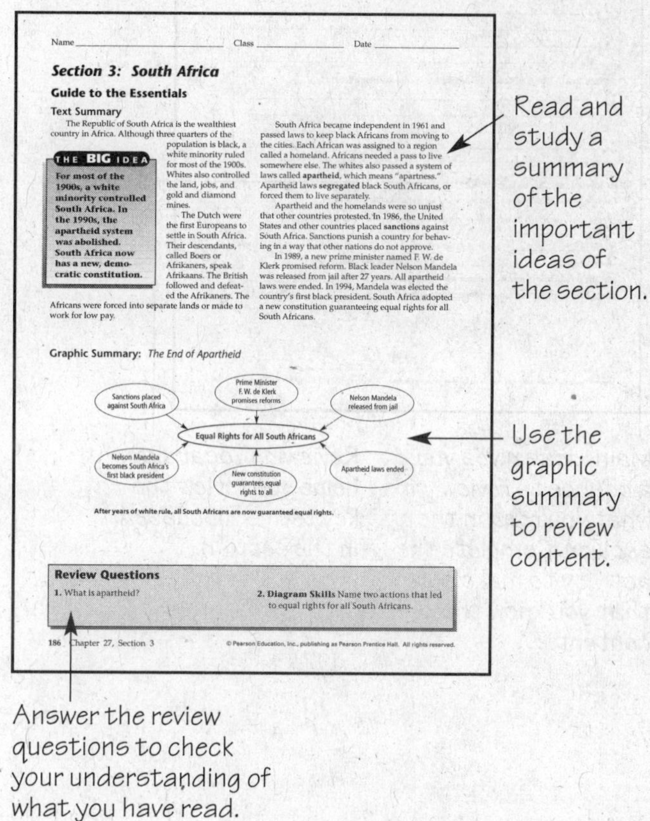

At times, some of the Vocabulary Worksheets will have writing activities. These activities will help you use the words you have learned and help you develop your composition skills.

Guided Reading and Review

The Guided Reading and Review worksheets will help you understand what you have read after you complete the assigned reading.

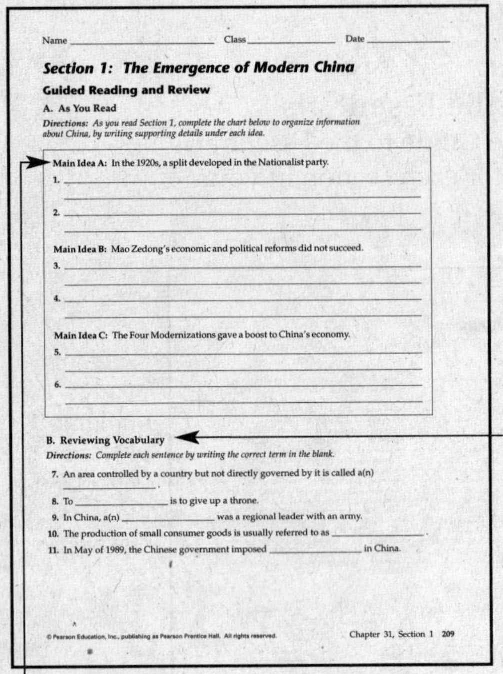

Name ______ Class ______ Date ______

Section 1: The Emergence of Modern China

Guided Reading and Review

A. As You Read

Directions: As you read Section 1, complete the chart below to organize information about China, by writing supporting details under each idea.

Main Idea A: In the 1920s, a split developed in the Nationalist party.

1. ______
2. ______

Main Idea B: Mao Zedong's economic and political reforms did not succeed.

3. ______
4. ______

Main Idea C: The Four Modernizations gave a boost to China's economy.

5. ______
6. ______

B. Reviewing Vocabulary

Directions: Complete each sentence by writing the correct term in the blank.

7. An area controlled by a country but not directly governed by it is called a(n) ______.
8. To ______ is to give up a throne.
9. In China, a(n) ______ was a regional leader with an army.
10. The production of small consumer goods is usually referred to as ______.
11. In May of 1989, the Chinese government imposed ______ in China.

 Chapter 31, Section 1 209

Main Ideas gives you a chance to review what you read in the section. Complete the activity to make sure that you know the content.

Reviewing Vocabulary helps you review the key terms discussed in the section.

Chapter Test

Once you finish a chapter, the Chapter Test worksheet is a good way to see if you have mastered the chapter content. Use the Guide to the Essentials worksheet to review those ideas you did not understand on the chapter test.

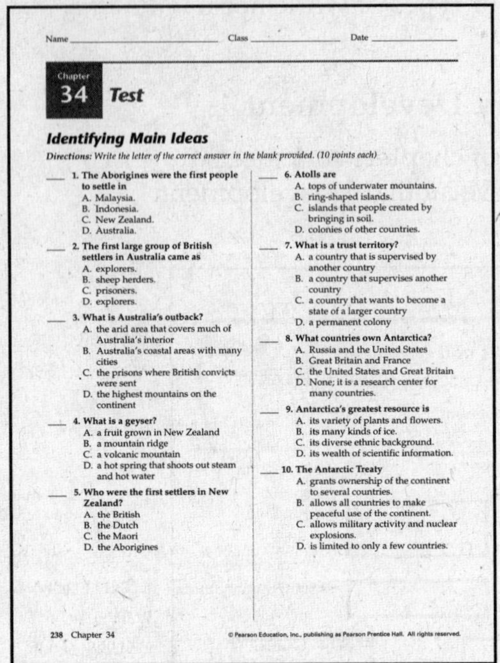

Name ______ Class ______ Date ______

Chapter 34 **Test**

Identifying Main Ideas

Directions: Write the letter of the correct answer in the blank provided. (10 points each)

____ **1. The Aborigines were the first people to settle in**
A. Malaysia.
B. Indonesia.
C. New Zealand.
D. Australia.

____ **2. The first large group of British settlers in Australia came as**
A. explorers.
B. sheep herders.
C. prisoners.
D. explorers.

____ **3. What is Australia's outback?**
A. the arid area that covers much of Australia's interior
B. Australia's coastal areas with many cities
C. the prisons where British convicts were sent
D. the highest mountains on the continent

____ **4. What is a geyser?**
A. a fruit grown in New Zealand
B. a mountain ridge
C. a volcanic mountain
D. a hot spring that shoots out steam and hot water

____ **5. Who were the first settlers in New Zealand?**
A. the British
B. the Dutch
C. the Maori
D. the Aborigines

____ **6. Atolls are**
A. tops of underwater mountains.
B. ring-shaped islands.
C. islands that people created by bringing in soil.
D. colonies of other countries.

____ **7. What is a trust territory?**
A. a country that is supervised by another country
B. a country that supervises another country
C. a country that wants to become a state of a larger country
D. a permanent colony

____ **8. What countries own Antarctica?**
A. Russia and the United States
B. Great Britain and France
C. the United States and Great Britain
D. None; it is a research center for many countries.

____ **9. Antarctica's greatest resource is**
A. its variety of plants and flowers.
B. its many kinds of ice.
C. its diverse ethnic background.
D. its wealth of scientific information.

____ **10. The Antarctic Treaty**
A. grants ownership of the continent to several countries.
B. allows all countries to make peaceful use of the continent.
C. allows military activity and nuclear explosions.
D. is limited to only a few countries.

238 Chapter 34

Name ______________________ Class ______________ Date ______________

Chapter 1

Exploring Geography

Vocabulary

acid rain
continent
core
crust
erosion
glacier
hemisphere
mantle

Vocabulary Development

Directions: *Imagine that you are a geographer studying the earth. Write a journal entry of one or more paragraphs describing what you do. Use at least five of the listed vocabulary words. Be specific in your paragraph(s) to help your readers appreciate the excitement of your discoveries.*

Name ______________________ Class ______________ Date ______________

Section 1: The Study of Geography

Guide to the Essentials

Text Summary

THE BIG IDEA

Geographers use five themes, or ideas, to organize their study of the earth and its people.

Geography is the study of where people, places, and things are located and how they relate to each other. Geographers use a variety of geographic tools, including maps, charts, and computer and satellite technologies. Geographers use concepts, or ideas, to organize the way they think about geography.

Many geographers use five main themes to study geography. The theme of location describes where a place is found. A location may be an **absolute location,** or its position on the globe. **Relative location** describes where a place is in relation to another place. An example of relative location is, "Mexico is south of the United States."

The theme of place describes how areas are alike or different. Places can be described by their physical features or in terms of their human characteristics, or how people live there.

The third geographic theme deals with regions. A region is a group of places with at least one thing in common. Geographers divide the world into many different regions based on various criteria.

The theme of movement describes the ways people, goods, and ideas move from one place to another. Geography has an important effect on movement.

The final geographic theme examines how people use and change their environment. People expand areas by building homes, roads, and factories, which have positive and negative effects on the surroundings.

Graphic Summary: *The World: Continents and Oceans*

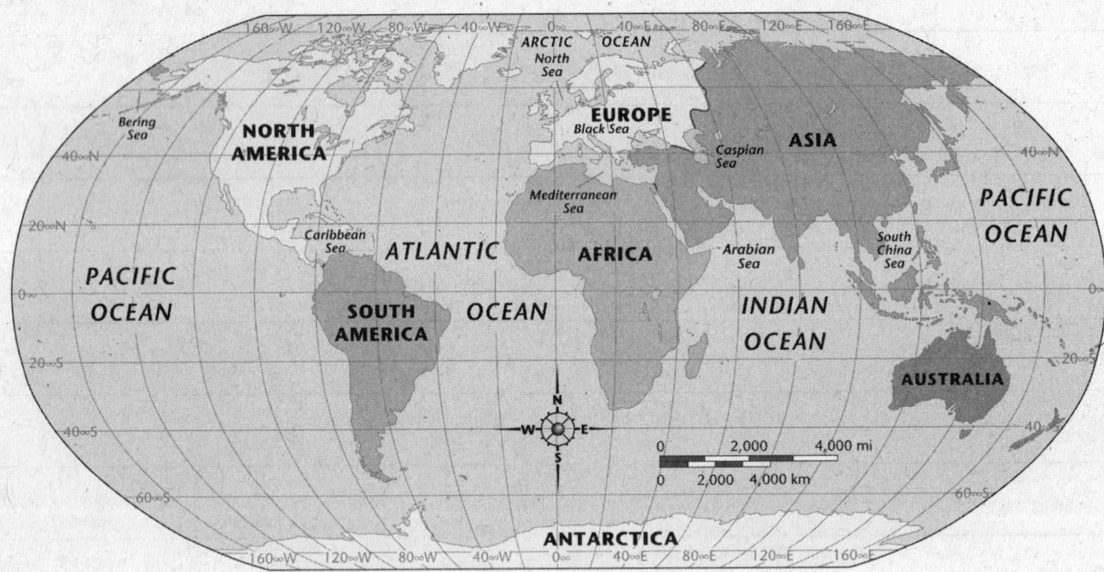

The earth's land is divided into seven continents.

Review Questions

1. Name the five themes of geography.

2. **Map Skills** Which two continents are bordered on the west by the Atlantic Ocean?

Name ______________________ Class ______________ Date ______________

Section 1: The Study of Geography

Guided Reading and Review

A. As You Read

Directions: *As you read Section 1, answer the following questions.*

1. What tools do geographers use to understand the world? ______________
2. What is a geographic concept? ______________
3. List 10 geographic concepts. ______________
4. What are two ways geographers describe the location of a place? ______________

   ____
5. What does the character of a place consist of? ______________
6. What are the three types of regions? ______________
7. What is the movement of a place? ______________

   ____
8. What are some examples of negative effects of human-environment interaction?

   ____

B. Reviewing Vocabulary

Directions: *Complete each sentence by writing the correct term in the blank.*

9. The position of a place on the globe is its ______________ location.
10. The ______________ of a place consists of its physical characteristics and human characteristics.
11. A central place and the surrounding places affected by it make up a(n) ______________ region.
12. ______________ is the study of where people, places, and things are located and how they relate to each other.
13. A viewpoint that is influenced by one's own culture and experience is ______________.
14. The location of a place compared to other places is its ______________ location.
15. People's feelings and attitudes about an area define a(n) ______________ region.
16. A(n) ______________ uses computer technology to collect, manipulate, analyze, and display data about the earth's surface.
17. An area in which a certain characteristic is found everywhere is a(n) ______________ region.
18. The Equator divides the earth into two halves or ______________.

Name ______________________ Class ______________ Date ______________

Section 2: Changes Within the Earth

Guide to the Essentials

Text Summary

Forces of nature, like volcanoes, are constantly changing the earth. Geology is the study of the earth's history and physical structure.

The center of the earth is called the **core.** It is made of very hot metal. The inner core is probably solid, while the outer core is liquid. The **mantle** is a thick layer of rock around the core. The **crust** is the earth's rocky outside layer. It is very thin, like cake icing.

THE BIG IDEA

The earth is always changing. Changes that take place inside the earth cause changes in the shape of the land.

More than 70 percent of the earth's surface is covered by water, mostly oceans and seas. The seven **continents** are the largest areas of land.

Forces inside the earth shape the earth's landforms. Volcanoes, for example, are mountains that form when molten, or melted, rock inside the earth breaks through the crust. On the surface, the molten rock flows as lava.

Breaks in the earth's crust cause faults. Sudden movement along a fault can cause an earthquake.

Most geologists believe that the earth's landmasses have broken apart, rejoined, and moved apart again. According to the theory of **plate tectonics,** the earth's crust and upper mantle are broken into moving plates. These plates can pull apart, crash into each other, or slide past each other. Oceans and continents ride on top of the plates.

Graphic Summary: *The Earth's Layers*

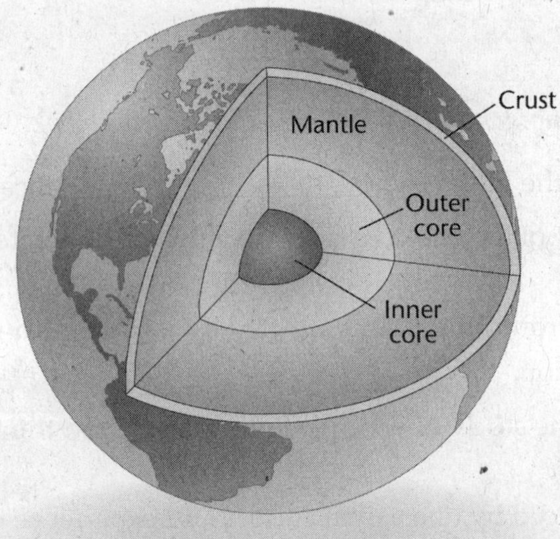

Scientists believe that the earth has several layers.

Review Questions

1. How much of the earth's surface is water?

2. Diagram Skills What are the four layers of the earth?

Name ______________________ Class ______________ Date ______________

Section 2: Changes Within the Earth

Guided Reading and Review

A. As You Read

Directions: *As you read Section 2, complete the chart below concerning internal forces of the earth.*

Cause	Effect
Molten rock breaks through the earth's surface.	**1.** ______________________
Large, sudden rock movements occur along a fault.	**2.** ______________________
Two plates pull away from each other.	**3.** ______________________
An oceanic plate meets a continental plate.	**4.** ______________________
Two continental plates collide.	**5.** ______________________

B. Reviewing Vocabulary

Directions: *Complete each sentence by writing the correct term in the blank.*

6. The center of the earth is called the ______________________.

7. A thick layer of rock called the ______________________ is around the earth's core.

8. The earth's ______________________ is a thin rocky surface.

9. Soil, rocks, landforms, and other surface features make up the ______________________.

10. The ______________________ is the layer of air, water, and other substances above the surface of the earth.

11. The water in oceans, lakes, rivers, and under the ground makes up the ______________________.

12. The ______________________ is the world of plants, animals, and other living things that occupy the land and waters of the planet.

13. ______________________ are the large landmasses in the earth's oceans.

14. Landforms are classified by differences in ______________________—that is, differences in elevation.

15. ______________________ is a theory that the earth's outer shell is not one piece of rock.

16. The idea that all continents were once a single landmass but are now separate is called the ______________________.

17. The ______________________ is a circle of volcanic mountains around the Pacific Ocean.

Name ______________________ Class ______________ Date ______________

Section 3: Changes on the Earth's Surface

Guide to the Essentials

Text Summary

THE BIG IDEA

Two forces that change the surface of the earth are weathering and erosion.

The surface of the earth is constantly changing. The forces that change the earth's surface are usually grouped into two categories: weathering and erosion.

Weathering is the process of breaking down rock into smaller pieces. **Mechanical weathering** breaks down or weakens rocks physically. Ice is the chief cause of mechanical weathering. Ice widens cracks and splits rocks.

Chemical weathering changes the chemical makeup of rocks. Water and carbon dioxide are the main causes of chemical weathering. They combine to form an acid that can dissolve rocks.

Erosion is the movement of weathered materials, such as soil, sand, and gravel, from one place to another. Moving water is the major cause of erosion. The water carries pieces of rock that act like sandpaper, grinding away the surface of rocks. Then the moving water carries away the bits of rocks and soil and deposits them elsewhere.

Wind is another cause of erosion. Winds lift away soil that has little to hold it. Then the winds deposit the soil elsewhere. Sand in the wind can carve or smooth the surfaces of rocks.

Glaciers, or slow-moving sheets of ice, are another cause of erosion. They wear away land and move rocks and soil to other places. Glaciers have carved out lakes and valleys.

Graphic Summary: *Weathering and Erosion*

	WEATHERING		EROSION		
	MECHANICAL	CHEMICAL	MOVING WATER	WIND	GLACIERS
WHAT IT DOES	• Physically breaks down large pieces of rock	• Changes a rock's chemical makeup	• Cuts into rock and wears it away • Carries pieces of rock to other places	• Carries soil away and deposits it elsewhere	• Carry dirt, rocks, and boulders • Wear away land
EXAMPLES	• Frozen water expands and enlarges cracks • Seeds fall into cracks and grow into trees that split the rocks	• Acid created by water and carbon dioxide can dissolve rocks • Acid rain eats away rock surfaces	• Carves canyons and valleys • Creates flood plains and deltas	• Dust bowls are formed by loss of soil • Rich farmland is created by new deposits of soil	• Carved out the Great Lakes

Weathering and erosion are the main causes of change in the earth's surface.

Review Questions

1. What is the difference between weathering and erosion?
2. **Chart Skills** What are two kinds of weathering?

Name ______________________ Class ______________ Date ______________

Section 3: Changes on the Earth's Surface

Guided Reading and Review

A. As You Read

Directions: *The two categories of external forces that change the earth's surface are shown below. As you read Section 3, fill in the boxes with examples of each.*

Weathering	
Mechanical Weathering	**Chemical Weathering**
1. ______________ ______________	**3.** ______________ ______________
2. ______________ ______________	**4.** ______________ ______________

Erosion		
5. ______________ ______________	**6.** ______________ ______________	**7.** ______________ ______________

B. Reviewing Vocabulary

Directions: *Read the statements below. If a statement is true, write T in the blank provided. If it is false, write F.*

_____ **8.** The process of weathering breaks down rock at or near the earth's surface.

_____ **9.** Mechanical weathering strengthens rocks.

_____ **10.** Chemical weathering cannot alter a rock's chemical makeup.

_____ **11.** Acid rain is a form of mechanical weathering.

_____ **12.** The movement of the earth's weathered materials is known as erosion.

_____ **13.** Moving water carries sediment—small particles of soil, sand, and gravel.

_____ **14.** Windblown deposits of mineral-rich dust and silt are called loess.

_____ **15.** Glaciers are an agent of weathering.

_____ **16.** Rocks and debris left behind by glaciers are called moraines.

Name ____________________ Class ____________ Date ____________

Chapter 1 Test

Identifying Main Ideas

Directions: *Write the letter of the correct answer in the blank provided. (10 points each)*

____ **1. Which of the following is the study of places, how they affect people, and how people change them?**
A. geography
B. movement
C. region
D. climate

____ **2. The theme of place describes**
A. exact location.
B. how areas are alike or different.
C. relative location.
D. how goods are moved.

____ **3. A group of places with at least one thing in common form a**
A. location.
B. relative location.
C. government.
D. region.

____ **4. Geology is the study of**
A. the earth's plants and animals.
B. how roads and factories are built.
C. how ships and airplanes carry people.
D. the earth's history and structure.

____ **5. What is the name of the center of the earth?**
A. core
B. fault
C. earthquake
D. lava

____ **6. The theory that the earth's crust is broken into moving plates is called**
A. geography.
B. absolute location.
C. plate tectonics.
D. the core.

____ **7. Weathering is the**
A. study of climates.
B. movement of glaciers.
C. study of erosion.
D. process of breaking down rock into smaller pieces.

____ **8. What is one effect of chemical weathering?**
A. chemical changes in rocks
B. formation of more ice
C. loss of glaciers
D. invention of sandpaper

____ **9. What are the three main causes of erosion?**
A. fire, air, and movement
B. water, wind, and glaciers
C. volcanoes, earthquakes, and tornadoes
D. rocks, soil, and sand

____ **10. Lakes and valleys have been carved out by**
A. chemical weathering.
B. wind.
C. mountains.
D. glaciers.

Name ______________ Class ______________ Date ______________

Chapter 2

Climates and Ecosystems

Vocabulary
biome
ecosystem
weather

Vocabulary Development

Directions: *To understand the meaning and context of a new word, it is helpful to explore the word in a word-map diagram. A word map asks three questions: "What is it?"; "What is it like?"; and "What are some examples?" Complete word maps for the vocabulary words listed to the right. One has been started for you.*

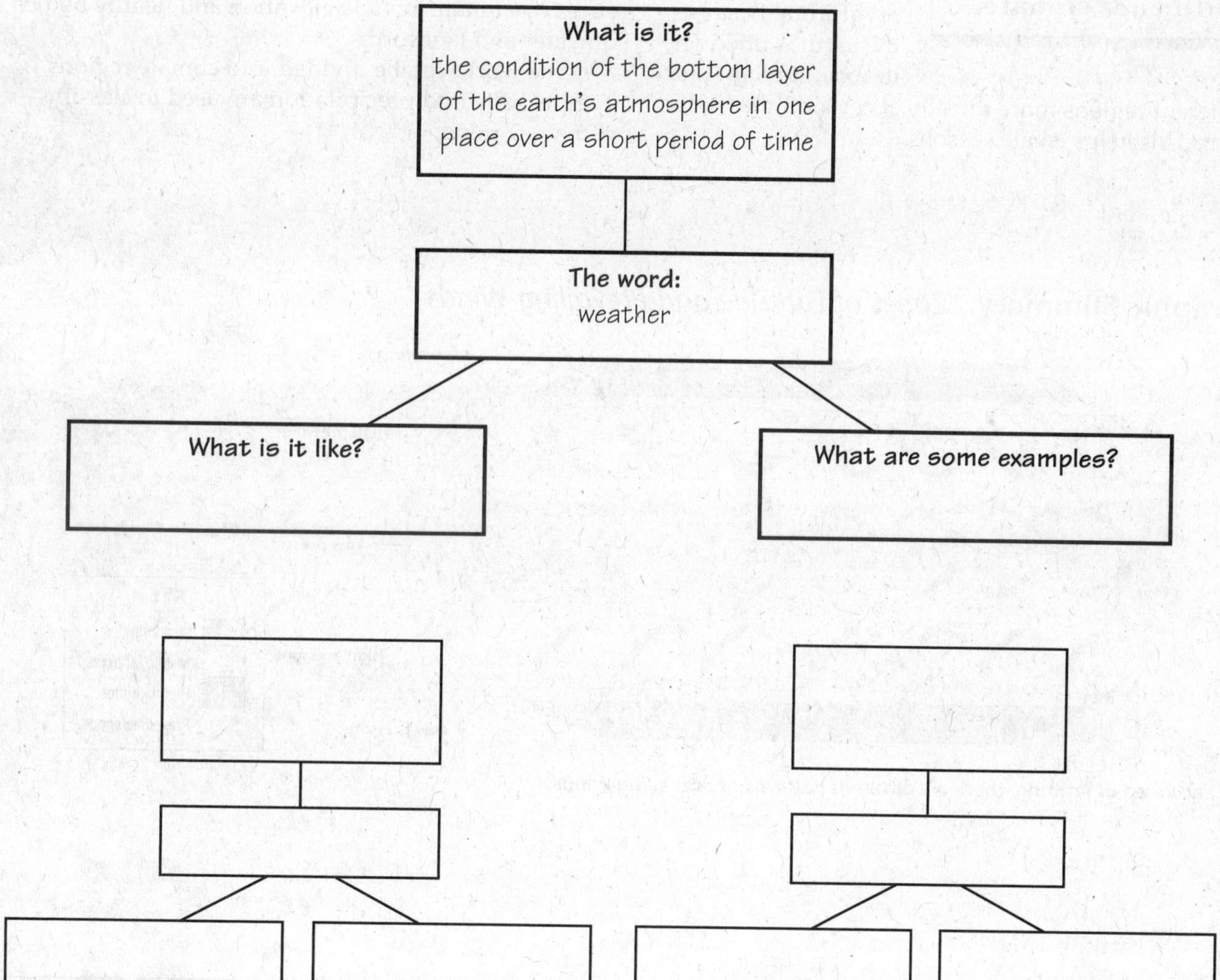

What is it?
the condition of the bottom layer of the earth's atmosphere in one place over a short period of time

The word:
weather

What is it like?

What are some examples?

Name ______________________ Class ______________ Date ______________

Section 1: *Weather and Climate*

Guide to the Essentials

Text Summary

THE BIG IDEA

Climate is the weather of an area over a long period of time. Location, latitude, elevation, and landforms influence climate.

Weather is the condition of the air in one place over a short period of time and is always changing. **Climate** is the kind of weather that an area has over a long period of time.

The sun is the source of the earth's climates. The earth moves around the sun in a yearly orbit, or path, which is called a **revolution**. Because the earth is tilted on its axis, sunlight hits different regions more directly at certain times of the year. This helps create seasons.

Latitude also affects climate. The sun's rays always fall most directly at or near the Equator. They are least direct near the North and South poles. As a result, most places near the Equator have warm climates while places farthest from the Equator are cold.

Prevailing winds, which occur in regular and predictable patterns, influence the climate of regions near them. Ocean currents, rivers of warm and cold water moving through the ocean, also affect climate.

Precipitation is all forms of water that fall to the earth's surface. The amount of precipitation a place receives has a major affect on its climate. Other influences on climate include elevation and nearby bodies of water and landforms.

The world can be divided into climate regions. Temperature and precipitation are used to classify climate regions.

Graphic Summary: *Zones of Latitude and Prevailing Winds*

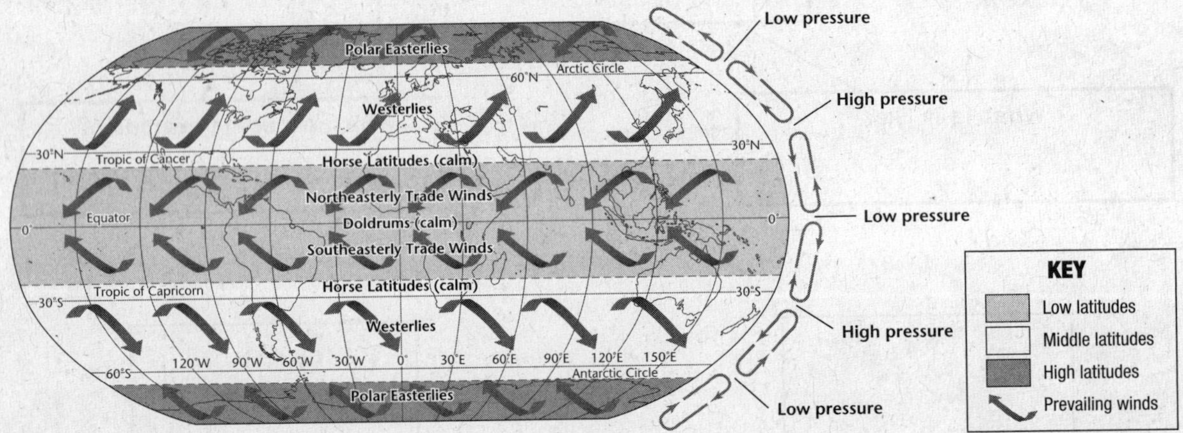

In each area of latitude, there are different patterns of prevailing winds.

Review Questions

1. Name three things that affect climate.

2. Map Skills In what directions do the prevailing winds move in the low latitudes?

Name ______________________ Class ______________ Date ______________

Section 1: Weather and Climate

Guided Reading and Review

A. As You Read

Directions: *As you read Section 1, complete the chart below. List the aspects of the earth's weather and climate indicated by the descriptions.*

Description	Identification
This reflects some heat back into space and traps some heat near the earth.	**1.** ______________
This process distributes the heat from the sun around the earth.	**2.** ______________
This occurs when cooler air cannot retain all its vapor.	**3.** ______________
These features affect surrounding climates because their temperatures are slow to change.	**4.** ______________
This is the most common type of precipitation.	**5.** ______________

B. Reviewing Vocabulary

Directions: *Complete each sentence by writing the correct term in the blank.*

6. ______________ is the condition of the bottom layer of the earth's atmosphere in one place over a short period of time.

7. ______________ refers to the weather patterns of an area over a long time.

8. The earth spins like a top in a movement called ______________.

9. The earth orbits the sun, completing one ______________ in a year.

10. Two seasons are marked by the summer and winter ______________.

11. The spring and fall seasons are marked by a(n) ______________.

12. ______________ is all forms of water that fall on the earth.

13. Air masses are known as ______________.

14. Climates of interior regions of a landmass, marked by warm or hot summers and cold, snowy winters, are called ______________.

Name ______________________ Class ______________ Date ______________

Section 2: Ecosystems

Guide to the Essentials

Text Summary

An **ecosystem** is formed by the interaction of plant life, animal life, and the physical environment in which they live. The four ecosystems are forest, grassland, desert, and tundra. Geographers use the term **biome** to describe major types of ecosystems that can be found in various regions throughout the world.

THE BIG IDEA

There are four kinds of ecosystems. They are forest, grassland, desert, and tundra.

Forest regions include many different types of biomes. A tropical rain forest has broadleaf evergreens, which keep their leaves all year. Rain forests grow where the temperature is warm and great amounts of rain fall. Forests of the middle latitudes consist mostly of broadleaf **deciduous** trees, which shed their leaves, usually in the fall. **Coniferous** forests may also grow in the colder parts of the middle latitudes and are named after the cones that protect their seeds. They have long, thin "needles" rather than broad, flat leaves. Most forests are a mixture of biomes. Another distinctive forest biome is **chaparral,** which includes small evergreen trees and low bushes, or shrub.

The characteristics of grasslands vary depending on their latitudes. Tropical grasslands, or **savannas,** grow in warm lands near the Equator. Temperate grasslands are found in cooler climates.

Desert ecosystems consist of plant and animal life that can survive with little water.

In **tundra** regions, temperatures are cool or cold. Plant life in this type of region survives in cold temperatures and short growing seasons and without sunlight for most of the winter.

Graphic Summary: *Forest Biomes*

FOREST	LOCATION (EXAMPLE)	TYPE OF PLANTS
Tropical Rain Forest	near the Equator	broadleaf evergreens
Deciduous	Western Europe	broadleaf deciduous
Coniferous	northern North America	needle evergreens
Mixed	northern United States	broadleaf deciduous and needle evergreens
Chaparral	southern California	low bushes

There are many different types of forest biomes.

Review Questions

1. What are the four main ecosystems?

2. **Chart Skills** What kinds of plants are found in chaparral forests?

Name ________________ Class ________________ Date ________________

Section 2: Ecosystems

Guided Reading and Review

A. As You Read

Directions: *As you read Section 2, describe the ecosystems by filling in the chart below.*

Ecosystem	Climate	Vegetation
Tropical Rain Forest	1. ________	2. ________
Mid-Latitude Forest	3. ________	4. ________
Coniferous Forest	5. ________	6. ________
Tropical Grasslands	7. ________	8. ________
Temperate Grasslands	9. ________	10. ________
Desert	11. ________	12. ________
Tundra	13. ________	14. ________

B. Reviewing Vocabulary

Directions: *Read the statements below. If a statement is true, write T in the blank provided. If it is false, write F.*

_____ **15.** Deciduous trees shed their leaves during one season, usually autumn.

_____ **16.** Herbivores are animals that eat plants and meat.

_____ **17.** An ecosystem is formed by the interaction of plants, animals, and the physical environment in which they live.

_____ **18.** North America's temperate grasslands are prairies.

_____ **19.** Coniferous forests contain mostly broadleaf trees.

_____ **20.** Permafrost is a layer of soil just below the surface of the tundra that is always frozen.

_____ **21.** A biome is a major type of ecosystem.

_____ **22.** In tundra regions, the temperature is always very warm.

_____ **23.** A savanna is a tropical grassland.

_____ **24.** Carnivores are meat-eating animals.

_____ **25.** Chaparral is a type of grassland.

Name ______________________ Class ______________ Date ______________

Chapter 2 **Test**

Identifying Main Ideas

Directions: *Write the letter of the correct answer in the blank provided. (10 points each)*

____ **1. There are seasons because**
A. climate and weather are different.
B. the earth is tilted on its axis.
C. there are prevailing winds.
D. the earth is round.

____ **2. Where are the sun's rays most direct during all times of the year?**
A. near the North and South poles
B. the Northern Hemisphere
C. at or near the Equator
D. the middle latitudes

____ **3. Prevailing winds occur**
A. in regular and predictable patterns.
B. during different seasons.
C. only near the Equator.
D. below the oceans.

____ **4. Precipitation includes**
A. ocean currents, wind, rain.
B. ocean currents, snow, rain.
C. wind, rain, sleet.
D. rain, snow, hail.

____ **5. What two categories are used to classify climate regions?**
A. weather and latitude
B. winds and ocean currents
C. temperature and precipitation
D. landforms and elevation

____ **6. What is an ecosystem?**
A. the interaction of plant life, animal life, and the physical environment in which they live
B. major types of plant life that can be found throughout the world
C. a mix of similar groups of plants that naturally grow in one place and depend on one another
D. the physical conditions of the natural surroundings

____ **7. What is the most common type of tree in a mid-latitude forest?**
A. chaparral
B. coniferous trees
C. deciduous trees
D. trees with small leaves or needles

____ **8. Tropical grasslands**
A. grow near the Equator.
B. include chaparral.
C. grow in cool climates.
D. are like ocean currents.

____ **9. Desert ecosystems**
A. need a lot of water.
B. need little water.
C. include tropical forest.
D. include coniferous trees.

____ **10. Where are tundra ecosystems found?**
A. near the Equator
B. in warm climates
C. in cold climates
D. in deciduous forests

Name ______________________ Class ______________ Date ______________

Chapter 3

Population and Culture

Vocabulary
command economy
cultural convergence
culture
immigrant
market economy
population density
traditional economy
urbanization

Vocabulary Development

Directions: *Write the correct vocabulary word on the line to complete each sentence below.*

1. A(n) ______________ is also known as a subsistence economy.

2. A(n) ______________ is an economic system that is controlled by a single, central government.

3. ______________ is the average number of people in a square mile or a square kilometer.

4. ______________ is the growth of city populations.

5. A(n) ______________ refers to a person who moves into a country.

6. ______________ happens when the skills, arts, ideas, habits, and institutions of one culture come in contact with those of another culture.

7. A(n) ______________ is an economic system that gives great freedom to individuals and groups.

8. ______________ is the beliefs and actions that define a group of people's way of life.

Directions: *Write sentences to describe each of the economic systems listed below.*

traditional economy

____

____

____

market economy

____

____

____

command economy

____

____

____

Name ______________________ Class ______________ Date ______________

Section 1: The Study of Human Geography

Guide to the Essentials

Text Summary

Human geography studies population and culture, as well as languages, religions, customs, and economic and political systems. **Culture** is made up of people's beliefs, actions, and way of life.

> **THE BIG IDEA**
> **Population is distributed unevenly over the world. During the twentieth century, the world's population grew more rapidly than ever before.**

The world's population today is more than six billion. The population density in some places is much higher than in other places. **Population density** is the average number of people in a square mile or square kilometer.

The world's population has been growing very rapidly since the 1950s (see graph). This increase is not divided equally among countries or parts of countries. **Urbanization,** or the growth of city populations, is happening throughout the world.

Differences in population are often the result of differences in cultures. Social organization is the way members of a culture organize themselves into groups. In all cultures the family is the most important part of social organization. Groups of people who speak the same language often share the same customs. Religion supports the values that a group of people believe are important.

Both internal and external influences affect a culture. **Cultural convergence** occurs when customs of a society come in contact with those of another culture. **Cultural divergence,** on the other hand, refers to the restriction of a culture from outside cultural influences.

Graphic Summary: *World Population Growth: A.D. 1150 to 2050*

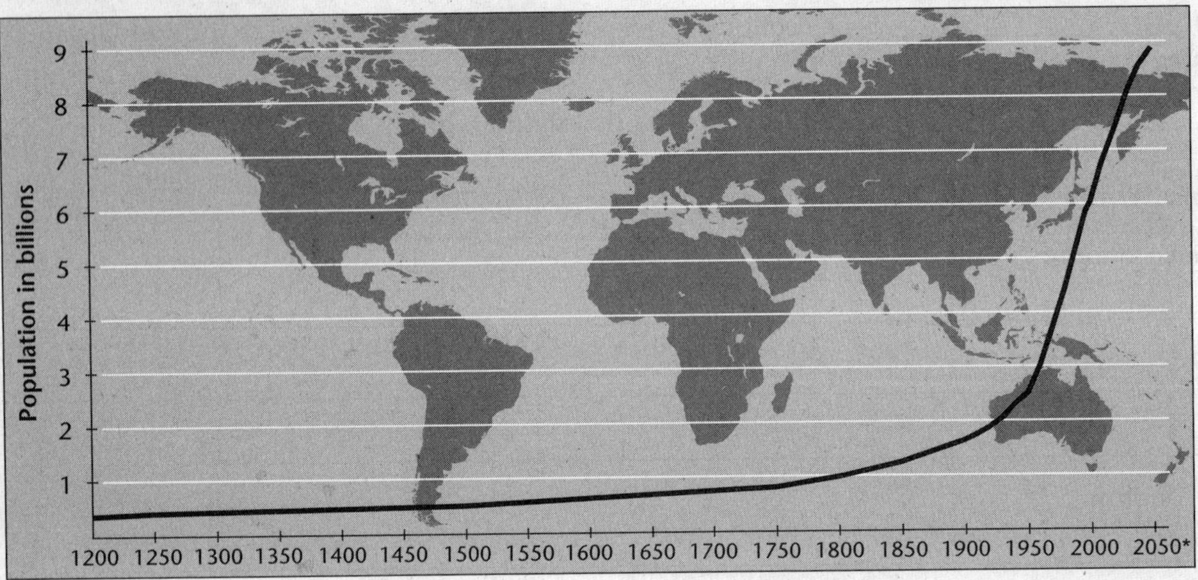

Source: United Nations Population Division
*Estimate

For many centuries, the world's population grew at about the same rate.

Review Questions

1. In what kinds of places would you expect to find the greatest population density?

2. **Graph Skills** What was the world's population in 1950?

Name ______________________ Class ______________ Date ______________

Section 1: The Study of Human Geography

Guided Reading and Review

A. As You Read

Directions: As you read Section 1, answer the following questions.

1. Why is the population density different in various parts of the world? ____

____

2. What are some possible negative effects of world population growth? What are possible positive effects?

____

____

3. List four of the elements of culture.

____

4. How can the movement of a group of people from one country to another cause cultural change?

____

____

B. Reviewing Vocabulary

Directions: Match the definitions in Column I with the terms in Column II. Write the correct letter in each blank.

Column I

_____ **5.** the number of live births each year per 1,000 people

_____ **6.** referring to the countryside

_____ **7.** a place where important ideas begin and spread out

_____ **8.** the average number of people in a square mile or kilometer

_____ **9.** people who leave a country to live elsewhere

_____ **10.** occurs when the skills, arts, ideas, habits, and institutions of one culture come in contact with those of another culture

_____ **11.** the growth of city population

_____ **12.** the beliefs and actions that define a group of people's way of life

_____ **13.** the process by which a cultural element is transmitted across some distance from one group or individual to another

_____ **14.** people who move into a country

_____ **15.** the result of the restriction of a culture from outside cultural influences

Column II

a. immigrants

b. culture

c. urbanization

d. culture hearth

e. rural

f. emigrants

g. population density

h. diffusion

i. cultural convergence

j. birthrate

k. cultural divergence

Name ______________________ Class ______________ Date ______________

Section 2: Political and Economic Systems

Guide to the Essentials

Text Summary

There are about 200 independent countries in the world. Four ideas define a place as a country: clearly defined territory, population, sovereignty, and government. **Sovereignty** is freedom from outside control.

THE BIG IDEA

Countries have different ways of organizing their governments and their economies.

Countries have different government systems. A country with a central government that rules the entire nation has a **unitary** system. A **federation** refers to a country in which the national government shares power with state governments. In a **confederation,** smaller levels of government keep most of the power and give the central government very limited powers.

Governments differ in authority. Leaders hold all, or nearly all, political power in an **authoritarian** government. Today the most common form of authoritarian government is a **dictatorship**, in which a person or small group holds most power. Dictators usually take power by military force.

Throughout history, the most common type of authoritarian government has been a **monarchy.** Monarchs are hereditary rulers, such as kings and queens, who were born into the ruling family.

In a **democracy,** people elect their leaders. Most democracies have representative governments in which adult citizens can vote for people to make laws.

A country's economic system determines how goods and services are produced and distributed. In a **traditional economy,** all goods and services produced are consumed in the family or village, leaving little surplus for trade. A **market economy** allows individuals or companies to make decisions concerning production and distribution. In a **command economy,** a central government controls the economic system.

Graphic Summary: *World Economic Systems*

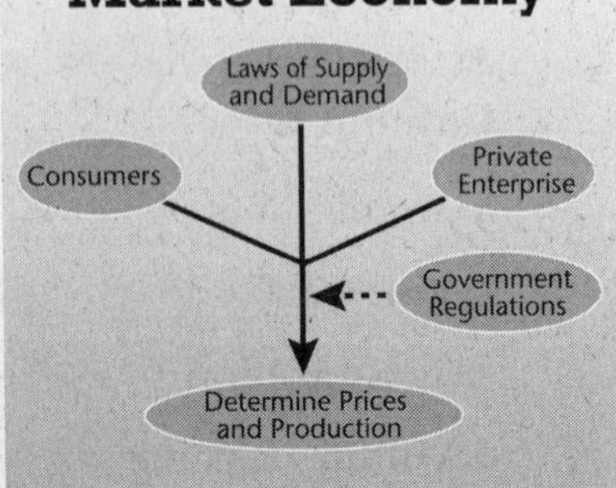

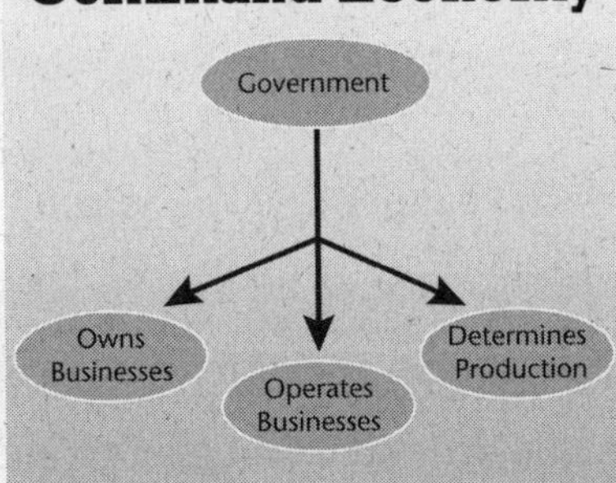

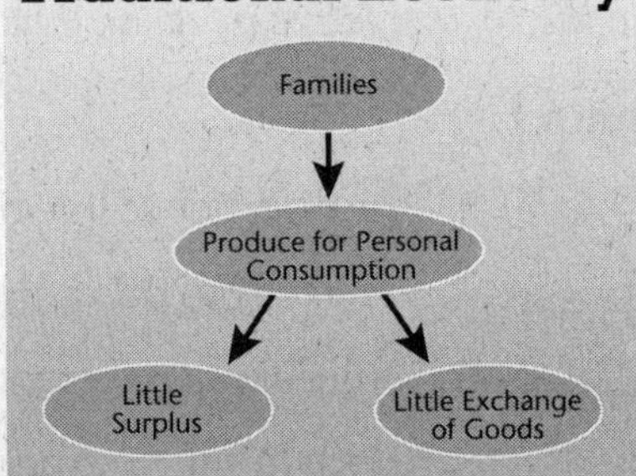

Each economic system has its own way of organizing economic activities.

Review Questions

1. How is the way a monarch gets power different from the leader of a democratic country?

2. **Diagram Skills** In which economic system is the government most involved?

Name ______________________ Class ______________ Date ______________

Section 2: Political and Economic Systems

Guided Reading and Review

A. As You Read

***Directions:** As you read Section 2, complete the chart below by ranking political or economic systems based upon the characteristic indicated.*

Political and Economic Systems	Rankings
Political systems: confederation, federation, unitary system Characteristic: most to least central government authority	**1.** ______________ **2.** ______________ **3.** ______________
Political systems: democracy, dictatorship Characteristic: most to least power of citizens	**4.** ______________ **5.** ______________
Economic systems: traditional economy, command economy, market economy Characteristic: most to least government control of the economy	**6.** ______________ **7.** ______________ **8.** ______________

B. Reviewing Vocabulary

***Directions:** Read the statements below. If a statement is true, write T in the blank. If it is false, write F.*

_____ **9.** Sovereignty refers to the land and water of a country.

_____ **10.** The United States is a democracy and a federation.

_____ **11.** Great Britain is both a confederation and a constitutional monarchy.

_____ **12.** A dictatorship is an authoritarian form of government.

_____ **13.** In a monarchy voters elect a king and a queen.

_____ **14.** A market economy is commonly associated with totalitarianism.

_____ **15.** A country may have a unitary government and a market economy.

_____ **16.** Many rural parts of less developed countries have traditional economies.

_____ **17.** Command economies often exist in democratic countries.

Name ______________________ Class ______________ Date ______________

Chapter **3**

Test

Identifying Main Ideas

Directions: Write the letter of the correct answer in the blank provided. (10 points each)

____ **1. Culture includes**
A. language, religion, and way of life.
B. the houses a group of people build.
C. a group's works of art.
D. all the items a group of people make.

____ **2. What is population density?**
A. the people who live in the most crowded parts of cities
B. the increase in the number of people from year to year
C. all the people alive in the world today
D. the average number of people in a square mile or square kilometer

____ **3. Which of the following statements is most accurate about the world's population growth?**
A. It has grown at a steady rate for the last 1,000 years.
B. It is growing more slowly now than 100 years ago.
C. It has grown more rapidly in the past 50 years than ever before.
D. It is not taking place in cities.

____ **4. Urbanization is the**
A. decline of city populations.
B. growth of country populations.
C. growth of city populations.
D. decline of country populations.

____ **5. What is the most important unit of social organization in all cultures?**
A. the family
B. social class
C. religion
D. gender

____ **6. Which has the most power in a unitary system of government?**
A. the central government
B. the state governments
C. power is shared equally
D. business owners

____ **7. Who holds the power in an authoritarian government?**
A. the people who vote
B. all individuals
C. the leader or leaders
D. a group who must be elected

____ **8. Which statement is true for all democracies?**
A. They are all ruled by a dictator.
B. The people elect the leaders.
C. The leader holds all political power.
D. They all have rulers who inherit power.

____ **9. Who makes decisions about producing goods and services in a market economy?**
A. The state makes all decisions.
B. The state makes most decisions.
C. Elected leaders make the decisions.
D. Individuals or companies make the decisions.

____ **10. Which of the following statements is true about a traditional economy?**
A. The government controls the economy.
B. The economy does not produce surplus goods for trade.
C. It is a free enterprise system.
D. Decisions are often made to achieve social or political goals.

Name ______________________ Class ______________ Date ______________

Chapter 4

Resources and Land Use

Vocabulary
export
fossil fuel
import
natural resource
nonrenewable resource
renewable resource
solar energy

Vocabulary Development

Directions: *All of the vocabulary words listed to the right describe either world resources or world economic activities. Write a sentence for each word that contains clues to help a reader understand the meaning. The first one is done for you.*

export

An export is an item that a country sends out to be sold in other countries.

fossil fuel

import

natural resource

nonrenewable resource

renewable resource

solar energy

Name ____________ Class ____________ Date ____________

Section 1: World Resources

Guide to the Essentials

Text Summary

THE BIG IDEA

People use natural resources to survive and meet their other needs. Modern societies depend on reliable sources of energy.

All people depend on **natural resources,** the materials that people take from the natural environment, for food, water, tools, and other needs. **Renewable resources** are those that the environment replaces. Sunlight, water, and soil are renewable resources.

Nonrenewable resources cannot be replaced once they are used. **Fossil fuels,** such as coal, oil, and natural gas, are nonrenewable. Many metals and other minerals cannot be replaced once they are used up. But objects made of them can be recycled so that the minerals can be used again.

Modern countries depend on energy from fossil fuels. Oil and natural gas are not spread out evenly around the world. Over half the world's known oil supply is in Southwest Asia. Coal is found in more places than oil or natural gas. But burning coal can cause air pollution.

Nuclear energy is produced by splitting uranium atoms to release their stored energy. Many people worry about leaks, explosions, and wastes from nuclear plants.

Many experts believe that countries must find renewable sources of energy. Water power uses the energy of falling water to create energy. **Geothermal energy** comes from the heat inside the earth. **Solar energy** is energy produced by the sun. It is not used much today, but it may provide the best source of energy for the future.

Graphic Summary: *Renewable and Nonrenewable Sources of Energy*

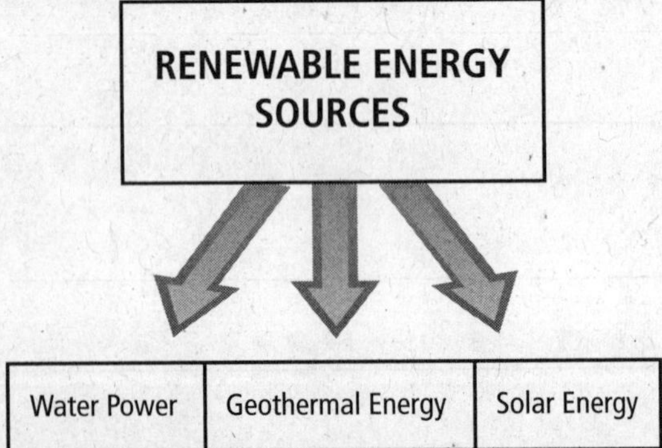

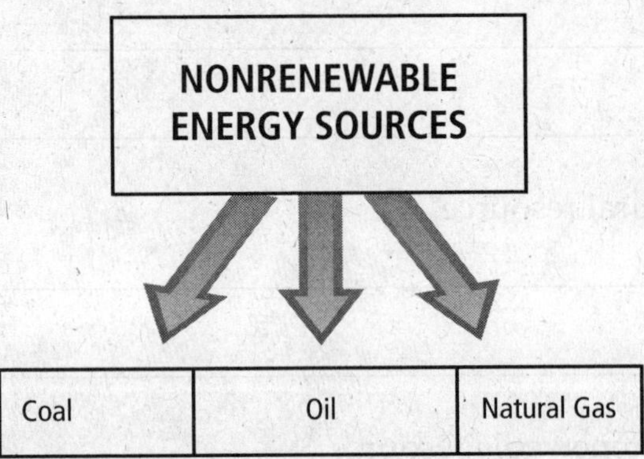

Energy sources that are renewable can be replaced.

Review Questions

1. How can recycling help with the problem of some nonrenewable resources?
2. **Diagram Skills** Why might a manufacturer prefer to depend on water power instead of oil?

Name ______________________ Class ______________ Date ______________

Section 1: World Resources

Guided Reading and Review

A. As You Read

Directions: As you read Section 1, complete the charts below about world resources.

Natural Resources
1. Examples of renewable resources are ______________________.
2. Examples of nonrenewable resources are ______________________.

Energy Sources	
Type	**Drawbacks, if any**
3. ______________	4. ______________
5. ______________	6. ______________
7. ______________	8. ______________
9. ______________	10. ______________
11. ______________	12. ______________

B. Reviewing Vocabulary

Directions: Complete each sentence by writing the correct term in the blank.

13. People have always used ______________, the materials from the natural environment, to help meet their needs.
14. Soil and water are examples of ______________.
15. Resources that cannot be replaced once they are used up are ______________.
16. Ancient plant and animal remains form ______________.
17. ______________ is produced by splitting uranium atoms.
18. People use ______________, or the energy from falling water, to power machines or generate electricity.
19. The earth's internal heat produces ______________.
20. Radiation from the sun produces ______________.

Name ____________________ Class ____________ Date ____________

Section 2: World Economic Activity

Guide to the Essentials

Text Summary

People acquire things they need to survive and luxuries they desire by earning a living. Geographers and economists classify these economic activities into four categories.

Primary economic activities rely directly upon natural resources, such as farming and mining. (See chart below.) Farming methods differ around the world. In less prosperous countries, farmers practice **subsistence farming.** They grow only enough for their own family or village. In countries with more advanced economies, farmers practice **commercial farming.** These farmers raise crops and animals to be sold for profit.

THE BIG IDEA

Economic activities are the ways people earn their living. Countries are at different stages of economic development.

When people use raw materials to produce new products, such as processing wheat into flour, they are engaging in **secondary economic activities. Tertiary activities** refer to service industries, such as health care. **Quaternary economic activities** focus on the acquisition, processing, and sharing of information, as in education.

Nations establish trading networks when they do not have the resources and goods they want. The goods that are sent out of a country are called **exports.** The goods that are brought into a country are called **imports.**

Economic activities and trade patterns influence a country's level of development. Modern industrial societies are considered developed countries, whereas countries with lower levels of prosperity are considered underdeveloped. Nations showing evidence of progress are considered developing. One way to measure a country's level of development is to look at the per capita gross domestic product (GDP), the total value of goods and services produced in a country within a year divided by the total population.

Graphic Summary: *Four Levels of Economic Activities*

	PRIMARY ACTIVITIES	SECONDARY ACTIVITIES	TERTIARY ACTIVITIES	QUATERNARY ACTIVITIES
LINK TO NATURAL RESOURCES	• Use natural resources directly	• Process natural resources	• Do not directly gather or process raw materials	• Do not need to be located near resources or a market
EXAMPLES	• Farming • Fishing • Mining • Forestry	• Processing flour from wheat • Making lumber from trees • Producing electrical power	• Doctors • Salespeople • Firefighters • Truck drivers	• Education • Government • Information Processing • Research

Economic activities can be grouped by how and if they use natural resources.

Review Questions

1. How does subsistence farming differ from commercial farming?

2. Diagram Skills What type of economic activity is firefighting?

Name ______________________ Class ______________ Date ______________

Section 2: World Economic Activity

Guided Reading and Review

A. As You Read

Directions: *As you read Section 2, complete the following charts.*

Economic Activities	
Types	**Examples**
Primary	**1.** ______________________
Secondary	**2.** ______________________
Tertiary	**3.** ______________________
Quaternary	**4.** ______________________

Economic Development	
Type of Country	**Characteristics**
Developed	**5.** ______________________
Underdeveloped	**6.** ______________________
Developing	**7.** ______________________

B. Reviewing Vocabulary

Directions: *Define the following terms.*

8. primary economic activity ______________________

9. subsistence farming ______________________

10. commercial farming ______________________

11. secondary economic activity ______________________

12. cottage industry ______________________

13. commercial industry ______________________

14. tertiary economic activity ______________________

15. quaternary economic activity ______________________

16. export ______________________

17. import ______________________

Name ______________________ Class ______________ Date ______________

Chapter 4

Test

Identifying Main Ideas

Directions: *Write the letter of the correct answer in the blank provided. (10 points each)*

____ **1. What is a renewable resource?**
A. a resource that cannot be reused
B. a resource you pay for
C. a resource that the environment will replace
D. a resource that comes from fossils

____ **2. Which of the following forms of energy comes from fossil fuels?**
A. oil
B. solar power
C. geothermal energy
D. water power

____ **3. What part of the world has over half the world's known oil supply?**
A. North America
B. Western Europe
C. Southern Africa
D. Southwest Asia

____ **4. Why are countries trying to find alternatives to nonrenewable energy sources?**
A. Nations without nonrenewable sources want to put those with these sources out of business.
B. Once nonrenewable sources are gone, there are no more sources of this energy.
C. Once nonrenewable sources are depleted, they are very expensive to produce again.
D. Nonrenewable sources will never be depleted, so there is no need for alternatives.

____ **5. What do you call energy that comes from the heat inside the earth?**
A. solar power
B. nuclear energy
C. geothermal energy
D. fossil fuel

____ **6. What kind of economic activities are fishing and mining?**
A. tertiary activities
B. primary activities
C. secondary activities
D. quaternary activities

____ **7. In which type of country would farmers most likely practice commercial farming?**
A. underdeveloped
B. developing
C. developed
D. democratic

____ **8. Why do nations import from and export to other nations?**
A. to convince people to immigrate
B. to fulfill an economic category
C. to continue good relations
D. to trade for the resources and goods they want

____ **9. What is per capita gross domestic product (GDP)?**
A. the salary a person earns each year
B. the total value of goods and services produced in a country in a year divided by the total population
C. all the products a country produces from raw materials
D. each person's share of a country's products and services

____ **10. Who would use most of a subsistence farmer's crops?**
A. the farmer's family and village
B. the people who buy the crops
C. commercial farmers
D. people around the world

Name ______________________ Class ______________ Date ______________

Chapter 5

Regional Atlas: Introduction to the United States and Canada

Vocabulary
colony
continental divide
Industrial Revolution
literacy
suburb
tributary

Vocabulary Development

Directions: *Using what you learned in Chapter 5, read each sentence below and decide whether the underlined word is used correctly. Indicate your answer by circling either "Correct" or "Incorrect." If the sentence is incorrect, write your own sentence that uses the word properly.*

1. A colony is any territory physically joined to a ruling power.

Correct Incorrect

____

2. The Industrial Revolution in the United States allowed factories to produce large quantities of goods.

Correct Incorrect

____

3. The Rocky Mountains form the continental divide that separates rivers flowing toward opposite sides of the continent.

Correct Incorrect

____

4. A tributary is a major river into which streams and smaller rivers flow.

Correct Incorrect

____

5. A suburb is a small city with many industries.

Correct Incorrect

____

6. Literacy is the ability to read and write.

Correct Incorrect

____

Name ______________________ Class ______________ Date ______________

Regional Atlas: The United States and Canada

Guide to the Essentials

Text Summary

Scientists believe that the first people to populate North America migrated from Asia and are known today as Native Americans. They were followed by the Europeans and Africans. English settlers established 13 **colonies,** territories separated from but subject to a ruling power. Eventually, the settlers broke ties with Great Britain to form the United States of America. Canada also ended ties with Great Britain to become a democracy.

THE BIG IDEA

The United States and Canada are two vast nations that share most of North America. Both are wealthy, developed nations with rich natural resources.

The physical features of both nations include high mountain chains in the west, plains in the central area, and lower mountains in the east. The Rocky Mountains form the **continental divide,** a boundary that separates rivers flowing toward opposite sides of a continent. The variety of ecosystems includes arctic tundra, several types of forests, grasslands, and desert scrub. While Canada has a colder climate than the United States, both countries have climate differences between east and west.

The United States has over 275 million people, whereas Canada has approximately 31 million. At least three fourths of people in both countries live in urban areas. The **standard of living,** a measurement based on available education, housing, health care, and nutrition, is considered high in both nations. Americans and Canadians have long life expectancies and extensive education systems, which contribute to high rates of **literacy,** or the ability to read and write.

Technological development has made high-tech industries an influential part of both economies. The United States and Canada are two of the world's largest energy producers and consumers. Although the United States has an abundance of fossil fuels, it still must import energy, whereas Canada is self-sufficient in its energy needs.

Graphic Summary:
The United States and Canada

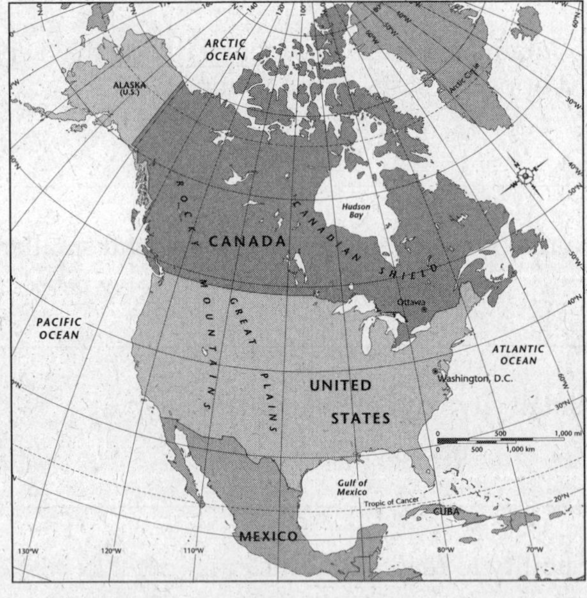

The United States and Canada cover most of North America.

Review Questions

1. Name two features shared by the United States and Canada.

2. **Map Skills** Which oceans border the United States and Canada?

Name ______________ Class ______________ Date ______________

Regional Atlas: *The United States and Canada*

Guided Reading and Review

A. As You Read

Directions: *As you work through the Regional Atlas, complete the chart below by writing two supporting details under each main idea.*

Main Idea A: The United States and Canada share a number of physical features.

1. ______________

2. ______________

Main Idea B: Latitude, elevation, and distance from oceans affect the climates of the United States and Canada.

3. ______________

4. ______________

Main Idea C: The size of the populations of Canada and the United States differs, but in some ways the populations of both nations are similar.

5. ______________

6. ______________

Main Idea D: Both the United States and Canada have a wide variety of resources and economic activities.

7. ______________

8. ______________

B. Reviewing Vocabulary

Directions: *Define the following terms.*

9. colony ______________

10. annex ______________

11. cede ______________

12. civil war ______________

13. Industrial Revolution ______________

14. continental divide ______________

15. drainage basin ______________

Name ____________________ Class ______________ Date ______________

Chapter 5 Test

Identifying Main Ideas

Directions: *Write the letter of the correct answer in the blank provided. (10 points each)*

____ **1. Who were the first people to populate North America?**
A. Canadians
B. Europeans
C. Africans
D. Native Americans

____ **2. Which term describes a territory separated from but subject to a ruling power?**
A. annex
B. colony
C. tributary
D. striation

____ **3. Which physical feature is located in the central portions of both Canada and the United States?**
A. high mountain chains
B. low mountains
C. plains
D. canyons

____ **4. What is the continental divide?**
A. a mountain in eastern North America
B. a river system that includes the Great Lakes
C. the Mississippi River
D. a boundary that separates rivers flowing toward opposite sides of a continent

____ **5. Which statement does *not* describe the climates of the United States and Canada?**
A. Canada has a colder climate.
B. Both countries have climate differences between east and west.
C. Canada has a warmer climate.
D. The United States has a warmer climate.

____ **6. What is the standard of living like in the United States and Canada?**
A. high in both countries
B. much higher in the United States
C. much higher in Canada
D. very low in both countries

____ **7. What factor most contributes to high rates of literacy in each nation?**
A. large populations
B. good economies
C. small populations
D. extensive education systems

____ **8. What proportion of Americans and Canadians live in urban areas?**
A. one quarter
B. three fourths
C. one half
D. nine tenths

____ **9. Which industry is an influential part of both economies?**
A. agricultural industries
B. manufacturing industries
C. service industries
D. high-tech industries

____ **10. Which statement correctly describes energy production and consumption in these countries?**
A. Canada imports energy, whereas the United States is self-sufficient.
B. The United States imports energy, whereas Canada is self-sufficient.
C. Both countries are self-sufficient.
D. Both countries import energy.

Name ______________________ Class ______________ Date ____________

Chapter 6

A Profile of the United States

Vocabulary
canal
free enterprise
gross national product
hierarchy
hinterland
metropolitan area
telecommunication

Vocabulary Development

Directions: *Match each vocabulary word in Column A with the correct definition in Column B.*

Column A	Column B
1. gross national product	**a.** artificial waterway
2. canal	**b.** a city and its surrounding suburbs
3. telecommunication	**c.** areas influenced by the city nearest to them
4. free enterprise	**d.** total value of a nation's output of goods and services
5. metropolitan area	**e.** rank
6. hierarchy	**f.** communication by electronic means
7. hinterland	**g.** another term for capitalism

Directions: *Write a short paragraph using at least four of the vocabulary terms on the list.*

Name ________________ Class ________________ Date ________________

Section 1: A Resource-Rich Nation

Guide to the Essentials

Text Summary

THE BIG IDEA

Rich natural resources, hardworking people, a free-enterprise system, and systems of transportation and communications have led to the economic success of the United States.

The United States is the world's fourth largest country in area and the third largest in population. It has a higher **gross national product (GNP)** than any other country. GNP is the total value of goods and services that a country produces in a year.

One reason for the wealth of the United States is that it is rich in natural resources. Farmers grow crops on the country's rich soils. Forests supply lumber for housing, furniture, paper, and other products. Mineral resources include fossil fuels—coal, oil, and natural gas. Other mineral riches include copper, gold, lead, titanium, uranium, and zinc.

The United States built transportation systems to help move raw materials and finished products. In the 1800s, steamboats and canals made water routes faster and cheaper. Later, railroads, automobiles, and an interstate highway system improved travel over land.

Communications improved with the invention of the telegraph and telephone. Today people and businesses are communicating using computers, satellites, and other forms of **telecommunication,** or communication by electronic means.

The political system has also been vital to the economic success of the United States. It reflects one of the country's most important shared values—the belief in individual equality, opportunity, and freedom. These values are aided by an economic system of **free enterprise,** which lets individuals own, operate, and profit from their own businesses.

Graphic Summary: *United States Economic Success*

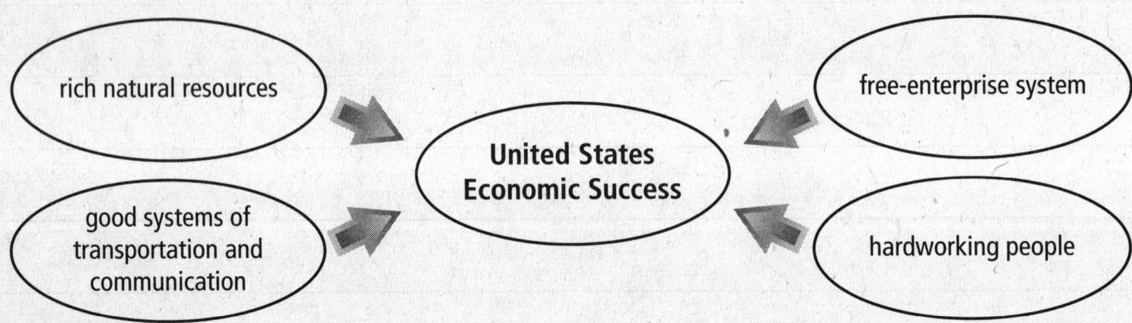

Many factors have led to the economic success of the United States.

Review Questions

1. Name three natural resources that have helped the United States to become wealthy.

2. **Diagram Skills** What four factors have contributed to the economic success of the United States?

Name ______________________ Class ______________ Date ______________

Section 1: A Resource-Rich Nation

Guided Reading and Review

A. As You Read

Directions: *As you read Section 1, complete the chart below by describing the factors that have contributed to the economic success of the United States.*

Factor	Descriptions
Major natural resources	**1.** ______________ **2.** ______________ **3.** ______________
Technological advances In water transportation In land transportation In communication	 **4.** ______________ **5.** ______________ **6.** ______________
American shared values	**7.** ______________
American economic system	**8.** ______________

B. Reviewing Vocabulary

Directions: *Define the following terms.*

9. gross national product ______________

10. canal ______________

11. telecommunication ______________

12. free enterprise ______________

Name ______________________ Class ______________ Date ______________

Section 2: A Nation of Cities

Guide to the Essentials

Text Summary

THE BIG IDEA

U.S. cities have grown because of location, transportation, economy, and people's choices. Different-size cities have different purposes.

The United States is a nation of city dwellers. About 80 percent of the people live in **metropolitan areas**, cities and their suburbs.

The location of a city is important to its growth. But as the nation's economy changed, so did the factors that made a place a good location.

Transportation is one factor. The first U.S. cities were Atlantic Ocean ports, where goods were shipped to and from Europe. As settlers moved inland, they shipped their crops on rivers, and river cities grew. By the mid-1800s, cities were being built along the expanding railroads. Automobiles gave people more freedom of movement. Many people and businesses moved from cities to suburbs, areas on the outer edges of cities.

As transportation improved, people had more choices about where they would live and work. Many people moved to cities in the South and West, where winters are warmer than in the Northeast. Cities like New York and Chicago remained important because of their many jobs and different activities.

Farms, towns, and cities all have a part in the nation's economy. Each depends on the others. There is a **hierarchy**, or ranking, of places according to their function. Smaller places serve a small area, while larger cities may serve the entire country and even much of the world.

Graphic Summary: *Urban Hierarchy*

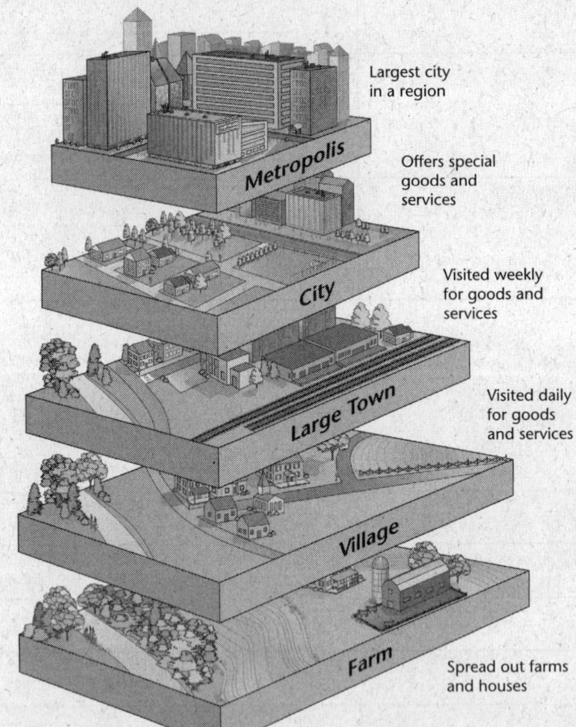

Each kind of place serves an important purpose in the urban hierarchy.

Review Questions

1. Why did the first U.S. cities develop near the Atlantic Ocean?

2. **Diagram Skills** Which place serves the smallest area?

Name ______________________ Class ______________ Date ______________

Section 2: A Nation of Cities

Guided Reading and Review

A. As You Read

Directions: *As you read Section 2, complete the chart below by writing three supporting details under each main idea.*

Main Idea A: Changes in transportation affected the growth of American cities.

1. ____

2. ____

3. ____

Main Idea B: Popular preferences and economic activities influence the growth of American cities today.

4. ____

5. ____

6. ____

Main Idea C: American cities can be organized in a hierarchy according to their function.

7. ____

8. ____

9. ____

B. Reviewing Vocabulary

Directions: *Define the following terms.*

10. metropolitan area ____

11. hierarchy ____

12. hinterland ____

Name ______________________ Class ______________ Date ______________

Chapter 6 Test

Identifying Main Ideas

Directions: *Write the letter of the correct answer in the blank provided. (10 points each)*

____ **1. Where does the United States rank among the nations in gross national product?**
A. first
B. second
C. third
D. fourth

____ **2. Where does the United States rank among the nations in population?**
A. first
B. second
C. third
D. fourth

____ **3. What kinds of natural resources helped the United States to become wealthy?**
A. steamboats, railroads, and automobiles
B. telephones, telegraphs, and computers
C. farmland, forests, and minerals
D. canals, satellites, and electronics

____ **4. What are telecommunications?**
A. written messages about phone calls
B. computers, telephones, and other electronic devices
C. television commercials
D. ads in magazines

____ **5. What is a free enterprise system?**
A. a way that people can give away goods and services
B. a system in which there is no charge for transportation
C. a system in which the state controls all new businesses
D. a system that allows people to own and run their own businesses

____ **6. What is a metropolitan area?**
A. a city that is growing
B. the area outside of a large city
C. a city that is part of another city
D. a large city together with its suburbs

____ **7. Where were the earliest U.S. cities located?**
A. on Atlantic Ocean ports
B. on Pacific Ocean ports
C. near railroads
D. near rivers

____ **8. Which of the following is an example of personal choice in deciding where to build a home or business?**
A. Shipping needs require the business to be on an ocean port.
B. People who like to swim set up a business in an area near a beach.
C. A hospital has nearby housing for its nurses.
D. A company told its employees they would have to move to a different factory.

____ **9. Which of the following is at the top of the urban hierarchy?**
A. farm
B. large town
C. village
D. metropolis

____ **10. Which of the following helps make a location a good place for a city to grow?**
A. a small population
B. nearby farms
C. poor transportation
D. good transportation

Name ____________ Class ________ Date ________

Chapter 7

Regions of the United States

Vocabulary

aqueduct
bayou
growing season
megalopolis
Sunbelt
tundra

Vocabulary Development

Directions: *Imagine that you are a tourist visiting the United States. Write a journal entry of one or more paragraphs describing what you see. Use at least five of the listed vocabulary words. Be specific in your paragraph(s) to help your readers appreciate the excitement of your travels.*

Name ______________________ Class ______________ Date ______________

Section 1: The Northeast

Guide to the Essentials

Text Summary

The United States government divides the country into four major regions: the Northeast, South, Midwest, and West. The Northeast has fewer natural resources than the other regions. Its rocky soil and steep hills make farming difficult. Coal, found in Pennsylvania, is its main mineral resource.

THE BIG IDEA

Water helped the Northeast to grow, providing transportation routes, fishing grounds, and water power for industry. This region now has many cities and a high population density.

But the waters of the Northeast have made it a center of trade, business, and industry. The North Atlantic Ocean is a rich source of fish. Excellent harbors helped ports to grow. The region's fast-flowing rivers provided power for early factories that made shoes, cloth, and other goods. River valleys became the routes for boats, wagons, railroads, and then highways. By the early 1900s, the Northeast was the world's most productive manufacturing region.

Cities on the Atlantic Ocean became international ports and shipbuilding centers. Their populations grew as people moved to the cities to work in new industries. Large numbers of European immigrants settled in the cities of the Northeast.

As cities grew they began to spread and run together. The far suburbs of one city reached to the suburbs of another. By the 1960s the area from Boston to Washington, D.C., became known as a **megalopolis**, or very large city made of several cities and their suburbs. Today about 40 million people, one seventh of the country's population, live in this megalopolis.

Some Northeast cities are losing population. As a result, city governments receive less in taxes and can provide fewer services.

Graphic Summary: *The Northeast*

Many large cities are found in the states of the Northeast.

Review Questions

1. Name two ways that rivers were important in helping the Northeast to grow.

2. **Map Skills** Which seven states of the Northeast border the Atlantic Ocean?

Name ______________________ Class ______________ Date ______________

Section 1: The Northeast

Guided Reading and Review

A. As You Read

Directions: *As you read Section 1, complete the chart below by writing three supporting details under each main idea.*

Main Idea A: The most valuable natural resource of the Northeast is its waters.

1. ____

____

2. ____

____

3. ____

____

Main Idea B: The cities of the Northeast grew in the 1800s and the early 1900s.

4. ____

____

5. ____

____

6. ____

____

B. Reviewing Vocabulary

Directions: *Complete the sentence by writing the correct term in the blank.*

7. A very large city created when the outer edges of one city reach the outer edges of another city is called a ______________.

Name ______________________ Class ______________ Date ______________

Section 2: The South

Guide to the Essentials

Text Summary

The South includes the city of Washington, D.C., the nation's capital. The region is rich in resources and has become a popular place to live and work.

> **THE BIG IDEA**
>
> **The South's warm climates and rich soils helped it prosper. Southern cities are growing rapidly as people move to the Sunbelt from other regions.**

The South is warmer than other regions. It receives plenty of precipitation. Mixed forests grow in the warm, wet climate. The western part of the region, Oklahoma and western Texas, are semiarid.

Native Americans grew crops in the rich soil of the region. Some Europeans built huge plantations and used enslaved workers to grow tobacco, rice, and cotton. Farming is still important in the South.

Texas's oil industry began in 1901, and oil is still important to the region. Some of the largest oil reserves in the United States are located in the South. In the 1950s, new businesses began coming to the South. The space industry developed in Florida, Alabama, and Texas. Some businesses moved from the Northeast to take advantage of the South's lower land and labor costs.

Thousands of people moved to the South in search of jobs. The region's mild climate also helped it to attract tourists and retired people. The states of the South and West became known as the **Sunbelt**.

The South has a very diverse population. Among the region's major cities are New Orleans, Miami, Atlanta, Houston, Dallas, and Washington, D.C.

Graphic Summary: *The South*

The South is bordered by both the Gulf of Mexico and the Atlantic Ocean.

Review Questions

1. What are two reasons for the South's rapid growth?

2. **Map Skills** Which states border the Gulf of Mexico?

Name ______________________ Class ______________ Date ______________

Section 2: The South

Guided Reading and Review

A. As You Read

Directions: *As you read Section 2, complete the chart below. In the right column, supply effects for each of the causes listed in the left column.*

Cause	Effect
Location near the Equator	1. ______________
Weather systems moving out of the Gulf of Mexico and the Caribbean	2. ______________
Subtropical climate and rich soils of most of the region	3. ______________
Rocky soil and steep slopes of Appalachia	4. ______________
Fast-moving streams of the Piedmont and large oil reserves	5. ______________
Cheaper land and lower labor costs	6. ______________
People looking for job opportunities and retirement locations	7. ______________
Migration of African Americans and Hispanics to the South	8. ______________

B. Reviewing Vocabulary

Directions: *Read the statements below. If a statement is true, write T in the blank. If it is false, write F.*

_____ **9.** A mangrove is a kind of tropical tree that grows in swampy ground along coastal areas.

_____ **10.** A marshy inlet of a lake or a river is known as a bayou.

_____ **11.** The fall line is an imaginary line between the Rocky Mountains and the Atlantic coastal plain.

_____ **12.** The band of southern states stretching from the Carolinas to Texas is called the Sunbelt.

Name ______________________ Class ______________ Date ______________

Section 3: The Midwest

Guide to the Essentials

Text Summary

The Midwest is often called "the nation's breadbasket" because the region's farms are among the most productive in the world. The export of farm products contributes to the wealth of the United States.

THE BIG IDEA

The climate and soil of the Midwest have made it a rich agricultural region. Industries grew because of transportation and natural resources.

Differences in climate and soil affect farming. There are also differences in the **growing season**, the average number of days between the last frost of spring and the first frost of fall. The growing season in southern Kansas is more than 200 days, while near the Canadian border it is less than 120 days.

The warmer, wetter areas of Illinois, Indiana, and Iowa raise corn, soybeans, and hogs. In the drier Great Plains states to the west, farmers grow wheat, oats, and sunflowers. The cooler northern parts of the region produce hay and dairy cattle. Technology has helped farmers grow more crops with fewer workers.

Business in many Midwestern cities and towns depends on farming. The Chicago Board of Trade is the largest **grain exchange**—a place where buyers and sellers make deals for grain.

Natural resources made the area a center of heavy manufacturing, oil and coal production, steel mills, and the auto industry. Water transportation helped industries and cities grow. Many large cities are on major rivers or the Great Lakes. The railroads also play an important part in shipping grain, livestock, and meat.

Graphic Summary: *The Midwest*

Four of the five Great Lakes are in the Midwest.

Review Questions

1. Why is the Midwest called "the nation's breadbasket"?

2. **Map Skills** Which six states of the Midwest border the Great Lakes?

Name ______________________ Class ______________ Date ______________

Section 3: The Midwest

Guided Reading and Review

A. As You Read

Directions: *As you read Section 3, organize information about Midwest farm products by completing the chart below.*

Place	Crops and Livestock
Warmer, wetter parts of Indiana, Illinois, and Iowa	**1.** ______________________
Drier Great Plains states	**2.** ______________________
States such as Wisconsin along the northern margins	**3.** ______________________

Directions: *As you continue to read, write down three supporting details for each main idea below.*

Main Idea A: Farming has changed from a small family enterprise to big business.

4. ______________________

5. ______________________

6. ______________________

Main Idea B: For several reasons, the Midwest has become the home to much heavy manufacturing.

7. ______________________

8. ______________________

9. ______________________

B. Reviewing Vocabulary

Directions: *Read the statements below. If a statement is true, write T in the blank. If it is false, write F.*

______ **10.** The dark-colored organic material created from the decay of plants and animals is called humus.

______ **11.** The growing season is the average amount of rainfall an area receives from early spring to late fall.

______ **12.** The place where grain is loaded, cleaned, mixed, and stored is called a grain elevator.

______ **13.** A grain exchange is a place where buyers and sellers store grain.

Name ______________ Class ______________ Date ______________

Section 4: The West

Guide to the Essentials

Text Summary

Water is the major factor affecting the West's natural resources, economic activity, and population density. Some areas have plenty of water, others have too little. Most of the region has either a semiarid or arid climate. Yet the western side of the mountains receives enough rain and has rich forests. Hawaii has a wet, tropical climate and tropical rain forests. Northern Alaska is mostly **tundra**, a cold, dry, treeless plain.

> **THE BIG IDEA**
> **The West's most outstanding feature is its landscape. The supply of water affects natural vegetation, economic activity, and where people live.**

Gold, silver, uranium, and other minerals are found in the Rocky Mountains and in the Sierra Nevada. People once came to the region hoping to get rich by finding gold and silver. Others set up businesses to serve the miners. Oil and natural gas are also found in the region. Forestry and fishing are major industries.

Cities in the West grew when the first transcontinental railroad was completed across the country in 1869. Los Angeles, California, is now the second largest city, after New York, in the United States. To support its growing population, Los Angeles must bring in water through **aqueducts**, pipes that carry water over long distances.

Alaska is the largest state but has a small population. Some places can be reached only by boat or airplane. Hawaii, made up of many islands in the Pacific Ocean, is located more than 2,000 miles (3,218 km) from the United States mainland.

Graphic Summary: *The West*

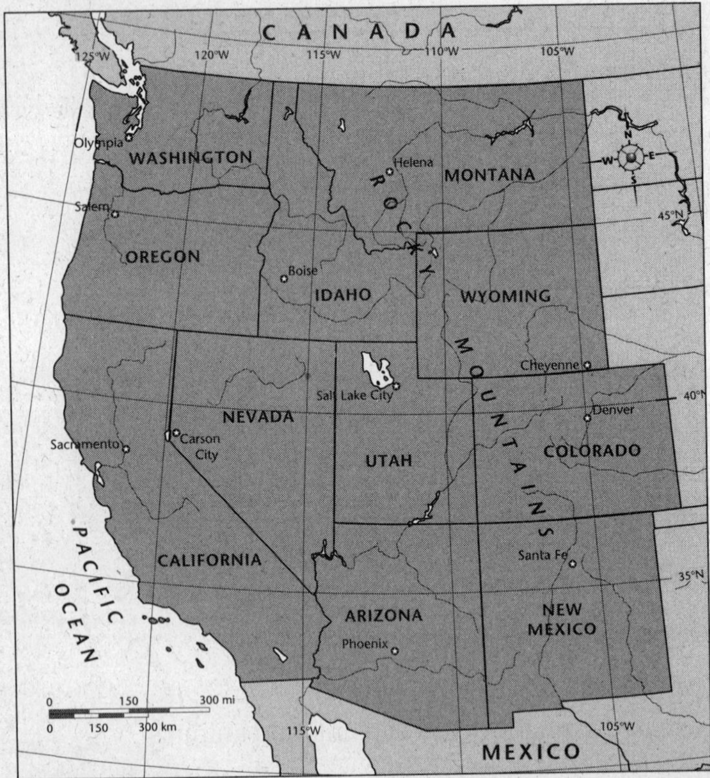

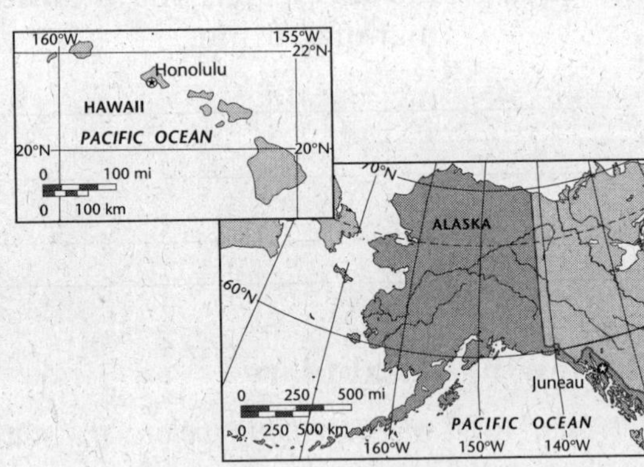

Mountains cover all the states in the West.

Review Questions

1. How does Los Angeles provide enough water for its population?
2. **Map Skills** What ocean borders the West?

Name ______________________ Class ______________ Date ______________

Section 4: The West

Guided Reading and Review

A. As You Read

Directions: *As you read Section 4, complete the chart below. In the right column, supply a resource, activity, or characteristic described by each sentence in the left column.*

Description	Resources, Activities, or Characteristics
The abundance or scarcity of this resource is the major factor affecting the West.	1. ______________
Along with uranium, these metals are resources that led to the growth of Western towns.	2. ______________
The discovery of this resource transformed the economy of Alaska in the 1960s.	3. ______________
This economic activity is important in the Pacific Coast states, as well as Hawaii and Alaska.	4. ______________
Nearly half of this comes from the Pacific Northwest.	5. ______________
The completion of this promoted the growth of Western cities.	6. ______________
Both Hawaii and Alaska are unique among Western states for this reason.	7. ______________

B. Reviewing Vocabulary

Directions: Complete the sentence by writing the correct term in the blank.

8. ______________ is a dry, treeless plain that sprouts grasses and mosses only in summer when the top layer of soil thaws.

9. A large pipe that carries water over long distances is called a(n) ______________.

Name ______________ Class ______________ Date ______________

Chapter 7

Test

Identifying Main Ideas

Directions: Write the letter of the correct answer in the blank provided. (10 points each)

____ **1. What helped the Northeast grow?**
A. gold, silver, uranium, and other minerals
B. lots of good soil
C. a semiarid climate
D. water for transportation, fishing, and water power

____ **2. What is a megalopolis?**
A. a large city
B. a small city with modern technology and good transportation
C. several large cities and their suburbs, which run into one another
D. several large cities that have poor populations

____ **3. Which two features helped the South to grow?**
A. good soil and a warm climate
B. mineral wealth and a dry climate
C. good soil and mountains
D. warm climate and rich fishing areas

____ **4. What is a fairly new industry in the South?**
A. cotton farms
B. the space industry
C. cotton mills
D. copper mining

____ **5. What is the Sunbelt?**
A. a region where people depend on solar power for energy
B. the warm area of the South and the West
C. a place where people study the sun's effect on the earth
D. the part of the earth that gets the most sun all year

____ **6. Which statement is true of the Midwest's farms?**
A. They are some of the most productive farms in the world.
B. They do not help the United States economy.
C. They do not use up-to-date technology.
D. Their main crop is cotton.

____ **7. What is a grain exchange?**
A. a place where grain is stored
B. a farm where grain is grown
C. a store where grain is sold
D. a place where buyers and sellers make deals for grain

____ **8. What climate is most common in the West?**
A. wet and rainy
B. arid or semiarid
C. tundra
D. tropical

____ **9. What factor in the West is most important in where people and businesses are located?**
A. the supply of water
B. the supply of minerals
C. forests
D. the fishing industry

____ **10. What is an aqueduct?**
A. a good supply of anything
B. an arid or semiarid region
C. a pipe for carrying oil
D. a pipe for carrying water long distances

Name ____________ Class ____________ Date ____________

Chapter 8 Canada

Vocabulary
bedrock
maritime
province
separatism
secede

Vocabulary Development

When you come across a word you do not know, you can often figure out its meaning from the word's context. The context is the parts of the sentence or paragraph that provide clues to the unfamiliar word's definition.

Directions: *Look at the sentences below. Then, write your own definition of each underlined word based on the context clues contained in each sentence. After doing this, check your definition against the definition provided in your textbook.*

1. The ten provinces of Canada have more political power than the fifty states of the United States.

____

____

2. Marked by hundreds of bays, inlets, and harbors, the Atlantic Provinces rely on maritime industries.

____

____

3. The Canadian Shield—an area of exposed bedrock, gravel, and sand—remains a wilderness of forests, lakes, and rivers.

____

____

4. Many people from Quebec favor separatism because of Quebec's unique French history and culture.

____

____

5. A referendum in 1995 to allow Quebec to secede from the rest of Canada failed.

____

____

Name ____________________ Class ______________ Date ______________

Section 1: Regions of Canada

Guide to the Essentials

Text Summary

Canada's ten provinces are similar to U.S. states, but with more power to govern themselves.

The four Atlantic provinces are called **maritime** provinces, meaning they border the sea. These small provinces are hilly, covered with forests, and have many good bays and inlets. The Grand Banks provide excellent fishing, but some areas have been overfished.

THE BIG IDEA

Canada has five regions, rugged landscapes, and a cold climate. Quebec and Ontario are Canada's heartland.

The heart of Canada's population and economy is in Ontario and Quebec, the Great Lakes–St. Lawrence area. It has three land areas: the Canadian Shield, with poor soil, a cold climate, and abundant minerals; the Hudson Bay Lowland, a wetlands between the Canadian Shield and Hudson Bay; and the St. Lawrence Lowlands, with rich soil, a mild climate, and 60 percent of Canada's population.

The three Prairie Provinces produce most of Canada's wheat and cattle. Oil and natural gas in Alberta provide wealth for the region. More than half the people in the Prairie Provinces live in cities, most of which lie along the railroads.

British Columbia has plenty of natural resources, including salmon, forests, and minerals. Vancouver, its largest city, is Canada's main Pacific port.

The northern area, 40 percent of Canada's land, has a harsh climate and rough land that make it hard to reach mineral wealth. The area includes the Yukon Territory, Northwest Territories, and as of 1999, Nunavut. This newest province was carved from the Northwest Territories as part of a land claim settlement with the native peoples.

Graphic Summary: *Regions of Canada*

Region	Province or Territory
Atlantic Provinces	New Brunswick Newfoundland Nova Scotia Prince Edward Island
Great Lakes and St. Lawrence Provinces	Ontario Quebec
Prairie Provinces	Alberta Manitoba Saskatchewan
British Columbia	British Columbia
Northern Territories	Northwest Territories Nunavut Yukon Territory

Canada has five distinct regions.

Review Questions

1. In which region do more than half of Canada's people live?

2. **Map Skills** What are Canada's three Prairie Provinces?

Name ______________________ Class ______________ Date ______________

Section 1: Regions of Canada

Guided Reading and Review

A. As You Read

Directions: As you read Section 1, fill in the chart below by providing details about the regions of Canada.

Atlantic Provinces

Names: **1.** ______________ **2.** ______________

3. ______________ **4.** ______________

Major landforms/landscapes: **5.** ______________

Economic activities: **6.** ______________

The Great Lakes and St. Lawrence Provinces

Names: **7.** ______________ **8.** ______________

Major landforms/landscapes: **9.** ______________

10. ______________

11. ______________

Economic activities: **12.** ______________

Prairie Provinces

Names: **13.** ______________ **14.** ______________ **15.** ______________

Major landforms/landscapes: **16.** ______________

Economic activities: **17.** ______________

British Columbia and the Northern Territories

Names: **18.** ______________ **19.** ______________

20. ______________ **21.** ______________

Major landforms/landscapes: **22.** ______________

23. ______________

Economic activities: **24.** ______________

B. Reviewing Vocabulary

Directions: Define the following terms.

25. province ______________

26. maritime ______________

27. lock ______________

28. bedrock ______________

Name ______________________ Class ______________ Date ______________

Section 2: The Search for a National Identity

Guide to the Essentials

Text Summary

THE BIG IDEA

Canadians have strong ties to their countries of origin, especially Britain and France. The government tries to encourage strong ties to Canada as well as diversity.

Canada's lack of national unity mainly results from diversity among its people. Canada's history helps to explain this challenge of unity.

Many Canadians identify more strongly with regional and ethnic groups than with the nation. The Inuit and the Native Americans first populated the land when their ancestors migrated to North America thousands of years ago. The British and French arrived in the 1500s and began colonizing the region, devastating the native population with European diseases and warfare.

France and Britain battled over the land and fought four wars in North America. By 1763, France surrendered all of its land. French colonists were allowed to remain in Canada, and in 1774 the British government passed laws to ensure they would be able to maintain their own language, laws, and culture.

Britain continued to rule Canada directly until 1867. Then Canada was given its own government, but many decisions were still made by Britain. In 1931, Canada became a fully independent country. The government agreed to protect the rights of French-speaking citizens.

Although French and English are both official languages, only 15 percent of Canadians speak both. The majority of French-speakers live in the province of Quebec. French Canadians feel discriminated against, claiming they are denied jobs because they are of French descent. Many want Quebec to **secede**, or withdraw, from the rest of Canada. This movement, called **separatism**, would make Quebec an independent country.

Although most Canadians have British or French ancestors, there are many immigrants from other parts of Europe as well as from Asia.

Graphic Summary: *Ethnic Composition of Canada*

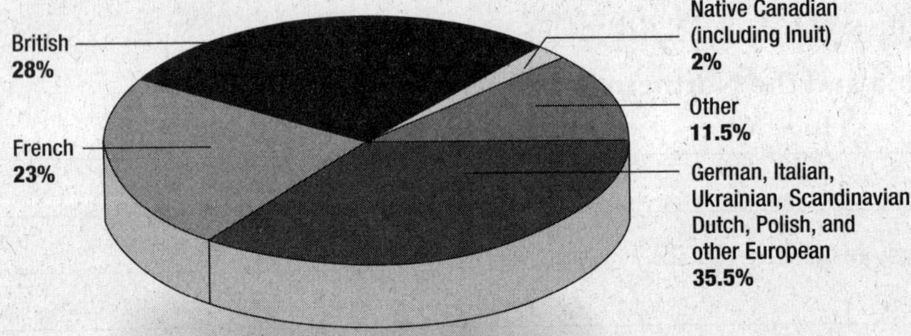

Most Canadians trace their roots to the countries of Europe.

Review Questions

1. What do separatists in Quebec want?

2. **Graph Skills** What country in Europe is the original place of origin for most Canadians?

Name ______________________ Class ______________ Date ______________

Section 2: The Search for a National Identity

Guided Reading and Review

A. As You Read

Directions: *As you read Section 2, fill in the chart below by supplying the missing information.*

Question	Answer(s)
What is the ancestry of the largest ethnic group in Canada?	**1.** ______________
What two groups of people were the first to live in Canada?	**2.** ______________ **3.** ______________
Which country surrendered all of its claim to Canadian territory after the British and French wars of the 1700s?	**4.** ______________
When did Canada become a completely independent country?	**5.** ______________
In which province do most French-speaking Canadians live?	**6.** ______________
What are Canada's official languages?	**7.** ______________ **8.** ______________
What do the separatists seek?	**9.** ______________
From what regions of the world have immigrants most recently been coming to Canada?	**10.** ______________

B. Reviewing Vocabulary

Directions: *Define the following terms.*

11. separatism ______________________________

____

12. secede ______________________________

____

Name ____________ Class ____________ Date ____________

Section 3: Canada Today

Guide to the Essentials

Text Summary

Canada is a prosperous nation with a stable government and a high standard of living. Yet it faces many challenges.

One challenge for Canada is extracting natural resources without harming the environment. Another challenge is urbanization. Today, 77 percent of the nation's population lives in cities. Canada must find a way to provide housing and services, control pollution, and prevent overcrowding in these urban areas.

THE BIG IDEA

Canada's size and location promote cooperation with the United States and the rest of the world. Yet Canada still faces the challenges of geography.

Canada and the United States share the longest undefended border in the world. Travelers pay **customs**, or fees, to bring goods from one country to the other. These nations also connect on a cultural level. People living close to the border can enjoy radio and television programs from stations in both countries. Also, professional sports leagues include teams from both nations.

Another important link between Canada and the United States is economics. Canada buys nearly 25 percent of all U.S. exports, and the United States buys about 85 percent of Canadian exports. While these countries have many ties, Canadians consider the relationship uneven. Canadians are generally aware of events happening in the United States, while Americans tend to know little about Canada.

Canada's major ports on the Atlantic and Pacific oceans make it a major trading partner with many nations of the world. Canada has a special relationship with fellow member nations of the Commonwealth of Nations. Canada also works to keep peace in many parts of the world.

Graphic Summary: *Comparing the United States and Canada*

Country	Population	Life Expectancy (years)	Per Capita GDP (in U.S. $)
Canada	32,507,874	79.9	29,700
United States	293,027,571	77.4	37,800

Source: *The World Factbook 2004*

The population of the United States is about nine times that of Canada. Both countries have a high standard of living.

Review Questions

1. What challenge does Canada face in developing its natural resources?

2. **Chart Skills** Which country has a higher per capita GDP?

Name ______________________ Class ______________ Date ______________

Section 3: Canada Today

Guided Reading and Review

A. As You Read

Directions: *As you read Section 3, complete the chart below by writing two supporting details under each main idea.*

Main Idea A: Canada faces many challenges with its natural resources and urbanization.

1. ____

2. ____

Main Idea B: Canada has several important links with the United States.

3. ____

4. ____

Main Idea C: Canada maintains its links with the world in several ways.

5. ____

6. ____

B. Reviewing Vocabulary

Directions: *Define the following terms.*

7. customs ____

8. tariff ____

9. NAFTA ____

Name ______________________ Class ______________ Date ______________

Chapter **8** **Test**

Identifying Main Ideas

Directions: *Write the letter of the correct answer in the blank provided. (10 points each)*

____ **1. What region has more than half of Canada's people?**
A. Atlantic Provinces
B. Ontario and Quebec
C. Prairie Provinces
D. Northwest Territories

____ **2. What does maritime mean?**
A. hilly and rocky
B. covered with forests
C. near the ocean
D. small

____ **3. Where do most of the people in the Prairie Provinces live?**
A. near the ocean
B. on wheat farms
C. on cattle ranches
D. in cities

____ **4. Why are many of Canada's minerals hard to reach?**
A. They are found in a harsh climate.
B. Canada does not have machinery to remove them.
C. The land is owned by Britain.
D. Nobody knows where they are.

____ **5. What happened to the French-speaking people after Britain defeated France?**
A. They had to leave the land.
B. They could stay if they stopped speaking French.
C. They could stay and keep their language and culture.
D. They formed their own country.

____ **6. What do separationists in Quebec want?**
A. to become an independent country
B. to make English-speaking Canadians learn to speak French
C. to have their own province
D. to live in other parts of Canada

____ **7. Which of the following is a challenge for Canada?**
A. trade with the world
B. animal protection
C. energy production
D. urbanization

____ **8. Why do Canadians consider their relationship with the United States uneven?**
A. Canada buys U.S. products, but the United States does not buy Canada's.
B. Canadians must pay customs on U.S. goods, but Americans do not have to pay customs on Canadian goods.
C. Canadians usually know more about the United States than U.S. citizens know about Canada.
D. Canadian professional sports teams cannot compete against teams in the United States.

____ **9. Which feature helps link Canada to the rest of the world?**
A. location of its major ports on both the Atlantic and the Pacific oceans
B. its vast size
C. its proximity to the United States
D. its diverse population

____ **10. What are customs on goods?**
A. the prices paid for goods
B. labels that explain how to use goods
C. an agreement that no taxes will be paid on goods from another country
D. fees paid when goods are brought from one country to another

Name ______________________ Class ______________ Date ______________

Chapter 9

Regional Atlas: Introduction to Latin America

Vocabulary

caudillo
cay
conquistador
coral
cultural convergence
El Niño
hurricane
mestizo
mulatto
pampas

Vocabulary Development

Directions: *Divide the vocabulary words listed into the four categories below, based on each word's significance in the chapter you have just read about Latin America.*

History	Physical Characteristics	Climates	People and Culture

Directions: *Write a sentence on each of the following topics using what you have learned in Chapter 9. Use two vocabulary words in each sentence.*

Topic: History

____

____

Topic: Physical Characteristics

____

____

Topic: Climates

____

____

Topic: People and Culture

____

____

Name ______________________ Class ______________ Date ______________

Regional Atlas: Latin America

Guide to the Essentials

Text Summary

> **THE BIG IDEA**
>
> **Latin America includes Mexico, Central America, the Caribbean islands, and South America. The region has a variety of climates, landforms, and resources. All the countries were once European colonies.**

Native Americans formed the Inca, Aztec, and Mayan empires in Latin America. Explorers from Spain and Portugal conquered these complex societies and much of Latin America. As a result, many Latin Americans are **mestizos**, people of mixed Native American and European descent. Others are descendants of Africans who were brought to work as slaves on Latin American plantations.

In the 1700s and 1800s, Latin Americans fought for independence, which created republics but not democracy. In the 1900s, Latin Americans struggled for reform, eventually bringing about democratic governments and economic gains in a number of countries.

Mountains dominate much of Latin America, but the region also includes the **pampas**, grassy plains in southeastern South America. The Amazon rain forest is one of the largest ecosystems in the world. Islands, some of which are the tops of underwater mountains, are found in the Caribbean.

Atmospheric and ocean currents affect Latin America's climate. These currents can create **tropical storms**, with winds of at least 39 miles per hour. These can become **hurricanes**, with winds of at least 74 miles per hour, which devastate islands and coastal regions.

As in other parts of the world, three major economic systems are found in Latin America. A **market economy** allows economic decisions to be determined by supply and demand, while the government makes those decisions in a **command economy.** Under a **traditional economy**, families produce goods and services for their own use.

Graphic Summary: *Latin America*

Latin America stretches from Mexico's northern border to the southern tip of South America.

Review Questions

1. What are the three different economic systems in Latin America?

2. **Map Skills** What bodies of water border Central America?

Name ______________________ Class ______________ Date ______________

Regional Atlas: Latin America

Guided Reading and Review

A. As You Read

Directions: *As you work through the Regional Atlas, complete the chart below by writing two details about each Latin American topic listed.*

Physical Characteristics	**1.** ______________ **2.** ______________
Climates	**3.** ______________ **4.** ______________
Ecosystems	**5.** ______________ **6.** ______________
People and Cultures	**7.** ______________ **8.** ______________
Economics, Technology, and Environment	**9.** ______________ **10.** ______________
Types of Economic Systems	**11.** ______________ **12.** ______________

B. Reviewing Vocabulary

Directions: *Define the following terms.*

13. conquistador ______________

14. cultural convergence ______________

15. *caudillo* ______________

16. pampas ______________

17. cay ______________

18. coral ______________

19. tropical storm ______________

20. hurricane ______________

Name ______________________ Class ______________ Date ______________

Chapter 9

Test

Identifying Main Ideas

Directions: *Write the letter of the correct answer in the blank provided. (10 points each)*

____ **1. What geographic feature dominates Latin America?**
A. Amazon rain forest
B. mountains
C. pampas
D. islands

____ **2. Some Caribbean islands are**
A. the tops of underwater mountains.
B. in the mountains.
C. part of El Niño.
D. near the Amazon River.

____ **3. What is the pampas?**
A. the uppermost layer of a rain forest where tree branches meet
B. the skeletons of tiny sea animals
C. grassy plains in southeastern South America
D. the lowland area drained by a river and its tributaries

____ **4. Under what kind of economy does the government make all economic decisions?**
A. market economy
B. traditional economy
C. command economy
D. democratic economy

____ **5. Who were the first people to live in Latin America?**
A. Spanish
B. Portuguese
C. mestizos
D. Native Americans

____ **6. From which two countries did most Europeans come to Latin America?**
A. England and France
B. Spain and Portugal
C. Germany and Italy
D. Belgium and Spain

____ **7. What is a mestizo?**
A. a Latin American Indian
B. a person who was born in Europe and lives in South America
C. a person of mixed European and Native American descent
D. a person whose ancestors came from Africa

____ **8. What is a hurricane?**
A. a tropical storm with winds of only 10 miles per hour
B. a warm water current in the Pacific Ocean
C. a cold water current in the Atlantic Ocean
D. a tropical storm with winds of at least 74 miles per hour

____ **9. Who were brought to work as slaves on Latin American plantations?**
A. Amazonians
B. mestizos
C. Mexicans
D. Africans

____ **10. Which place is one of the largest ecosystems in the world?**
A. the Amazon rain forest
B. the mountains of western South America
C. Central America
D. Mexico

Name ______________ Class ______________ Date ______________

Chapter 10

Mexico

Vocabulary
cash crop
hacienda
irrigation
migrant worker
peninsula
plateau
sinkhole
subsistence farming

Vocabulary Development

Directions: *Match each term in Column A with the correct definition in Column B.*

Column A	Column B
1. cash crop	**a.** an area of high, flat land
2. hacienda	**b.** a strip of land surrounded by water on three sides
3. irrigation	**c.** the artificial watering of farmland by storing and distributing water from reservoirs or rivers
4. migrant worker	**d.** forms when the roof of a cavern collapses
5. peninsula	**e.** growing only enough crops to meet a family's needs
6. plateau	**f.** farm crop grown for sale and profit
7. sinkhole	**g.** large, Spanish-owned estate of land
8. subsistence farming	**h.** landless peasant who travels from place to place to cultivate or harvest crops

Directions: *Categorize the vocabulary words as either geography terms or culture terms in the diagram below.*

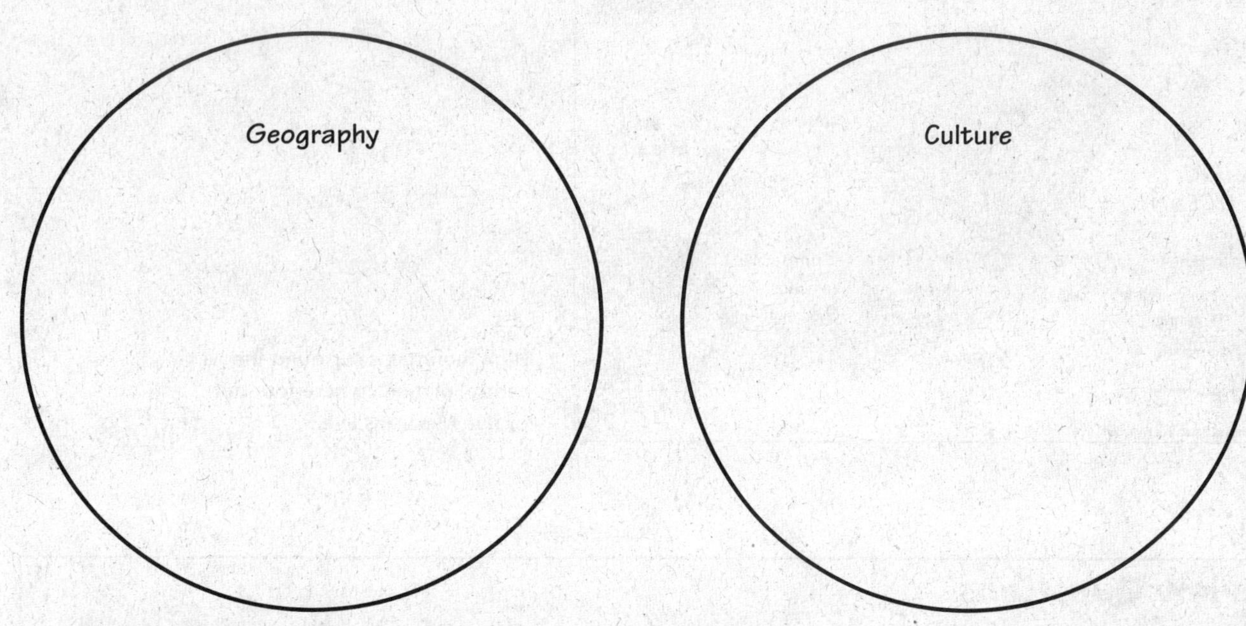

Name ______________________ Class ______________ Date ______________

Section 1: Geography of Mexico

Guide to the Essentials

Text Summary

THE BIG IDEA

The central plateau is Mexico's heartland. Most of Mexico is mountainous. The coastal areas are different from the rest of the country.

Mountains dominate Mexico's geography. The Sierra Madre Occidental—the western Sierra Madre—is Mexico's largest mountain range. On the east, the Sierra Madre Oriental runs parallel to the eastern coast. The central plateau—the Plateau of Mexico—is Mexico's largest region and lies between the two mountain ranges. About four fifths of Mexico's people live on the plateau. It has large cities, rich farmland, and plenty of rain. Large numbers of people have moved to Mexico City in search of a better life.

Many active volcanoes border the southern edge of the central plateau. Earthquakes often shake the land, killing people and causing serious damage. Although the southern part of the central plateau is in the tropics, its climate is not tropical. That is because the plateau's high elevation keeps temperatures mild.

The plains of the northern Pacific coast are hot and dry. Farmers use **irrigation**, the artificial watering of farmland, to raise wheat, cotton, and other crops. By contrast, the Baja California **peninsula**, a strip of land sticking out into the ocean, is mostly mountainous desert.

Along the southern Pacific coast, mountains lie close to the ocean. The tropical climate and beautiful scenery have made tourism an important business. The Gulf coastal plain is rich in oil and natural gas. The Yucatán Peninsula is mostly flat. Ancient Mayan ruins attract tourists.

Graphic Summary: *Mexico: Political and Physical*

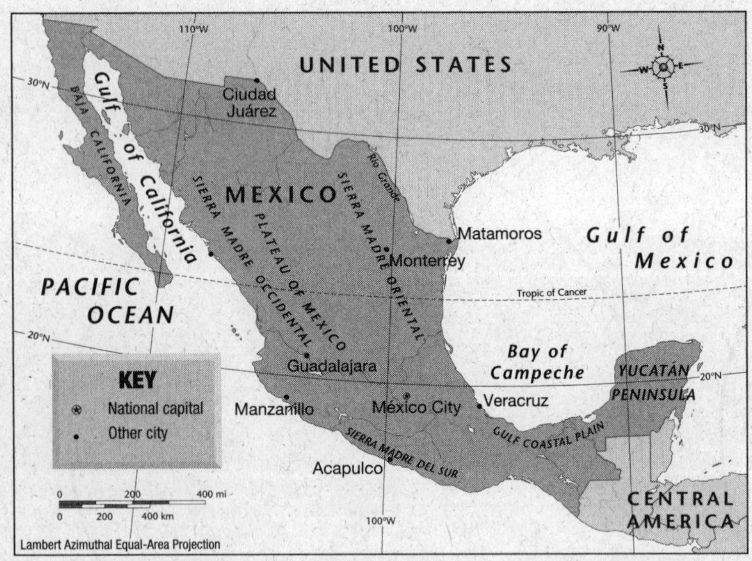

High mountains surround the central plateau, where four out of five Mexicans live.

Review Questions

1. In what part of Mexico do most of its people live?
2. **Map Skills** What peninsula is in northwestern Mexico?

Name ______________________ Class ______________ Date ______________

Section 1: Geography of Mexico

Guided Reading and Review

A. As You Read

Directions: *As you read Section 1, complete the chart by describing the physical and human features of each region of Mexico.*

Region	Physical and Human Features
Central Plateau	**1.** ______________________
Northern Pacific Coast	**2.** ______________________
Southern Pacific Coast	**3.** ______________________
Gulf Coastal Plain	**4.** ______________________
Yucatán Peninsula	**5.** ______________________

B. Reviewing Vocabulary

Directions: *Define the following terms.*

6. plateau ______________________

7. peninsula ______________________

8. irrigation ______________________

9. sinkhole ______________________

Name ______________________ Class ______________ Date ______________

Section 2: A Place of Three Cultures

Guide to the Essentials

Text Summary

THE BIG IDEA

Three cultures—Indian, colonial Spanish, and modern Mexican—form Mexico today. Most Mexicans live in cities. Poverty is a problem in both cities and rural areas.

The Aztecs built the most powerful empire in early Mexico. Spanish soldiers conquered the Aztecs in 1521. They built Mexico City on the ruins of the Aztec capital of Tenochtitlán. Mexico became part of the Spanish colony of New Spain.

In 1810, Miguel Hidalgo, a priest, began a rebellion against Spanish rule. Mexico won independence in 1821 but was ruled by military dictators.

After the Mexican Revolution, which lasted from 1910 to 1920, Mexico had a new constitution. It established a democratic republic. However, one political party held power until 2000.

The government bought land from large landowners and gave it to people who did not have any land. This policy is called **land redistribution**. Most of the reclaimed land is owned by the members of rural communities that practice subsistence farming. Approximately one third of Mexico's farms are huge commercial farms. They raise **cash crops**, farm crops grown for sale and profit.

Millions of Mexicans have no land and cannot find work. Many become **migrant workers** who travel from place to place where extra workers are needed to help grow and harvest crops.

Three quarters of Mexico's population live in urban areas. Most are very poor, although there is a growing middle class. Two of Mexico's most important industries are oil and tourism. Factories along the U.S. border assemble goods sold in the United States.

Graphic Summary: *The Three Cultures of Mexico*

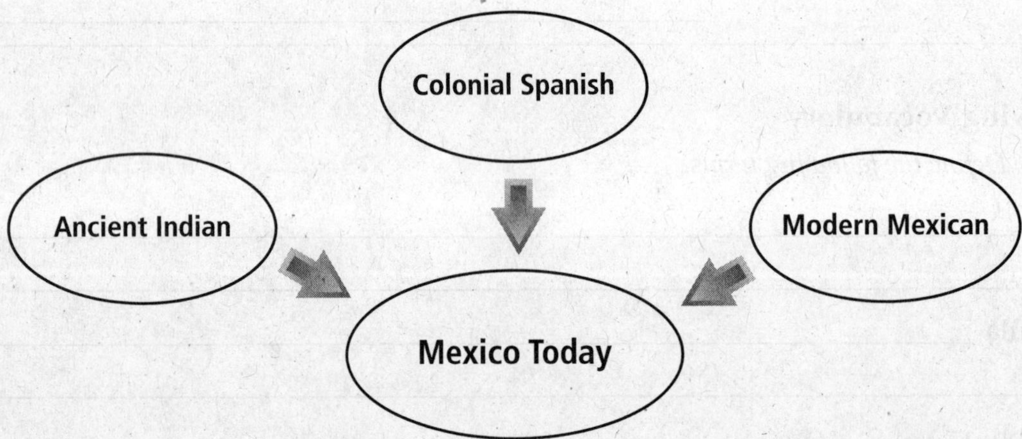

Three cultures have made Mexico what it is today.

Review Questions

1. Name two of Mexico's most important industries.

2. **Diagram Skills** What are the three cultures that make up Mexico today?

Name ______________________ Class ______________ Date ______________

Section 2: A Place of Three Cultures

Guided Reading and Review

A. As You Read

Directions: As you read Section 2, answer the following questions.

1. How did Spain make Mexico a colony? ______________________________

2. How did Mexico become a democracy? ______________________________

3. How has rural life in Mexico changed since 1920? ______________________________

4. What are Mexico's major industries? Why? ______________________________

B. Reviewing Vocabulary

Directions: Match the definitions in Column I with the terms in Column II. Write the correct letter in each blank.

Column I

_____ 5. farmland owned collectively by farmers

_____ 6. commercial farms

_____ 7. large, Spanish-owned estates of lands run as farms or ranches

_____ 8. growing only enough crops to meet a family's needs

_____ 9. people who travel from place to place to do seasonal work on farms

_____ 10. factories that assemble products almost exclusively for consumers in the United States

_____ 11. a government policy of breaking up haciendas and distributing the land

_____ 12. farm produce grown for sale in local or world markets

_____ 13. a free trade agreement between Canada, the United States, and Mexico

Column II

a. haciendas
b. land redistribution
c. *ejidos*
d. subsistence farming
e. *latifundios*
f. cash crops
g. migrant workers
h. NAFTA
i. *maquiladoras*

Name ______________________ Class ______________ Date ______________

Chapter

10 Test

Identifying Main Ideas

Directions: Write the letter of the correct answer in the blank provided. (10 points each)

____ **1. Most Mexicans live in**
A. the central plateau.
B. the Sierra Madre Occidental.
C. the Sierra Madre Oriental.
D. Baja California.

____ **2. What keeps temperatures mild in Mexico's central plateau?**
A. irrigation
B. elevation
C. ocean breezes
D. rain

____ **3. What makes the plains of the northern Pacific coast good for farming?**
A. It has a mild climate and plenty of rain.
B. Farmers use irrigation to water the crops.
C. Many rivers water the land.
D. Farmers bring in soil from other parts of Mexico.

____ **4. An important industry in the southern Pacific coast is**
A. farming.
B. oil.
C. tourism.
D. ranching.

____ **5. What is an important mineral resource in the Gulf coastal plain?**
A. gold
B. tin
C. coal
D. oil

____ **6. What was New Spain?**
A. a part of Mexico
B. a colony of Spain
C. the Aztec capital city
D. the Spanish capital city

____ **7. Until 2000, Mexico's government was controlled by**
A. the Aztecs.
B. the Spanish.
C. New Spain.
D. one political party.

____ **8. What event made Mexico an independent country?**
A. the rebellion against Spain that began in 1810
B. the Mexican Revolution that began in 1910
C. the land distribution that gave land to landless farmers
D. the conquest of the Aztecs

____ **9. What is land redistribution?**
A. planting new crops
B. dividing large farms and giving land to people without land
C. taking land from small farmers to create large farms
D. raising cash crops on large farms

____ **10. A migrant worker is a person who**
A. works in the tourist industry.
B. moves to a city to work in a factory.
C. travels from place to place to work on farms and harvest crops.
D. belongs to a farming community that practices subsistence farming.

Name ______________________ Class ______________ Date ______________

Chapter 11

Central America and the Caribbean

Vocabulary
archipelago
coral island
guerrilla
isthmus
leeward
windward

Vocabulary Development

Directions: *Write the correct vocabulary term on the line to complete each sentence below.*

1. A(n) ________________ is a narrow strip of land, with water on both sides, that connects two larger bodies of land.
2. A(n) ________________ is an opponent to a government who organizes armed forces outside the regular army.
3. ________________ refers to land that faces the wind.
4. A(n) ________________ is a group of islands.
5. A(n) ________________ is an island in the Caribbean created by the remains of tiny sea animals called coral polyps.
6. ________________ refers to land that faces away from the wind.

Directions: *Write a paragraph that describes the physical characteristics of Central America and the Caribbean. Use at least five vocabulary terms in your paragraph.*

____

____

____

____

____

____

____

____

____

____

____

Name ______________________ Class ______________ Date ______________

Section 1: Central America

Guide to the Essentials

Text Summary

THE BIG IDEA

Central America has many landscapes and climates. Most people are poor farmers, but power is held by a small number of very rich people. This has led to violent political conflicts.

Central America is an **isthmus**, a narrow strip of land connecting two larger land areas. The larger areas are the continents of North America and South America.

In 1914, the Panama Canal opened. It allowed ships to cross the isthmus and travel between the Atlantic and Pacific oceans. Ships no longer had to travel around the tip of South America.

Seven small countries make up Central America (see map). There are three major landforms—mountains, the Caribbean lowlands, and the Pacific coastal plain. Each region has a different climate. The rugged mountains, the core of the region, are difficult to cross and have caused transportation problems.

Central America's population includes Indians, Europeans (mostly Spanish), mestizos, and people of African descent. Most Central Americans are poor farmers with little political power. The wealthiest people, Europeans and mestizos, are mainly plantation owners. They dominate government in the region. There is a small but growing middle class.

Armed conflicts have been part of Central America's history. A shortage of farmland is one cause of unrest. Another cause is that governments mainly serve the interests of the wealthy. People opposed to those governments have sometimes organized **guerrilla** movements, armed forces outside the regular army. Guerrillas often fight in small bands against the government-controlled army. Cease-fires in several countries have brought hopes of peace.

Graphic Summary: *Central America*

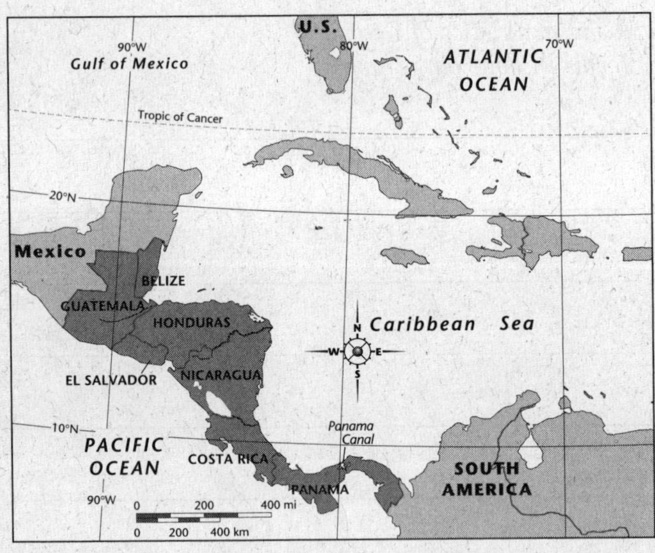

Central America is made up of seven small countries.

Review Questions

1. What is the main occupation of most people in Central America?

2. **Map Skills** Which five countries of Central America border both the Pacific Ocean and the Caribbean Sea?

Name ______________________ Class ______________ Date ______________

Section 1: Central America

Guided Reading and Review

A. As You Read

Directions: *As you read Section 1, complete the chart below about Central America by supplying the missing question or answer.*

Question	Answer(s)
1. ______________________	a mountainous core; Caribbean lowlands; the Pacific coastal plain
What are the four main groups of people of Central America?	**2.** ____________ **3.** ____________ **4.** ____________ **5.** ____________
What classes exist in Central America today?	**6.** ______________________
What are the two extremes of Central American farms?	**7.** ______________________ **8.** ______________________
9. ______________________	shortage of farmland; unequal distribution of farmland; favored treatment of the wealthy

B. Reviewing Vocabulary

Directions: *Complete each sentence by writing the correct term in the blank.*

10. Panama is an ______________, a narrow strip of land with water on both sides that connects two larger bodies of land.

11. ______________ forces are armed units not part of a country's regular army.

Name ______________________ Class ______________ Date ______________

Section 2: The Caribbean Islands

Guide to the Essentials

Text Summary

The Caribbean islands are divided into three groups: the Greater Antilles, the Lesser Antilles, and the Bahamas. Most islands lie in the tropics.

THE BIG IDEA

The Caribbean islands, located in the tropics, have three main island groups. Many people leave the islands to find work.

The Bahamas form an **archipelago**, or group of islands. Most Lesser Antilles islands form another archipelago. The Greater Antilles includes the four largest islands—Cuba, Jamaica, Hispaniola, and Puerto Rico. Hispaniola is divided into two countries—Haiti and the Dominican Republic.

Mountainous islands are the tops of volcanic mountains. Some volcanoes are still active. The flatter islands are **coral islands**. They were created by the remains of tiny sea animals called coral polyps.

Sea and wind affect the climate. Ocean water keeps temperatures mild and humidity high. Winds affect the amount of rainfall. Islands that face the wind, or **windward** islands, get a lot of rain. The **leeward** islands face away from the winds and receive much less rain.

Many Caribbean people are descendants of Africans who were enslaved by European colonists and brought to work on plantations. Other people are descendants of immigrants from Asia who came after slavery ended. Many people are descended from Europeans or native Indians.

Many Caribbean people depend on farming. They grow sugar, bananas, coconuts, cocoa, rice, and cotton. Others work in industries related to farming, such as packaging rice products. The islands' beauty attracts tourists, but few islanders benefit from tourism. Many people leave the islands to find work or escape political unrest.

Graphic Summary: *The Caribbean Islands*

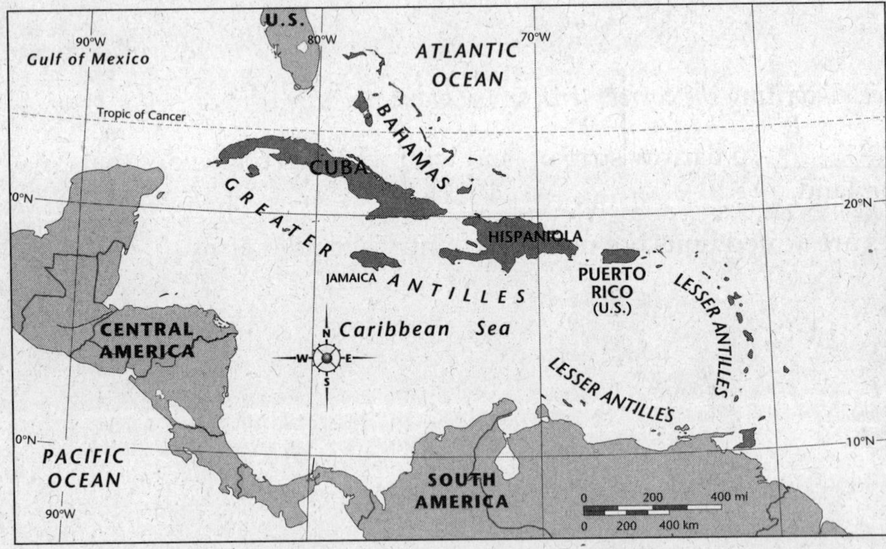

Many islands make up the Caribbean island region.

Review Questions

1. Which islands get more rain, windward islands or leeward islands?

2. **Map Skills** What bodies of water surround the Caribbean islands?

Name ______________________ Class ______________ Date ______________

Section 2: The Caribbean Islands

Guided Reading and Review

A. As You Read

Directions: *As you read about the Caribbean islands in Section 2, fill in the charts below with details for each category listed.*

Caribbean Island Groups		
Three Major Groups	**Types of Island Formations**	**Climate of Islands**
1. ______________	**4.** ______________ ______________	**7.** ______________ ______________ ______________ ______________
2. ______________	**5.** ______________ ______________	
3. ______________	**6.** ______________ ______________	

People of the Islands (non-Europeans)	
8. ______________	**9.** ______________

Interaction and Movement	
Economic Activities	**Reasons for Migration**
10. ______________	**12.** ______________ ______________ ______________
11. ______________	

B. Reviewing Vocabulary

Directions: *Complete each sentence by writing the correct term in the blank.*

13. The Bahamas are a group of islands, or a(n) ______________.

14. All of the Bahamas are ______________, islands formed by the remains of tiny, soft-bodied sea animals.

15. The side of the Caribbean islands that *faces* the wind—or the ______________ side—receives heavy rainfall.

16. On the side of the Caribbean islands *away* from the wind—the ______________ side—the amount of rainfall is much less.

Name ____________________ Class ____________ Date ____________

Chapter 11 Test

Identifying Main Ideas

Directions: *Write the letter of the correct answer in the blank provided. (10 points each)*

____ **1. What is the name for a narrow strip of land that connects two larger land areas?**
A. canal
B. isthmus
C. mountains
D. coastal plain

____ **2. One cause of conflict in Central America has been**
A. too much farmland.
B. democratic governments.
C. a shortage of farmland.
D. too few people.

____ **3. The mountains of Central America**
A. are on the coasts.
B. cause transportation problems.
C. make transportation easy.
D. are in only two countries.

____ **4. Which sentence best describes most of the people of Central America?**
A. They are very poor farmers with little political power.
B. They are wealthy people who own large plantations.
C. They are members of a large middle class.
D. They are members of the army.

____ **5. What is a guerrilla?**
A. an animal found only in Central America
B. a member of a government army
C. a member of a group that fights against the army
D. a wealthy owner of a Central American plantation

____ **6. What is an archipelago?**
A. a group of islands
B. any large island
C. an island that receives a lot of rain
D. an island that receives little rain

____ **7. Which two countries make up the island of Hispaniola?**
A. Jamaica and Cuba
B. Haiti and the Dominican Republic
C. Puerto Rico and Jamaica
D. Haiti and Jamaica

____ **8. What kind of rainfall would you expect on the leeward side of an island?**
A. much more than on the windward side
B. much less than on the windward side
C. strong rains all the time
D. no rainfall

____ **9. After slavery ended in the Caribbean, many immigrants arrived from**
A. Africa.
B. Asia.
C. North America.
D. Australia.

____ **10. Why do many people in the Caribbean leave their islands?**
A. Island soil is not good for farming.
B. Tourists use all the land.
C. Volcanoes erupt too often.
D. They leave to find work.

Name ________________ Class ________________ Date ________________

Chapter 12

Brazil

Vocabulary

- deforestation
- ecotourism
- escarpment
- favela
- gasohol
- plantation
- sertão

Vocabulary Development

Directions: *Using what you learned in Chapter 12, answer the following questions. Use one of the vocabulary words listed to the right in each answer.*

1. Why was much of the interior of Brazil underdeveloped and sparsely populated?

2. Why is the land of the northeast region often devastated by heavy rains?

3. What happens to many uneducated Brazilians who move to São Paolo?

4. Where do many poor rural workers find employment?

5. What was one development that resulted from the high cost of imported oil in the 1970s?

6. What is one threat to the plant and animal life in the Amazon rain forest?

7. What is one industry in Brazil that has been developed to encourage economic growth and preserve the rain forest?

Section 1: The Land and Its Regions

Guide to the Essentials

Text Summary

THE BIG IDEA

Brazil is a giant country with nearly half of South America's people. The vast Amazon River basin is rich in plant and animal life.

Brazil has nearly half of South America's people and land. It has two main landforms—plains and plateaus. The huge Amazon River basin is a plains region. A narrow lowlands region follows the Atlantic coast.

A huge interior plateau drops sharply to the plains. The drop forms an **escarpment,** or steep cliff, between the two levels. The escarpment created a barrier to Brazil's interior for many years. Inland from the coast lies the ***sertão***, or interior plateau.

Portuguese settlers started sugar plantations along the coast of the northeast in the 1500s. They brought enslaved Africans to do the work. Poverty in this region is great because the soil is poor and rain is uncertain.

Brazil's southeast is the smallest region and economic heartland. Many crops grow on its fertile soil. Coffee is the biggest and most important crop. About 40 percent of Brazilians live in this region, mostly in or near two cities—Rio de Janeiro and São Paulo. The cities attract poor people from rural areas who are looking for a better life. But many end up in slum communities called ***favelas***. Houses there are often built of mud, tin, and wood boards.

Brazil's capital, Brasília, is in the Brazilian Highlands. It was built to attract people to this area, which is on the central plateau.

The Amazon River basin is home to thousands of kinds of plants and animals. Only about 10 percent of Brazilians live there, including about 200,000 Indians.

Graphic Summary: *Brazil*

Brazil is the largest country in South America and has many of the largest cities.

Review Questions

1. What region is Brazil's economic heartland?

2. **Map Skills** What city is located on the Amazon River?

Name ______________________ Class ______________ Date ______________

Section 1: The Land and Its Regions

Guided Reading and Review

A. As You Read

Directions: *As you read Section 1, complete the chart on Brazil's regions by supplying key details on each topic listed.*

Regions	Details
The Northeast Region	
Settlement of the coast	**1.** ______________________
Climate of the *sertao*	**2.** ______________________
People's lives in the *sertao*	**3.** ______________________
The Southeast Region	
Percent of Brazil's land area	**4.** ______________________
Percent of Brazil's population	**5.** ______________________
Farming conditions	**6.** ______________________
Major crops	**7.** ______________________
Major cities	**8.** ______________________
Conditions in the cities	**9.** ______________________
The Brazilian Highlands	
Location	**10.** ______________________
History of Brasília	**11.** ______________________
The Amazon River Region	
Percent of Brazil's land area	**12.** ______________________
Percent of Brazil's population	**13.** ______________________

B. Reviewing Vocabulary

Directions: *Define the following terms.*

14. escarpment ______________________

15. *sertao* ______________________

16. *favela* ______________________

Name ______________________ Class ______________ Date ______________

Section 2: Brazil's Quest for Economic Growth

Guide to the Essentials

Text Summary

Brazil is a country of extremes. It is rich in natural resources but has much poverty. The country is taking steps to modernize its economy. The growth of industry has helped to create a middle class.

> **THE BIG IDEA**
>
> **Brazil is developing new industries and encouraging people to move to the interior to reduce poverty. Some development has hurt the environment.**

Many of the poorest Brazilians live in urban *favelas*. Others are small farmers who live in the northeastern *sertão*, a region with poor soil and uncertain rainfall.

To attack poverty, Brazil's government has increased industry and encouraged people to settle in the interior. The government has built steel mills, oil refineries, and hydroelectric dams. It built the new capital of Brasília in the Brazilian Highlands and built thousands of miles of new roads. To encourage people to move to the interior, the government gave away land and mining permits.

Manufacturing now makes up more than one third of Brazil's gross domestic product. The development of **gasohol**, a new fuel that mixes gasoline with ethanol, which comes from sugar cane, allows Brazil to grow its own fuel rather than import expensive foreign oil. About half of the people work in service industries such as hotels, restaurants, stores, and government.

Economic change has been good for Brazil, but it has had some unexpected bad effects. *Favelas* have grown larger as more people have moved to the cities. New settlers in the Amazon Basin cut down forests to plant crops. They learned, however, that the rain forest had kept the soil from washing away. Today the soil is no longer good for farming. **Deforestation**, or the permanent removal of woodland, threatens thousands of species of plants and animals in the Amazon. The government is now working to stop this threat.

Graphic Summary: *Percentage of Brazilians Living in Cities, 1974–2005*

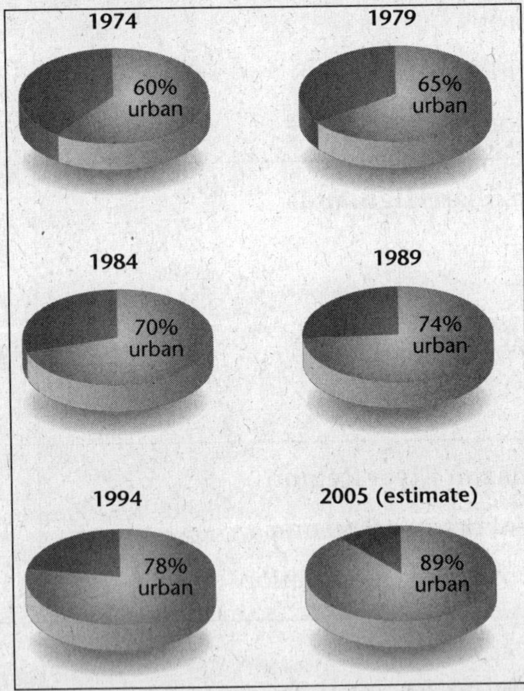

The percentage of Brazilians moving to cities has been increasing steadily.

Review Questions

1. What has Brazil done to encourage the development of the country's interior region?

2. **Graph Skills** How did the percentage of people living in cities change from 1974 to 1994?

Name ______________________ Class ______________ Date ______________

Section 2: Brazil's Quest for Economic Growth

Guided Reading and Review

A. As You Read

Directions: *As you read Section 2, complete the chart about Brazil's economic development by supplying the missing information.*

Question	Answers
What are two major causes of rural poverty in Brazil?	**1.** ____________ **2.** ____________
Name three ways the government boosted the growth of industry in Brazil during the 1940s and the 1950s.	**3.** ____________ **4.** ____________ **5.** ____________
Name three ways the government encouraged the development of Brazil's interior.	**6.** ____________ **7.** ____________ **8.** ____________
Identify three signs of the success of Brazil's development program.	**9.** ____________ **10.** ____________ **11.** ____________
Identify two drawbacks to Brazil's development program.	**12.** ____________ **13.** ____________

B. Reviewing Vocabulary

Directions: *Define the following terms.*

14. plantation ____________

15. gasohol ____________

16. deforestation ____________

17. ecotourism ____________

Name ______________________ Class ______________ Date ______________

Chapter **12** *Test*

Identifying Main Ideas

Directions: *Write the letter of the correct answer in the blank provided. (10 points each)*

____ **1. What is an escarpment?**
A. an area of thick rain forest plants
B. a river basin
C. a sharp cliff between different levels of land
D. a plateau area

____ **2. What was the main crop of Portuguese plantations in Brazil's northeast?**
A. coffee
B. sugar
C. cocoa
D. rubber

____ **3. Which area of Brazil is its economic heartland?**
A. the Amazon River basin
B. the Brazilian Highlands
C. the northeast
D. the southeast

____ **4. A home in a *favela* would probably be made of**
A. marble and glass.
B. bricks and cement.
C. steel bars.
D. tin and mud.

____ **5. About how many Indians live in the Amazon river basin?**
A. 2,000
B. 20,000
C. 200,000
D. 2,000,000

____ **6. To encourage people to move to the interior, Brazil built a new capital and**
A. many roads.
B. railroads.
C. rain forests.
D. *favelas*.

____ **7. Another way the government encouraged people to move to the interior was by giving away**
A. land.
B. free railroad tickets.
C. a year's salary.
D. hydroelectric dams.

____ **8. Gasohol is made from a mixture of**
A. gasoline and oil.
B. gasoline and ethanol.
C. natural gas and ethanol.
D. natural gas and gasoline.

____ **9. When farmers cleared the rain forests to create farms, they discovered that**
A. crops grew very quickly.
B. there were minerals under the soil.
C. the soil was not good for farming.
D. many kinds of animals ate their crops.

____ **10. What role is Brazil's government playing in deforestation?**
A. It is cutting down trees to grow crops.
B. It is helping industries develop in the Amazon Basin.
C. It is trying to stop it.
D. It is developing ethanol from the trees that are being removed.

Name ____________________ Class ____________ Date ____________

Chapter 13

Countries of South America

Vocabulary

- altiplano
- estuary
- pampas
- páramo
- piedmont
- selva
- timber line

Vocabulary Development

Directions: *Imagine that you are a tour guide in South America. Write a journal entry of one or more paragraphs about the countries of this continent. Use at least five of the listed vocabulary words. Be specific in your paragraph(s) to be sure your reader appreciates the beauty and diversity of this region.*

Name ______________________ Class ______________ Date ______________

Section 1: The Northern Tropics

Guide to the Essentials

Text Summary

THE BIG IDEA

There are five countries to the north of Brazil. Each one has its own economy and its own mix of people.

The northern tropics, the five countries on the northern coast of South America, have both similarities and differences. Guyana, Suriname, and French Guiana together are called the Guianas. They share a tropical wet climate and a narrow coastal plain on the Atlantic Ocean. Their cultures are different from most of the rest of South America.

Many people in the Guianas are of Asian or African descent. Many others are **mulattoes**, people of mixed African and other ancestry. Most live by fishing or growing sugar cane and rice. Others mine **bauxite**, a mineral used in making aluminum.

Colombia and Venezuela have three physical regions—lowlands, mountains, and the **llanos**, or grassy plains. Climate depends on elevation. Different crops are grown at different elevations. (See diagram on right.)

Venezuela's economy is based on oil. Although Venezuela has huge oil reserves, oil is not a renewable resource. Therefore, Venezuela is also investing in other industries, including bauxite and iron mines, power plants, and factories.

Colombia's farmers depend mostly on one crop—coffee. A country that depends on one crop, such as coffee, faces problems if prices drop or coffee trees die. The government is trying to encourage the export of other crops. Colombia also grows two illegal crops—marijuana and cocaine. People who control the drug trade have a lot of power. Colombia and the United States are working to end the drug trade and its violence.

Graphic Summary: *Vertical Climate Zones in Latin America*

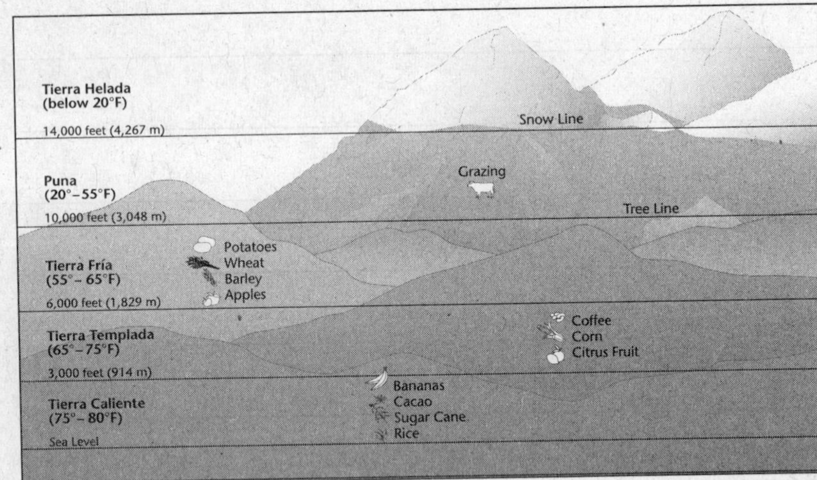

Climate changes with the elevation of the land. Some crops grow best at certain latitudes.

Review Questions

1. Which country in the northern tropics is rich in oil?

2. **Diagram Skills** What is the name for the climate zone where coffee is grown?

Name ______________________ Class ______________ Date ______________

Section 1: The Northern Tropics

Guided Reading and Review

A. As You Read

Directions: *As you read Section 1, complete the chart below to compare the Guianas and Venezuela. Then, answer the questions that follow.*

Country	Official Language	Ethnic Background of the Population	Basis of Economy
Guyana	**1.** ______________	**2.** ______________ ______________	**3.** ______________ ______________
Suriname	**4.** ______________	**5.** ______________ ______________	**6.** ______________ ______________
French Guiana	**7.** ______________	**8.** ______________ ______________ ______________	**9.** ______________ ______________ ______________
Venezuela	**10.** ______________	**11.** ______________ ______________	**12.** ______________ ______________

13. How are the landscapes of Venezuela and Colombia alike? ______________________________

____

14. On what cash crop does Colombia's economy depend? ______________________________

____

B. Reviewing Vocabulary

Directions: *Complete each sentence by writing the correct term in the blank.*

15. People of mixed African and other ancestry, or ______________________, are a major part of French Guiana's population.

16. ______________________ is the mineral used to make aluminum.

17. On either side of Venezuela's Orinoco River lies grassland called the ______________________.

18. In Colombia, the Andes Mountains have three parallel ranges called ______________________.

19. ______________________, or tenant farmers, in Colombia grow coffee but little food.

Name ______________________ Class ______________ Date ______________

Section 2: The Andean Countries

Guide to the Essentials

Text Summary

THE BIG IDEA

The Andes have had a great effect on the economies of Ecuador, Peru, Bolivia, and Chile. Different ethnic groups earn their livings in different ways.

The Andes form the backbone of South America, shaping the economies and lifestyles of the people in Ecuador, Peru, Bolivia, and Chile. It is the longest unbroken mountain chain in the world.

The Andes stretch from the Caribbean Sea to the southern tip of South America. A long narrow coastal plain lies between the Andes and the Pacific Ocean. In northern Chile, the coastal plain is occupied by the Atacama Desert, the driest place on earth. Between the peaks of the Andes are highland valleys and plateaus.

The climate in the Andes varies with elevation. At high elevations, only cold-weather plants grow. At the bottom of the eastern slopes are forested tropical lowlands called the *selva*.

People are drawn to the Andes because of its rich soil and wealth of minerals. The original inhabitants of the highlands were groups of Native Americans, who still make up between 25 and 55 percent of the populations of Bolivia, Ecuador, and Peru. These Indians follow a traditional lifestyle in the highlands, practicing subsistence agriculture.

The next largest group of inhabitants is mestizos, who speak Spanish and live in cities and towns. People of European background make up a small percentage of the population, but because they control most of the wealth, they have the most political power.

Chile is a long, narrow country and unlike other Andean nations, it has relatively few Indians. About two thirds of its people are mestizos. Another quarter is of European descent. Most Chileans live in the fertile Central Valley.

Graphic Summary: *South America*

Country	Population	Life Expectancy (years)	Per Capita GDP (in U.S. $)
Argentina	39,144,753	75.7	11,200
Bolivia	8,724,156	65.1	2,400
Brazil	184,101,109	71.4	7,600
Chile	15,823,957	76.3	9,900
Colombia	42,310,775	71.4	6,300
Ecuador	13,212,742	76.0	3,300
Guyana	705,803	62.4	4,000
Paraguay	6,191,368	74.6	4,600
Peru	27,544,305	69.2	5,200
Suriname	436,935	69.1	3,500
Uruguay	3,399,237	75.9	12,600
Venezuela	25,017,387	74.0	4,800

Source: *The World Factbook 2004*

The Andean countries vary greatly in population size and in GDP.

Review Questions

1. Which of the Andean countries has the smallest Indian population?

2. **Chart Skills** Which of the Andean countries has the smallest population?

Name ______________________ Class ______________ Date ______________

Section 2: The Andean Countries

Guided Reading and Review

A. As You Read

Directions: *As you read Section 2, complete the chart by answering the questions about the Andean countries.*

Question	Answers
Into what three areas do the Andes Mountains divide the Andean countries?	**1.** ______________ **2.** ______________ **3.** ______________
What are the two main natural resources of the Andean Highlands?	**4.** ______________ **5.** ______________
What two groups make up most of the populations of Ecuador and Peru?	**6.** ______________ **7.** ______________
What group makes up the majority of Chile's population?	**8.** ______________
What products does Chile's Central Valley send to U.S. supermarkets in the winter?	**9.** ______________

B. Reviewing Vocabulary

Directions: *Define the following terms.*

10. *altiplano* ______________________________

11. *páramo* ______________________________

12. timber line ______________________________

13. *selva* ______________________________

Name ______________________ Class ______________ Date ______________

Section 3: *The Southern Grassland Countries*

Guide to the Essentials

Text Summary

The three nations of southern South America are Uruguay, Paraguay, and Argentina. They are among the richest countries of the continent. The region is bound together by several large rivers that flow into the Río de la Plata. The Plata is an **estuary**, a broad river mouth formed where a flooded river valley meets the sea.

THE BIG IDEA

Several large rivers link the three nations of southern South America. Argentina and Uruguay are among the richest countries in South America.

The highest peaks of the Andes are in western Argentina. Lower down is the gently rolling **piedmont**, or foothills, region. The Gran Chaco is a hot, interior lowland in parts of Paraguay, Argentina, and Bolivia.

The **pampas** are temperate grasslands in Argentina and Uruguay. **Gauchos**, or cowboys, once herded cattle on the pampas. Now grains are grown there too. South of the pampas is Patagonia, a dry, old plateau. It has oil and bauxite and is good for raising sheep.

Paraguay has no seacoast, but the Río de la Plata provides an outlet to the Atlantic Ocean. Most Paraguayans are mestizos. Paraguay and Brazil worked together to build the Itaipu Dam, one of the world's largest hydroelectric projects.

Uruguay has good grasslands for raising livestock. The country produces wool, meat, and leather. Most of the people of Uruguay and Argentina are of European descent.

Argentina is the wealthiest country in South America. Most Argentineans live in cities. There are many factories and good harbors.

Graphic Summary: *Some Land Regions in Southern South America*

Region	Location	Description
Piedmont	western Argentina	low, gently sloping foothills
Gran Chaco	Paraguay, Argentina, Bolivia	hot, interior lowland
Pampas	Argentina, Uruguay	temperate grasslands
Patagonia	southern tip of Argentina and Chile	cold and dry plateau

The countries of southern South America have some special land regions.

Review Questions

1. What is the wealthiest country of South America?

2. **Chart Skills** In what countries is the Gran Chaco located?

Name ______________________ Class ______________ Date ____________

Section 3: The Southern Grassland Countries

Guided Reading and Review

A. As You Read

***Directions:** As you read Section 3, complete the charts below.*

Regions of Southern South America		
Region	**Location**	**Land and/or Climate**
Andean Region	**1.** ______________	**2.** ______________
Tropical Lowlands	**3.** ______________	**4.** ______________
Grasslands	**5.** ______________	**6.** ______________
Patagonia	**7.** ______________	**8.** ______________

Countries of Southern South America	
Paraguay	
Area where most people live	**9.** ______________
Basis of economy	**10.** ______________
Uruguay	
Ethnic background of population	**11.** ______________
Basis of economy	**12.** ______________
Argentina	
Ethnic background of population	**13.** ______________
Capital city	**14.** ______________

B. Reviewing Vocabulary

***Directions:** Match the definitions in Column I with the terms in Column II. Write the correct letter in each blank.*

Column I

_____ **15.** cowboys who herded cattle in the pampas

_____ **16.** broad river mouth

_____ **17.** foothills of the Andes

_____ **18.** grasslands of Argentina and Uruguay

Column II

a. estuary

b. piedmont

c. pampas

d. gauchos

Name ______________________ Class ______________ Date ______________

Chapter 13 Test

Identifying Main Ideas

Directions: Write the letter of the correct answer in the blank provided. (10 points each)

____ **1. How is the population of the Guianas different from other countries in Latin America?**
A. Most people in the Guianas are Native Americans.
B. About half the people in the Guianas are of European descent.
C. Almost all the people in the Guianas are of African descent.
D. The Guianas have many people of Asian descent.

____ **2. What is bauxite?**
A. a form of silver
B. a mineral used to make aluminum
C. an oil rig
D. an area good for ranching

____ **3. What does the word llano mean?**
A. a wide plain
B. an oil drill
C. a factory
D. a hydroelectric plant

____ **4. Why is it a problem for Colombia's economy to depend on coffee?**
A. People will not work on coffee farms.
B. If the price of coffee drops, Colombia will make less money.
C. If the price of coffee rises, Colombia will make less money.
D. People who sell drugs will not buy coffee.

____ **5. The Atacama Desert is**
A. in the rain forest.
B. on the Atlantic coast.
C. part of the coastal plain.
D. high in the Andes.

____ **6. How do most Indians make their living in the Andean countries?**
A. They work in factories.
B. They are government leaders.
C. They are subsistence farmers.
D. They own large farms.

____ **7. In which Andean country are two thirds of the people mestizos?**
A. Chile
B. Bolivia
C. Ecuador
D. Peru

____ **8. How have the pampas changed?**
A. Gauchos set up more ranches than ever before.
B. People built many large cities on the pampas.
C. Farmers are no longer using the pampas to grow wheat.
D. The pampas are now also used for growing grains.

____ **9. Which of the following is an estuary?**
A. Pampas
B. Patagonia
C. Río de la Plata
D. Piedmont

____ **10. The Gran Chaco is**
A. a dry, cold plateau.
B. a hot, interior lowland.
C. a foothills region.
D. a broad river mouth.

Name ____________________ Class ____________ Date ____________

Chapter 14

Regional Atlas: Introduction to Western Europe

Vocabulary
compulsory
cultural diffusion
euro
Industrial Revolution
prevailing westerlies
Renaissance
summits

Vocabulary Development

Directions: *Use the vocabulary words listed to fill in the blank in each sentence below.*

1. The period of new advances in science, technology, and the arts in Western Europe during the 1400s is known as the ____________.

2. The shift from human power to machine power is called the ____________.

3. Farming began to spread into Western Europe in about 5400 B.C. as a result of ____________.

4. The ____________ of the Alps contrast with the flat North European Plain.

5. The ____________ refers to the constant flow of air from west to east.

6. In 1999, the European Union introduced the ____________, a single currency to be used by member nations.

7. Education in Western European nations is required or ____________.

Directions: *Write a paragraph using at least three of the vocabulary words listed.*

Name ______________________ Class ______________ Date ______________

Regional Atlas: Western Europe

Guide to the Essentials

Text Summary

Migration and the process of **cultural diffusion**, in which peoples adopt the practices of their neighbors, have affected the history of Western Europe.

THE BIG IDEA

The countries of Western Europe are home to many cultures. The region is small but densely populated and its economy is based on industry and services.

Western Europe contains a variety of physical features. Oceans and seas surround much of Western Europe, while the **summits**, or highest points, of the Alps contrast with the flat North European Plain.

Temperate climates are caused by this region's proximity to the sea. The North Atlantic Drift, along with winds known as the **prevailing westerlies**, creates milder climates than those of other regions located at the same latitudes. The varying altitudes throughout Europe affect the vegetation and animal life of a region.

Western Europe occupies only 3 percent of the world's landmass, but it is one of the most densely populated regions in the world. Economic growth has encouraged people to migrate to Western Europe from all over the world in search of employment.

The growing use of machines during the 1800s became known as the **Industrial Revolution**. Industrialization and many natural resources helped transform this region from an agricultural society to an industrial society.

In the 1950s, six Western European nations formed a "common market" for their mutual economic benefit. As it expanded, it became the European Union (EU). In 1999, this union introduced the **euro**, a single currency to be used by member nations.

The idea of free nationwide education originated in Europe. In all Western European nations, education is **compulsory**, or required, for a certain number of years.

Graphic Summary: *Migration to Europe*

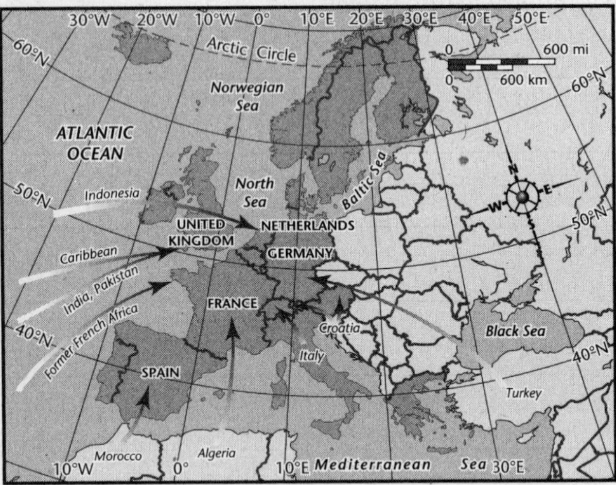

People migrate to Western Europe from all regions of the world.

Review Questions

1. Why is Western Europe one of the most densely populated regions in the world?
2. **Map Skills** According to the map, to which Western European country have Turkish citizens migrated?

Name ______________________ Class ______________ Date ______________

Regional Atlas: Western Europe

Guided Reading and Review

A. As You Read

Directions: *As you work through the Regional Atlas, complete the chart below by giving examples of each characteristic of Western Europe.*

Centers of Ancient Civilizations	Mountain Ranges
1. ______________	3. ______________
2. ______________	4. ______________
Peninsulas	**Rivers**
5. ______________	9. ______________
6. ______________	10. ______________
7. ______________	11. ______________
8. ______________	12. ______________
Major Climate Regions	**Major Ecosystems**
13. ______________	17. ______________
14. ______________	18. ______________
15. ______________	19. ______________
16. ______________	20. ______________
	21. ______________

B. Reviewing Vocabulary

Directions: *Complete each sentence by writing the correct term in the blank.*

22. Through the process of ______________, people adopt the practices of their neighbors.
23. The ______________ was a period of rebirth and rediscovery of knowledge in Western Europe that began in the 1400s.
24. The growing use of machines in the 1700s and 1800s was the ______________.
25. The ______________ is the highest point on a mountain.
26. The constant winds that blow from west to east in the earth's temperate zones are the ______________.
27. The ______________ is a single currency used by member nations of the European Union.
28. In Europe and the United States, school is ______________, or required, until a certain age.

Name ______________________ Class ______________ Date ______________

Chapter 14

Test

Identifying Main Ideas

***Directions:** Write the letter of the correct answer in the blank provided. (10 points each)*

____ **1. The process in which peoples adopt the practices of their neighbors is called**
A. cultural diffusion.
B. Industrial Revolution.
C. Renaissance.
D. migration.

____ **2. Which physical feature surrounds much of Western Europe?**
A. the Alps
B. oceans and seas
C. the Northern European Plain
D. rivers

____ **3. How does Western Europe's proximity to the sea affect this region's climate?**
A. It makes the region prone to hurricanes.
B. It makes the climate mild.
C. It makes the region prone to tsunamis.
D. It makes the climate very cold.

____ **4. The highest point of a mountain is called a**
A. summit.
B. peak.
C. slope.
D. base.

____ **5. What is the euro?**
A. another name given for Western European nations
B. the period when people migrated to Western Europe
C. a common market between countries
D. a single currency used by European Union member nations

____ **6. Which of the following have affected Western Europe's ecosystem?**
A. climate and history
B. economic activities
C. human influence and varying altitudes
D. migration and cultural diffusion

____ **7. Western Europe occupies how much of the world's landmass?**
A. 97 percent
B. 3 percent
C. 15 percent
D. 54 percent

____ **8. Which of the following has encouraged people to migrate to Western Europe in search of employment opportunities?**
A. economic growth
B. the Industrial Revolution
C. the formation of the European Union
D. the strong agricultural industry

____ **9. The European Union was formed by**
A. companies that do business in Western Europe.
B. people who work in factories in Western Europe.
C. all the countries in Europe.
D. six Western European nations that wanted a "common market" for their mutual economic benefit.

____ **10. A compulsory education is an education that is**
A. for people who want to pursue a profession in science.
B. required for a certain number of years.
C. based on mathematics.
D. for students who want to learn fine arts.

Name ______________________ Class ______________ Date ______________

Chapter 15

The British Isles and Nordic Nations

Vocabulary

blight
bog
cultural divergence
fjord
geothermal energy
moor
ore
tertiary economic activity

Vocabulary Development

Directions: *Divide the vocabulary words listed into the four categories below, based on each word's significance in the chapter you have just read.*

England	Scotland and Wales	The Two Irelands	Nordic Nations

Directions: *Write a sentence on each of the following topics using what you have learned in Chapter 15. Use two vocabulary words in each sentence.*

Topic: England

____

____

Topic: Scotland and Wales

____

____

Topic: The Two Irelands

____

____

Topic: Nordic Nations

____

____

Name ______________________ Class ______________ Date ______________

Section 1: England

Guide to the Essentials

Text Summary

THE BIG IDEA

Great Britain has been a center of trade and transportation. The Industrial Revolution began in Great Britain.

Great Britain is a large island that includes England, Scotland, and Wales. Together with Northern Ireland, they form the United Kingdom. Most people in the United Kingdom live in England.

England's Highlands are in the west. Land there is difficult to farm. The Midlands, once rich in coal, are the center of industry. The soil in the Lowlands is **fertile**, able to produce many crops. Lowland farms grow wheat and vegetables and raise sheep and cattle.

England's most important city is London. It is located on the Thames River. London is inland, but ocean ships can sail up the river.

The Industrial Revolution began in England. Factories first used water power to make cloth. Later they switched to coal as a source of power. England had major coal fields. It also had large amounts of iron **ore**, or rock containing a valuable mineral. The coal and iron were used to make steel.

The Industrial Revolution made Britain rich. It also made factory towns noisy and dirty. Britain led the world in industry until the late 1800s. Then, the United States and Germany began producing as much steel as Britain.

Much of Britain's coal is now gone. Today the country uses oil and natural gas found under the North Sea. Service industries are more important than factories. Britain's economy has been growing steadily.

Graphic Summary: *The British Isles*

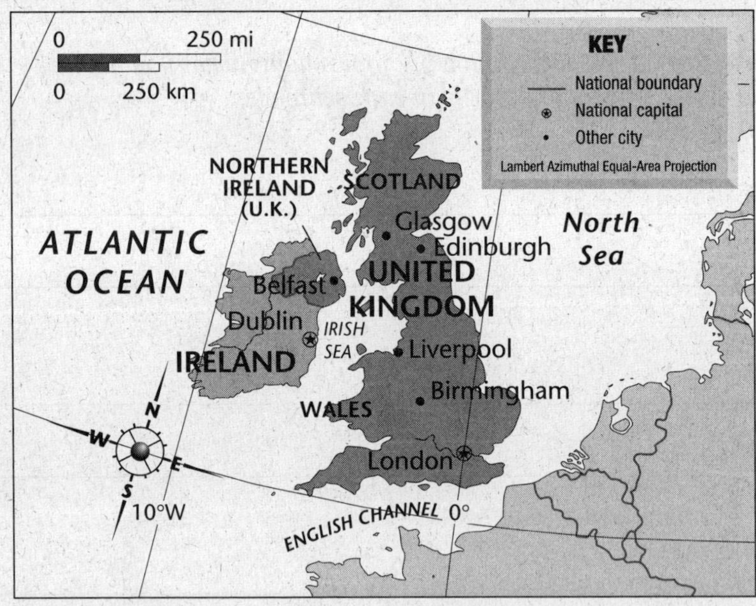

The British Isles include two large islands—Great Britain and Ireland.

Review Questions

1. What part of England is a center of industry?

2. **Map Skills** What places make up the United Kingdom?

Name ______________________ Class ______________ Date ______________

Section 1: England

Guided Reading and Review

A. As You Read

Directions: *As you read Section 1, complete the chart below by writing supporting details under each main idea.*

Main Idea A: England has three very different geographic regions.

1. Highlands: ______________________________

____

2. Midlands: ______________________________

____

3. Lowlands: ______________________________

____

Main Idea B: London's location has made it one of the most important commercial cities in the world.

4. ______________________________

____

5. ______________________________

____

Main Idea C: England was once the "workshop of the world," but today it is no longer a leading exporter of manufactured goods.

6. ______________________________

____

7. ______________________________

____

B. Reviewing Vocabulary

Directions: Match the definitions in Column I with the terms in Column II. Write the correct letter in each blank.

Column I	Column II
_____ 8. able to produce abundant crops	a. ore
_____ 9. rocky material containing a valuable mineral	b. fertile
_____ 10. service industry	c. tertiary economic activity

Name ______________________ Class ______________ Date ______________

Section 2: Scotland and Wales

Guide to the Essentials

Text Summary

THE BIG IDEA

Scotland and Wales have their own cultures, which are different from England's. Each is divided into highlands and lowlands.

Scotland was a separate country until it was united with England in 1707. It still keeps its own systems of law and education. Many Scots belong to the Presbyterian Church instead of the Church of England.

The Highlands region of Scotland is a large, high plateau with many lakes. Much of the Highlands are also covered with **moors**, plains with no trees. The moors have many **bogs**, areas of wet, spongy ground. Fishing and sheepherding are important industries in the Highlands.

Most of Scotland's people live in the Central Lowlands. In the 1800s, it was a center of industry. However, since the mid-1900s, many factories have closed and jobs were lost.

The Southern Uplands is close to Scotland's border with England. It is a sheep-raising region with many woolen mills.

Today, new industries are becoming important in Scotland. The discovery of oil in the North Sea brought new jobs. Computer and electronic businesses also have developed in some areas.

Wales has been united with England since 1284. Most of the Welsh people speak English, but many also speak Welsh.

Some of Great Britain's biggest coal mines are in Wales. By the mid-1900s, many mines and factories had to close because they were not modern. In the 1990s, new high-tech industries and tourism helped rebuild the economy of Wales.

Graphic Summary: *The United Kingdom*

The United Kingdom	area (sq. mi.)	Population	Largest City
England	50,302	49,807,082	London
Northern Ireland	5,452	1,663,300	Belfast
Scotland	30,418	5,111,000	Glasgow
Wales	8,019	2,927,000	Cardiff

Source: The World Almanac and Book of Facts 2001

England is the largest part of the United Kingdom.

Review Questions

1. Where do most people live in Scotland?

2. Chart Skills Which part of the United Kingdom has the second largest population?

Name ______________________ Class ______________ Date ______________

Section 2: Scotland and Wales

Guided Reading and Review

A. As You Read

Directions: *As you read Section 2, complete the chart below to compare and contrast Scotland and Wales.*

Feature	Scotland	Wales
Physical Characteristics	**1.** ______________ ______________ **2.** ______________ ______________	**7.** ______________ ______________ **8.** ______________ ______________
Economy	**3.** ______________ ______________ **4.** ______________ ______________	**9.** ______________ ______________ **10.** ______________ ______________
Culture	**5.** ______________ ______________ **6.** ______________ ______________	**11.** ______________ ______________ **12.** ______________ ______________

B. Reviewing Vocabulary

Directions: *Define the following terms.*

13. moor ______________________________

14. bog ______________________________

15. glen ______________________________

Name ______________________ Class ______________ Date ______________

Section 3: The Two Irelands

Guide to the Essentials

Text Summary

THE BIG IDEA

Ireland is an island that is divided into two political regions: Northern Ireland and the Republic of Ireland. The two parts share a history of conflicts.

Ireland is divided into Northern Ireland, which is part of the United Kingdom, and the Republic of Ireland, an independent country. Ireland's people are also divided by religion and culture.

The island's moist, marine climate keeps vegetation green. About one sixth of the land is covered by **peat**, a spongy material containing mosses and plants. Peat is used for fuel.

Invasions and war have shaped Ireland's history. Celtic tribes arrived first. They often defended themselves against Viking raids. After Normans from France conquered England in 1066, some took land in Ireland and forbade the use of Gaelic, the Celtic language. Eventually, English rulers began considering Ireland a possession of England.

In the 1500s, groups in Europe began a movement known as the Reformation, which led to a split from the Roman Catholic Church. Most English people became Protestants, whereas the Irish remained mostly Catholics. Conflict between Irish Protestants and Catholics led to **cultural divergence**, or deliberate efforts to keep the cultures separate.

In the 1840s, a plant disease known as a **blight** caused the Irish Potato Famine. The famine caused many deaths and resulted in anti-British feelings and immigration to the United States.

Many Irish wanted independence. After rebellions between 1916 and 1921, Ireland was divided into two parts. The six northeastern counties remained part of the United Kingdom. The rest eventually became independent as the Republic of Ireland in 1949.

A slight majority in Northern Ireland are Protestant. Most Catholics want to reunite all of Ireland, while most Protestants do not. Both sides have used violence. Steps toward peace began in 1994.

Graphic Summary: *Events in Ireland in the 1900s*

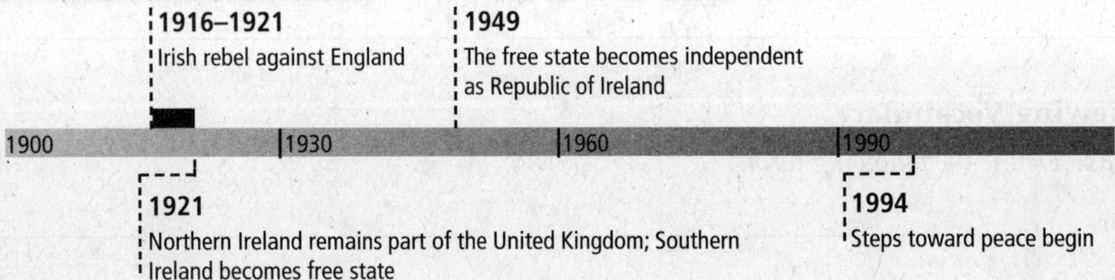

Ireland saw many changes in the 1900s.

Review Questions

1. What religions divide the people of Ireland?

2. **Timeline Skills** In what year did the Republic of Ireland become independent?

Name ______________________ Class ______________ Date ______________

Section 3: The Two Irelands

Guided Reading and Review

A. As You Read

Directions: *As you read Section 3, complete the chart by writing a brief description of each important development in Irish-English history.*

Date(s)	Major Developments in Irish-English History
300 B.C.	1. ______________________
800–1014	2. ______________________
1066	3. ______________________
1171	4. ______________________
1500s	5. ______________________
1840s	6. ______________________
1916–1921	7. ______________________
1949	8. ______________________
1994	9. ______________________

B. Reviewing Vocabulary

Directions: *Complete each sentence by including a definition of the italicized term.*

10. In Ireland, one source of fuel is *peat,* ______________________
____
______________________.

11. Conflict between Irish Protestants and Catholics led to *cultural divergence,* ______________________
____
______________________.

12. Ireland was devastated in the 1840s by a potato *blight,* ______________________
____
______________________.

Name ______________________ Class ______________ Date ______________

Section 4: *The Nordic Nations*

Guide to the Essentials

Text Summary

THE BIG IDEA

The five Nordic nations of northern Europe are united as a region by location and similar cultures.

The Nordic nations are Norway, Sweden, Finland, Denmark, and Iceland. All are located in the northern latitudes. The region has many peninsulas and islands. Landforms vary greatly. Denmark is very flat, while Norway is very mountainous.

The Scandinavian Peninsula includes most of Norway and Sweden. Its coasts have flooded valleys called **fjords** that were carved out by glaciers. Most fjords have steep walls. Some are so deep that oceangoing ships can sail into them.

Volcanoes and glaciers exist side by side in Iceland. Icelanders use **geothermal energy**, created by the heat inside the earth, to produce heat and electricity.

Location in the northern latitudes results in long winters and short summers. In midwinter, the sun shines only two or three hours a day. In midsummer, the sun shines more than 20 hours a day.

Much of the Nordic region has a surprisingly mild climate. Warm ocean currents keep the coasts free of ice. Mountains in Norway block the warm air, however, making areas east of the mountains cold and dry.

The Nordic nations have similar histories. Vikings sailed out of the region from 800 to 1050. The nations were often united. Except for Finnish, the languages of these countries have common roots. Most of the people belong to the Lutheran Church.

The Nordic countries all have strong **mixed economies.** That means the government operates some businesses, and private companies operate others.

Graphic Summary: *The Nordic Nations*

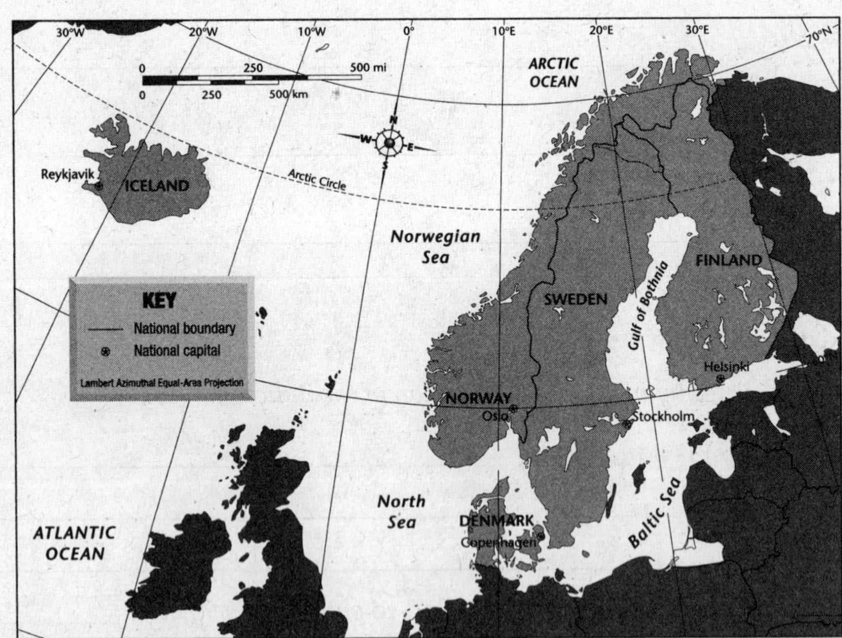

The Nordic nations share peninsulas and islands.

Review Questions

1. What is a mixed economy?

2. Map Skills Which three Nordic nations have land that lies north of the Arctic Circle?

Name ______________________ Class ______________ Date ______________

Section 4: The Nordic Nations

Guided Reading and Review

A. As You Read

Directions: *As you read Section 4, complete the chart below to summarize the physical and human characteristics of the Nordic nations.*

Feature	Descriptions
Landscape	**1.** ______________ **2.** ______________
Climate	**3.** ______________ **4.** ______________
Culture	**5.** ______________ **6.** ______________
Government and Economy	**7.** ______________ **8.** ______________

B. Reviewing Vocabulary

Directions: *Complete each sentence by writing the correct term in the blank.*

9. The Scandinavian coast has many steep-walled, deep-water valleys called ______________, which were formed by glaciers.

10. The people of Iceland have learned to take advantage of the island's geology to produce ______________.

11. The Nordic nations have ______________ that include elements of both free enterprise and socialism.

Name ____________________ Class ____________ Date ____________

Chapter 15 **Test**

Identifying Main Ideas

Directions: *Write the letter of the correct answer in the blank provided. (10 points each)*

____ **1. What area is part of the United Kingdom but is not part of Great Britain?**
A. Scotland and Wales
B. Northern Ireland
C. the Republic of Ireland
D. all of Ireland

____ **2. Where did the Industrial Revolution begin?**
A. the United States
B. Germany
C. England
D. Ireland

____ **3. What is a moor?**
A. wet, spongy ground
B. a plain with no trees
C. moss used for fuel
D. good farmland

____ **4. Where do most people in Scotland live?**
A. the Central Lowlands
B. the Southern Uplands
C. the Highlands
D. near the North Sea

____ **5. Why did many factories in Wales close in the mid-1900s?**
A. They were not modern enough.
B. There was no need for factory goods.
C. Tourism forced the factories to close.
D. There was no coal to power them.

____ **6. What is the main use for peat?**
A. food
B. fertilizer for crops
C. fuel
D. keeping the land green

____ **7. What is included in Northern Ireland?**
A. the Republic of Ireland
B. six counties that are part of the United Kingdom
C. six counties that are part of the Republic of Ireland
D. the independent part of Ireland

____ **8. Which of the following explains what makes the Nordic nations a region?**
A. They are located in the northern latitudes.
B. They are located in Europe.
C. All the people speak Finnish.
D. All the people belong to the Catholic Church.

____ **9. What is a fjord?**
A. a steep mountain
B. a long summer day with sun for more than 20 hours
C. a flooded valley with steep sides
D. a warm ocean current that keeps the climate mild

____ **10. The Nordic nations all have**
A. summer all year.
B. moors.
C. winter all year.
D. mixed economies.

Name ______________________ Class ______________ Date ______________

Chapter 16

Central Western Europe

Vocabulary
canton
confederation
decentralize
inflation
nationalize
neutral
perishable good
reparation

Vocabulary Development

Directions: *Match each vocabulary term in Column A with the correct definition in Column B.*

Column A	Column B
1. nationalize	a. a state in the country of Switzerland
2. confederation	b. transfer power to smaller regions of a country
3. reparation	c. not taking sides in conflicts between other countries
4. inflation	d. an item that does not stay fresh for a long period of time
5. decentralize	e. money for war damages
6. canton	f. to bring under state control
7. neutral	g. a loose political union
8. perishable good	h. sharply rising prices

Directions: *Categorize the vocabulary terms as either political terms or economic terms in the diagram below.*

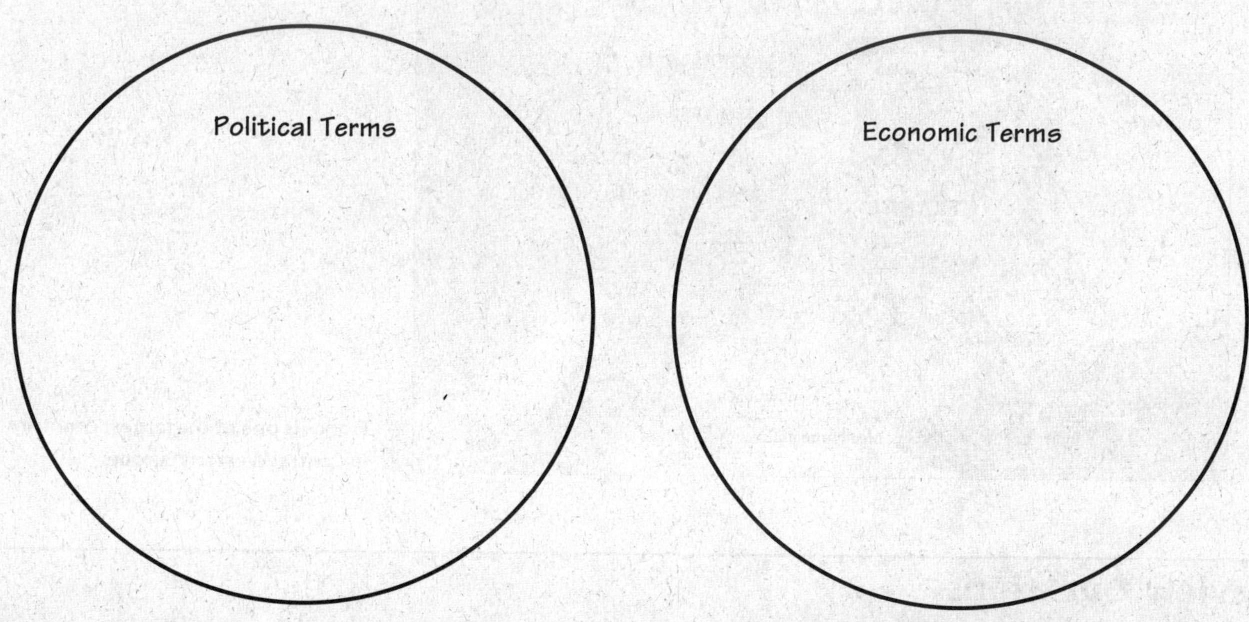

Name ______________________ Class ______________ Date ______________

Section 1: France

Guide to the Essentials

Text Summary

> **THE BIG IDEA**
> **France has a distinct identity based on its history, language, and culture. It also has a variety of physical and economic regions.**

Although France has a strong national identity, the people of each region have their own traditions and way of life. The Paris Basin in the north is the center of France's main manufacturing center. Paris, the capital city, is its center. The southwest is famous for wine grapes. Bordeaux is its main city.

In southern France, the Rhône River flows between two mountain areas. The Massif Central is west of the Rhône. The snow-covered Alps separate France from Italy. In 1965, a tunnel was built through the mountains.

Between the Alps and the Mediterranean Sea is a coastal land called the French Riviera. Its beautiful beaches attract many tourists. Marseille is the busiest seaport in France and the second busiest in Western Europe. The Rhine River, in eastern France, forms part of France's border with Germany. This region has large deposits of iron ore and coal.

For hundreds of years, France was ruled by kings. In 1789, the French Revolution ended the monarchy. Since then, France has had many forms of government. The French language helps to unify the French people. The French are proud of their philosophers and artists.

France is a wealthy nation but has faced some economic problems. A **recession**, or long decline in business activity, caused many people to lose their jobs in the 1990s.

Graphic Summary: *Central Western Europe*

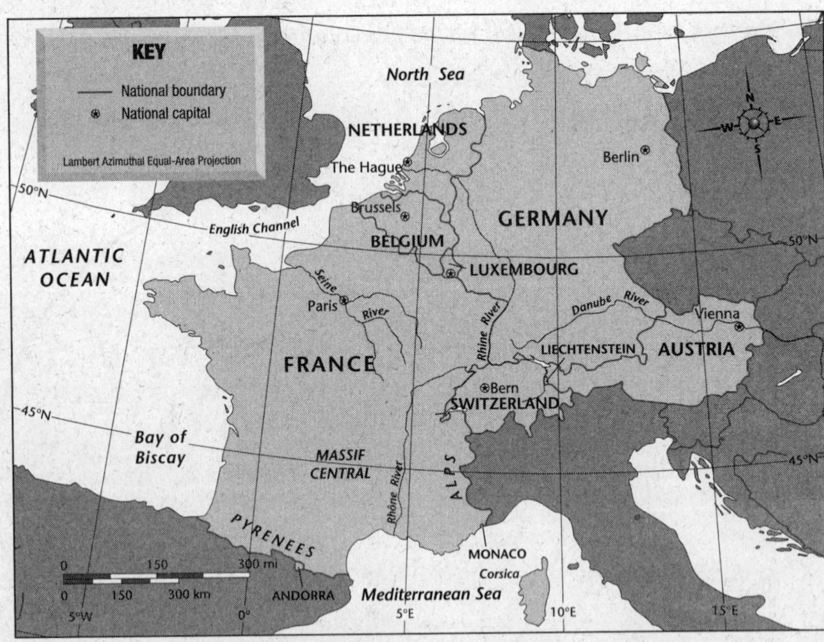

France is one of the largest countries in Central Western Europe.

Review Questions

1. Where is the center of France's manufacturing region?

2. **Map Skills** What five countries of Central Western Europe border France?

Name ______________________ Class ______________ Date ______________

Section 1: France

Guided Reading and Review

A. As You Read

Directions: *As you read Section 1, complete the chart below by describing the physical features and economy of each region of France.*

Region	Physical Geography	Economy
Northern France	1. ______________	2. ______________
Southwestern France	3. ______________	4. ______________
South central and southeastern France	5. ______________	6. ______________
Mediterranean coast	7. ______________	8. ______________
Rhine Valley	9. ______________	10. ______________

B. Reviewing Vocabulary

Directions: *Match the definitions in Column I with the terms in Column II. Write the correct letter in each blank.*

Column I

_____ **11.** regional variations in a language

_____ **12.** style of painting associated with Claude Monet and Pierre Auguste Renoir

_____ **13.** to place a business or industry under government control

_____ **14.** an extended period of little or no economic growth

Column II

a. nationalize

b. Impressionism

c. dialects

d. recession

Name ______________________ Class ______________ Date ______________

Section 2: Germany

Guide to the Essentials

Text Summary

THE BIG IDEA

Germany is Europe's leading industrial nation. It was united again in 1990 after having been two separate countries since the end of World War II.

The area that is now Germany was divided for hundreds of years into small states. Prussia began to unite the German states in the late 1700s. Germany was defeated in World War I and had to pay the winning countries **reparations**, money for war damages. The payments caused economic hardships and **inflation**, quickly rising prices. In 1929, many Germans lost their jobs during a worldwide economic depression.

In the early 1930s, Adolf Hitler and his Nazi party took power. Hitler blamed Jews and others for Germany's problems. In 1939, Germany invaded Poland, beginning World War II. The Nazis killed millions of Jews and other people in concentration camps. Germany was finally defeated in 1945.

After World War II, Germany was divided into Communist East Germany and democratic West Germany. In November 1989, the Berlin Wall, which had divided East and West Berlin, came down. The two countries reunited in October 1990.

Germany has three geographic regions. The south has high mountains, the center has hills, low peaks, and plateaus, and the north is flat.

Farming, manufacturing, and trade are important industries. The Rhine and Elbe rivers flow through one of the world's most important industrial centers. The Ruhr Valley, rich in coal, produces most of Germany's iron and steel. Germany rebuilt its economy after World War II. By 1999, it was the leading industrial country in Western Europe.

Graphic Summary: *Germany*

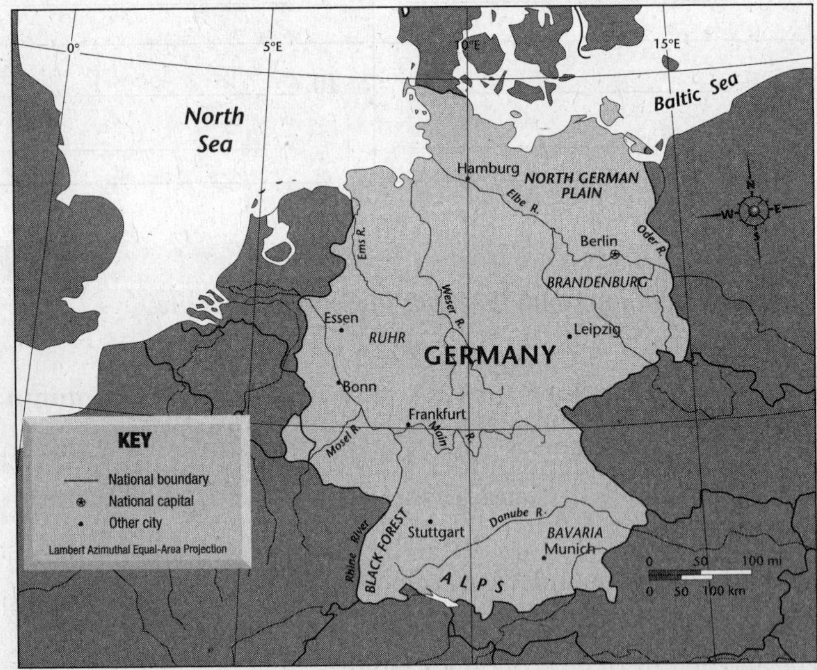

Germany's coast is on the North Sea and the Baltic Sea.

Review Questions

1. Why is the Ruhr Valley important to Germany?

2. **Map Skills** What mountain range is in southern Germany?

Name ______________________ Class ______________ Date ______________

Section 2: Germany

Guided Reading and Review

A. As You Read

Directions: *As you read Section 2, complete the chart below by identifying one or more major results of each event.*

Event	Aftermath
Charlemagne's death	**1.** ______________
Protestant Reformation	**2.** ______________
End of Franco-Prussian War	**3.** ______________
End of World War I	**4.** ______________
End of World War II	**5.** ______________
Overthrow of East Germany's government	**6.** ______________

Directions: *As you read Section 2, complete the chart below about the regions of Germany.*

Region	Physical Features	Economy
Northern	**7.** ______________	**8.** ______________
Central	**9.** ______________	**10.** ______________
Southern	**11.** ______________	**12.** ______________

B. Reviewing Vocabulary

Directions: *Define the following terms.*

13. confederation ______________

14. reparation ______________

15. inflation ______________

16. lignite ______________

Name ______________________ Class ______________ Date ______________

Section 3: The Benelux Countries

Guide to the Essentials

Text Summary

THE BIG IDEA

Belgium, the Netherlands, and Luxembourg are the Benelux countries. They are all small and have low, flat land.

The word Benelux comes from the first letters of Belgium, Netherlands, and Luxembourg. They are also called the Low Countries because so much of their land is low and flat. They are small in area, but their total population is almost as large as Canada's.

One fifth of the Netherlands is land taken from the sea. When the Romans conquered the area, they built **dikes**, walls of earth and rock, to hold back the sea. Later, the Dutch people reclaimed land by building dikes around a piece of land and pumping water out into canals. They call this reclaimed land a **polder**. Beginning in the 1200s, the Dutch used windmills to power the pumps that remove water from the land. The Dutch use more than half their land for agriculture.

Belgium has two main ethnic groups who speak different languages. The Walloons speak French. The Flemings speak Flemish, a dialect of Dutch. For many years, French was the only official language, even though more people spoke Flemish. In 1898, Flemish also became an official language. More recently, Belgium **decentralized** its government. It transferred power to smaller regions.

Luxembourg is the smallest Benelux country. Its people speak French, German, and Luxembourgish, a dialect of German. Luxembourg has one of the highest standards of living in Europe. It has many high-tech businesses and service industries. It trades mostly with other countries of the European Union.

Graphic Summary: *Countries of Central Western Europe*

Country	Population	Life Expectancy (years)	Per Capita GDP (in U.S. $)
Austria	8,174,762	78.8	30,000
Belgium	10,348,276	78.4	29,000
France	60,424,213	79.4	27,500
Germany	82,424,609	78.5	27,600
Liechtenstein	33,436	79.4	25,000
Luxembourg	462,690	78.6	55,100
Netherlands	16,318,199	78.7	28,600
Switzerland	7,450,867	80.3	32,800

Source: *The World Factbook 2004*

Luxembourg has the highest GDP in Central Western Europe.

Review Questions

1. How do the Dutch use the land they took from the sea?

2. **Chart Skills** Which Benelux country has the largest population?

Name ______________________________ Class __________________ Date __________________

Section 3: The Benelux Countries

Guided Reading and Review

A. As You Read

***Directions:** As you read Section 3, complete the chart below by writing three supporting details under each main idea.*

Main Idea A: The Dutch have intensely managed their environment.

1. ______________________________

2. ______________________________

3. ______________________________

Main Idea B: Conflict between two ethnic groups affects Belgian life.

4. ______________________________

5. ______________________________

6. ______________________________

Main Idea C: Luxembourg is a small but prosperous country.

7. ______________________________

8. ______________________________

9. ______________________________

B. Reviewing Vocabulary

***Directions:** Complete each sentence by writing the correct term in the blank.*

10. The Dutch have built ____________________ of earth and rock to hold back the water.

11. The land that the Dutch reclaimed from the sea is called a(n) ____________________ .

12. The Belgian government has passed laws to ____________________, giving greater authority to the governments in Wallonia, Flanders, and Brussels.

Name ______________________ Class ______________ Date ______________

Section 4: Switzerland and Austria

Guide to the Essentials

Text Summary

THE BIG IDEA

The people of Switzerland have very different cultural traditions from one another. Austria has been independent for a short time.

The Alps cover more than half the area of both Switzerland and Austria. Both countries are landlocked, meaning they do not have a coast on the sea.

Switzerland has three official languages: French, German, and Italian. The country is a confederation, a loose organization of states. It was formed in 1291 when three **cantons**, or states, united. Today, there are 26 cantons in the confederation. Each has its own language, religion, customs, and ways of making a living. Switzerland is **neutral**, and has not taken sides in wars between other countries in more than 200 years.

The Swiss have one of the world's highest standards of living. Milk from dairy farms is used in making chocolate and cheese. Switzerland is also known for products like watches, which need skilled labor.

Austria has had its present borders only since the end of World War I. For many years before then, it was part of the Austro-Hungarian Empire. The empire controlled much of Eastern Europe in the late 1800s. It collapsed after its defeat in World War I.

Austrians speak German. Most people live in the eastern lowlands, where land is flat or hilly. Austria has mineral resources, such as iron ore, which are used for industry. Other economic activities include dairy farming and manufacturing. Vienna, the capital, was once one of the world's largest cities.

Graphic Summary: *Refugees to Western Europe*

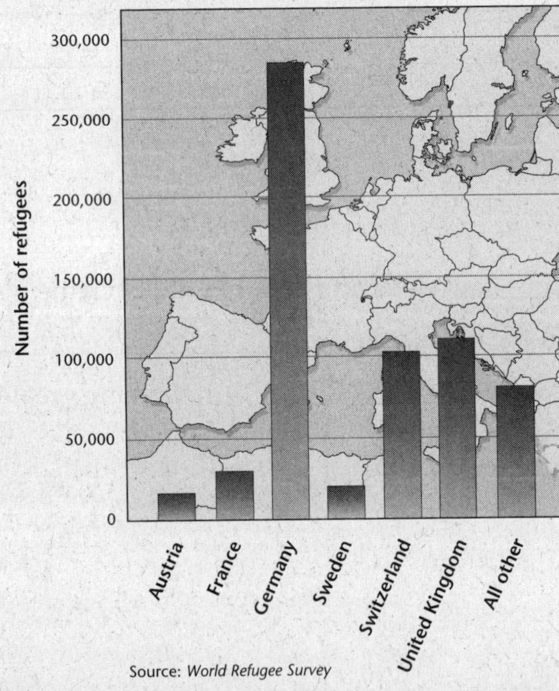

Austria and Switzerland's strong economies have enabled them to take in many refugees.

Review Questions

1. Which war brought an end to the Austro-Hungarian Empire?

2. **Graph Skills** About how many refugees have gone to Switzerland?

Name ______________________ Class ______________ Date ______________

Section 4: Switzerland and Austria

Guided Reading and Review

A. As You Read

Directions: *As you read Section 4, complete the charts below.*

Switzerland: Facts in Brief	
Official languages	**1.** ______________________
Form of government	**2.** ______________________
Agricultural exports	**3.** ______________________
Manufactured products	**4.** ______________________
Service industries	**5.** ______________________

Austria: Facts in Brief	
Historical highlights	**6.** ______________________
Industries	**7.** ______________________
Agriculture	**8.** ______________________
Mineral resources	**9.** ______________________
Capital city	**10.** ______________________

B. Reviewing Vocabulary

Directions: *Define the following terms.*

11. canton ______________________

12. neutral ______________________

13. perishable good ______________________

14. strip mining ______________________

Name ____________________ Class ____________ Date ____________

Chapter 16

Test

Identifying Main Ideas

Directions: *Write the letter of the correct answer in the blank provided. (10 points each)*

____ **1. What region of France is the main manufacturing center?**
A. the Paris Basin
B. the southwest
C. the Rhône Valley
D. the area around Bordeaux

____ **2. A tunnel through the Alps connects France and**
A. Germany.
B. the Netherlands.
C. Austria.
D. Italy.

____ **3. The river that forms part of the border between France and Germany is the**
A. Rhône.
B. Rhine.
C. Ruhr.
D. Elbe.

____ **4. What are reparations?**
A. a time of rising prices
B. money to pay for war damages
C. the work of bringing private companies under government control
D. repairs of government buildings

____ **5. What happened to Germany immediately after World War II?**
A. It was reunited as one country.
B. Many people lost their jobs after a worldwide depression.
C. It was divided into East Germany and West Germany.
D. The Berlin Wall came down.

____ **6. What is the leading industrial country in Western Europe?**
A. France
B. Germany
C. Switzerland
D. Luxembourg

____ **7. What is a polder?**
A. land that was lost to the ocean
B. land that was reclaimed from the sea
C. walls of earth to hold back the sea
D. a canal in the Netherlands

____ **8. What are the two languages of Belgium?**
A. French and German
B. German and Dutch
C. Dutch and Flemish
D. Flemish and French

____ **9. What is a confederation?**
A. a loose group of states
B. states united with a strong central government
C. a country that has no states
D. a country ruled by a stronger country

____ **10. How long has Austria had its present borders?**
A. since it was the Austro-Hungarian Empire
B. since the 1800s
C. since the end of World War I
D. since the end of World War II

Name ______________________ Class ______________ Date ______________

Chapter 17

Mediterranean Europe

Vocabulary
- dry farming
- graben
- inhabitable
- navigate
- seismic activity
- sirocco
- subsidence
- tsunami

Vocabulary Development

Directions: *Write a short paragraph using each group of words below. Use the topic given as the context for your paragraph.*

Topic: Spain has physical features that make it distinct from other nations in Europe.

Words: navigate/dry farming/sirocco

Topic: Italy has turned its geographic disadvantages into opportunities.

Words: seismic activity/subsidence

Topic: Greece is a mountainous land composed of many peninsulas and islands.

Words: graben/inhabitable/tsunami

Name ____________________ Class ______________ Date ______________

Section 1: Spain and Portugal

Guide to the Essentials

Text Summary

THE BIG IDEA

Spain and Portugal share the Iberian Peninsula. Mountains separate the peninsula from the rest of Europe.

Two countries—Spain and Portugal—dominate the Iberian Peninsula. The Pyrenees Mountains separate the peninsula from the rest of Europe. Reaching Spain by water is also difficult because steep cliffs rise along the coast.

The *Meseta*, or plateau, covers central Spain. Several rivers cross the Meseta, but only the Guadalquivir is **navigable**, deep and wide enough for ships.

Spain has a Mediterranean climate with mild, rainy winters and hot, dry summers. Little rain, however, reaches the Meseta, which is dry. Farmers there grow wheat and barley. **Siroccos**—hot, dry winds from northern Africa—make the southeast even drier.

Spain is developing new industries, such as transportation equipment. Bilbao and Barcelona are centers of industry. Madrid is the capital and largest city.

Many people in Spain identify with their regions. The Basques of northern Spain speak a language that is not related to any other European language. Some Basques want independence from Spain. People in other regions want more local control.

Portugal gets good rainfall for farming. Wheat, corn, and barley grow well. The country exports olive oil and cork.

Portugal became a trading nation in the 1100s. By the 1400s, Portuguese explorers had found routes around Africa to East Asia. Both Spain and Portugal had colonies in Latin America. Portugal also had colonies in Africa. They started to lose their colonies in the 1800s.

Graphic Summary: *Iberian Peninsula*

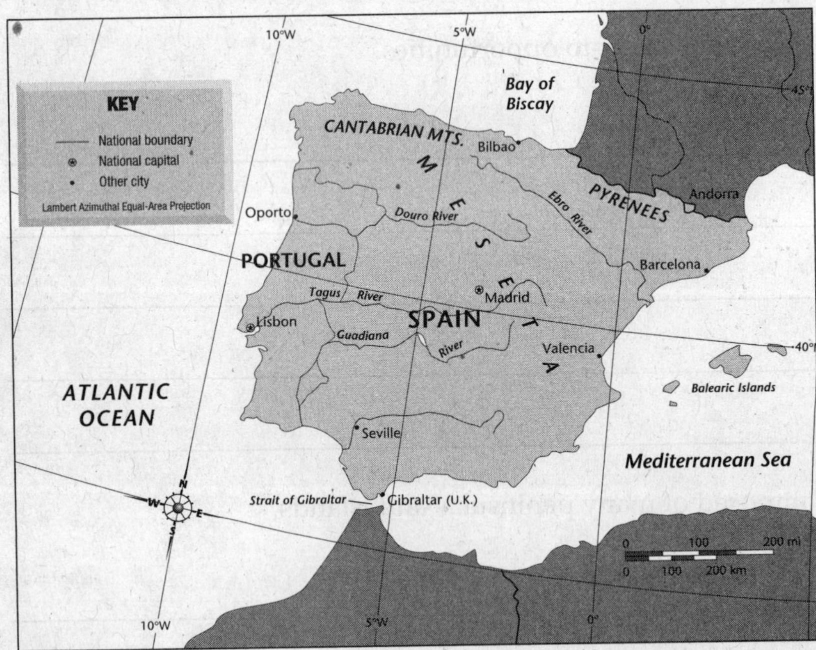

The countries of Spain and Portugal are located on the Iberian Peninsula.

Review Questions

1. On what peninsula are Spain and Portugal located?

2. **Map Skills** On what body of water is Lisbon located?

Name ______________________ Class ______________ Date ______________

Section 1: Spain and Portugal

Guided Reading and Review

A. As You Read

Directions: *As you read Section 1, complete the chart below by writing two supporting details under each main idea.*

Main Idea A: The Iberian Peninsula is separated from the rest of Europe by its physical characteristics.

1. ____

____

2. ____

____

Main Idea B: Portugal has had great influence overseas during its history.

3. ____

____

4. ____

____

Main Idea C: The economies of Spain and Portugal are moving away from agriculture and toward industry.

5. ____

____

6. ____

____

B. Reviewing Vocabulary

Directions: *Complete each sentence by writing the correct term in the blank.*

7. The Guadalquivir is the only Spanish river that is ______________.

8. Farmers in the Meseta use ______________ methods to grow wheat and barley, leaving the fields unplanted every one or two years to gather moisture.

9. Hot, dry winds from North Africa, called ______________, create semiarid conditions in southeast Spain.

10. Madrid is Spain's ______________, a center of economic activity and influence.

Name ______________________ Class ______________ Date ______________

Section 2: Italy

Guide to the Essentials

Text Summary

THE **BIG** IDEA

Italy is mountainous, but agriculture is important to the economy. Many Italians have moved to the industrial north to find jobs.

Many people recognize Italy's boot shape on a map. The Apennine Mountains run all the way down the Italian Peninsula. The Alps form the northern border.

Until the 1960s, more than one third of the population lived and worked on farms. Today only 10 percent of the people are farmers. Italian factories make automobiles, home appliances, and other metal goods. The European Union has given Italy a larger market for its goods.

After the Roman Empire collapsed, many Italian cities became independent states. As Christianity spread, the Roman Catholic Church gained control of large amounts of land.

In 1861, states in the north joined to form the country of Italy. Within ten years, the peninsula was united. There are still great differences among Italy's regions.

The heart of the northern region is the Po River valley. This is Italy's best farmland. About two thirds of Italy's factory goods are made there.

Central Italy includes Rome, the capital. Inside Rome is Vatican City, the center of the Roman Catholic Church. Cities in central Italy became famous during the **Renaissance,** a time of great art and learning that started in Italy in the 1300s.

Southern Italy includes the islands of Sicily and Sardinia. The poor soil makes farming hard. Many people have moved to the north to find jobs.

Graphic Summary: *Italy*

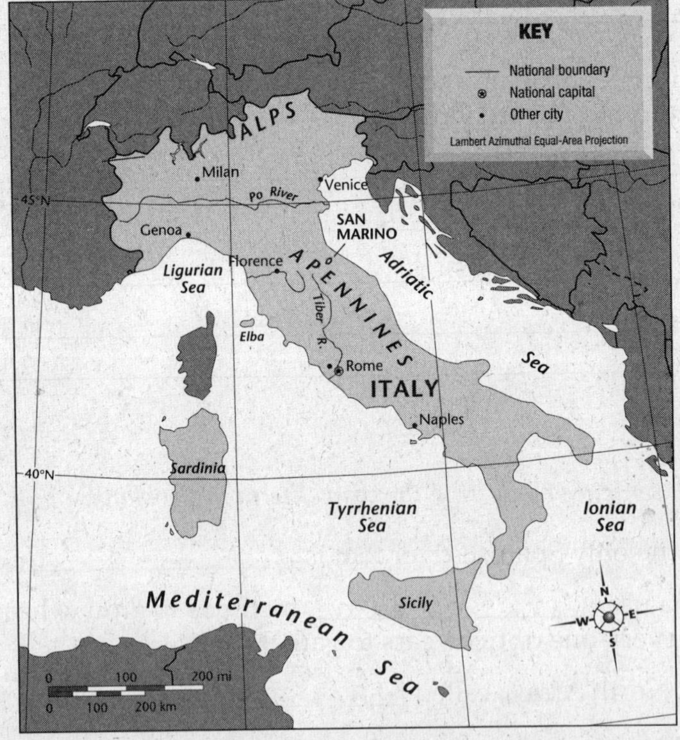

Italy is almost completely surrounded by water.

Review Questions

1. Why have many southern Italians moved to the north?

2. **Map Skills** What mountains form Italy's northern border?

Name ______________________ Class ______________ Date ______________

Section 2: Italy

Guided Reading and Review

A. As You Read

Directions: *As you read Section 2, complete the chart below by listing and describing the major cities in each region of Italy.*

Region	Major Cities	Description
Northern Italy	**1.** ______________	**2.** ______________
	3. ______________	**4.** ______________
	5. ______________	**6.** ______________
	7. ______________	**8.** ______________
Central Italy	**9.** ______________	**10.** ______________
	11. ______________	**12.** ______________
	13. ______________	**14.** ______________
Southern Italy	**15.** ______________	**16.** ______________

B. Reviewing Vocabulary

Directions: *Complete each sentence by writing the correct term in the blank.*

17. The Apennines Mountains experience a great deal of ______________, or many earthquakes and volcanic eruptions.

18. Venice suffers from ______________, a geological phenomenon in which the ground in an area sinks.

19. A great period of art and learning called the ______________ began in Italy in the 1300s and was diffused throughout Europe.

Name ______________ Class ______________ Date ______________

Section 3: Greece

Guide to the Essentials

Text Summary

History and geography make Greece part of the Mediterranean region. The culture that began in Greece developed further in Western Europe. Greece also has ties to Eastern Europe and Turkey, which it borders.

THE BIG IDEA

Greece is mountainous and has an agricultural economy. It has relied on the sea for trade throughout its history.

Greece includes some 2,000 islands. Most of the country is covered by mountains and rocky soil. Farmers raise sheep and goats on the slopes. Wheat, olives, and citrus fruits are grown on the narrow coastal plains.

Athens, the capital, is a modern city with ancient monuments. Over one third of all Greeks live in and near Athens.

Greece depends on the sea for trade. It has one of the world's largest fleets of ships as well as a shipbuilding industry. Fishing and tourism are also important.

The sea also keeps Greece connected to its islands. Fewer than two hundred of the islands are **inhabitable,** or able to support a permanent population. The island of Crete puzzles people. About thirty-five hundred years ago, it was a center of culture and trade. Around 1500 B.C., the culture declined. Nobody today can fully explain why.

Western culture has many of its roots in ancient Greece. From the second century B.C. to the fifth century A.D., Greece was part of the Roman Empire. Then it became part of the Byzantine Empire. The Turks ruled Greece for nearly 400 years until Greece gained its independence in 1829.

Graphic Summary: *Comparing Four Mediterranean Countries*

Country	Population	Life Expectancy (years)	Per Capita GDP (in U.S. $)
Greece	10,647,529	78.9	19,900
Italy	58,057,477	79.5	26,800
Portugal	10,524,145	77.3	18,000
Spain	40,280,780	79.3	22,000

Source: *The World Factbook 2004*

Greece and Portugal are similar in size of population and per capita GDP.

Review Questions

1. What makes Greece a part of the Mediterranean region?

2. **Chart Skills** Which country has the highest population? Which one has the lowest life expectancy?

Name ______________________ Class ______________ Date ______________

Section 3: Greece

Guided Reading and Review

A. As You Read

Directions: *As you read Section 3, organize information about cause and effect in Greece by completing the chart below.*

Cause(s)	Effect
1. ______________________ ______________________ **2.** ______________________ ______________________ **3.** ______________________ ______________________	Greece may be considered part of Mediterranean Europe.
The African and Eurasian tectonic plates meet in southern Greece.	**4.** ______________________
5. ______________________	Greece has experienced soil erosion.
More than one third of Greece's total population lives in and around Athens.	**6.** ______________________
7. ______________________	Greece relies heavily on trade over water; shipbuilding is a key industry.
Greece has experienced military conquests by other cultures.	**8.** ______________________

B. Reviewing Vocabulary

Directions: *Complete each sentence by writing the correct term in the blank.*

9. The Aegean Sea to the east of the Greek mainland occupies a sunken area of land called a(n) ______________.

10. Fewer than 200 of the islands south of Greece are ______________, or able to support permanent residents.

11. The giant waves that were once thought to have helped destroy Crete are called ______________.

Name ______________________ Class ______________ Date ______________

Chapter 17 Test

Identifying Main Ideas

Directions: Write the letter of the correct answer in the blank provided. (10 points each)

____ **1. What mountains separate the Iberian Peninsula from the rest of Europe?**
A. the Pyrenees
B. the Alps
C. the Apennines
D. the Meseta

____ **2. What is a sirocco?**
A. a form of money used in Spain
B. the kind of climate found in Iberia
C. a warm current of water
D. a hot wind from northern Africa

____ **3. How are the Basques different from other people in Spain?**
A. They speak a language that is not related to other languages of Europe.
B. They speak only Spanish.
C. They want stronger ties with the Spanish government.
D. They have better farmland than other people in Spain.

____ **4. Where did Portugal once have colonies?**
A. in North America and Antarctica
B. in North America and South America
C. in Africa and Latin America
D. in northern Asia

____ **5. Where are most of Italy's factories located?**
A. in the south of the country
B. in the center of the country
C. in the north of the country
D. in Sardinia and Sicily

____ **6. Where is Italy's best farmland?**
A. in the north, in the Po River valley
B. in the southern islands of Sardinia and Sicily
C. in the southern tip of Italy's boot
D. in the central part of the country

____ **7. What was the Renaissance?**
A. the period when Italy was united as one country
B. a time of great art and learning
C. a time when people had to move to find work
D. the age when most factories were opened

____ **8. Which has Greece always depended on for trade?**
A. airports
B. the European Union
C. the sea
D. highways

____ **9. Which place would be considered *uninhabitable*?**
A. a place with a large permanent population
B. a place that cannot support a permanent population
C. a place with a small permanent population
D. a place with many tourists

____ **10. What industry is important in Greece?**
A. manufacturing automobiles
B. road-building
C. airplane construction
D. shipbuilding

Name ______________________ Class ______________ Date ______________

Chapter 18

Regional Atlas: Introduction to Central Europe and Northern Eurasia

Vocabulary
- acid rain
- communism
- Eurasia
- ethnic group
- infant mortality
- inland sea
- life expectancy

Vocabulary Development

Directions: *Using what you learned in Chapter 18, answer the following questions with one of the vocabulary terms to the right. Include the definition of the term in your answer.*

1. What political system did the Soviet Union adopt after the Russian Revolution?

____

____

2. What name was given to the large single continent that includes both Europe and Asia?

____

____

3. How would you describe the cultures of Central Europe and Northern Eurasia?

____

____

4. What is one harmful result of industrial activities in Central Europe and Northern Eurasia?

____

____

5. What is the term for the number of children who die within the first year of life?

____

____

6. What kind of body of water is the Black Sea?

____

____

7. What is one problem in Romania that is a result of pollution and a weak health care system?

____

____

Name ______________________ Class ______________ Date ______________

Regional Atlas: Central Europe and Northern Eurasia

Guide to the Essentials

Text Summary

Central Europe and Northern Eurasia spans two continents in the Northern Hemisphere. The land is generally flat in the west and rises higher in the east and the south. The region is covered in broad plains, which allowed for movement throughout history.

> **THE BIG IDEA**
>
> **Central Europe and Northern Eurasia covers a vast area. There are great physical, cultural, and economic differences between the west and east.**

The climates of the region range from Mediterranean to subarctic. Irkutsk, Russia, has the coldest winters of any place in the world besides Antarctica.

The **tundra,** a treeless plain in arctic areas where short grasses and mosses grow, covers northern Russia. Coniferous forests, called **taiga,** and grasslands, called the **steppe,** are found across Central Europe and in Russia.

A history of migration has resulted in a **multiethnic** region, containing many ethnic groups. Although **communism,** a system in which the government controlled almost all aspects of political and economic life, restricted religion, Orthodox Christianity is an important faith in Central Europe.

In the 1980s, the fall of communism resulted in a move to capitalism. Industrial activities have led to pollution and acid rain. The fall of communism affected the level of health care in many nations.

Graphic Summary: *Central Europe and Northern Eurasia*

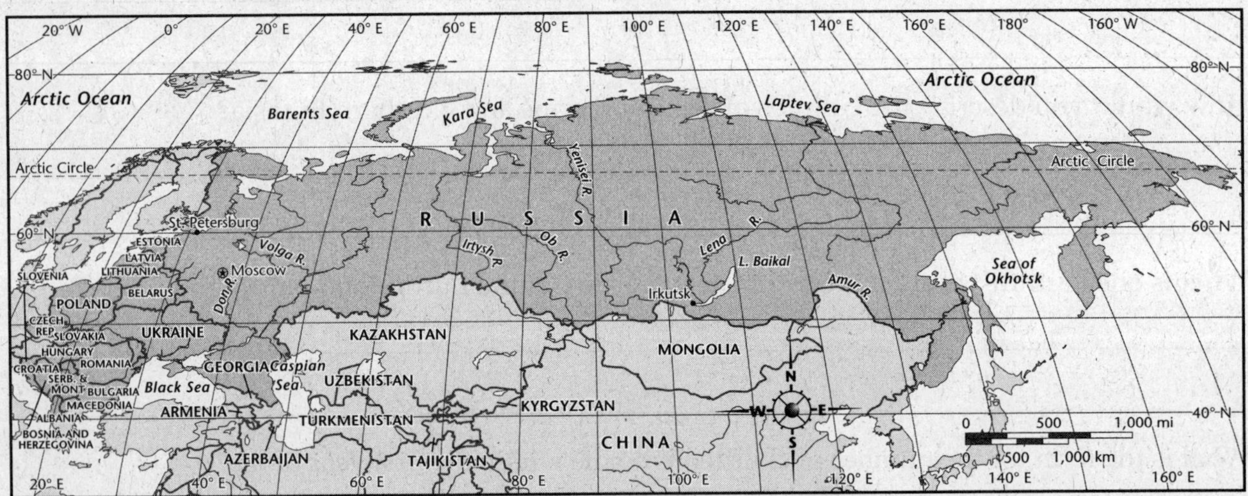

The borders of the countries of Central Europe and Northern Eurasia have changed often.

Review Questions

1. How has the geography of Central Europe and Northern Eurasia affected the movement of people across the region?
2. **Map Skills** What country of Central Europe and Northern Eurasia is the largest?

Name ______________________ Class ______________ Date ______________

Regional Atlas: Central Europe and Northern Eurasia

Guided Reading and Review

A. As You Read

Directions: *As you work through the Regional Atlas, complete the chart below by writing in details about Central Europe and Northern Eurasia for each topic listed.*

Topics	Details
Physical Characteristics	**1.** ______________ **2.** ______________
Major Climates	**3.** ______________ **4.** ______________
Major Ecosystems	**5.** ______________ **6.** ______________
Ethnic Groups	**7.** ______________ **8.** ______________
Major Economic Activities	**9.** ______________ **10.** ______________

B. Reviewing Vocabulary

Directions: *Define the following terms.*

11. domestication ______________

12. communism ______________

13. Eurasia ______________

14. inland sea ______________

15. tundra ______________

16. taiga ______________

17. steppe ______________

18. multiethnic ______________

19. ethnic group ______________

20. acid rain ______________

21. infant mortality ______________

22. maternal mortality ______________

23. life expectancy ______________

Name ____________________ Class ____________ Date ____________

Chapter 18 **Test**

Identifying Main Ideas

Directions: *Write the letter of the correct answer in the blank provided. (10 points each)*

____ **1. Central Europe and Northern Eurasia span**
A. four countries.
B. one continent.
C. two continents.
D. three countries.

____ **2. What common geographical feature of Central Europe and Northern Eurasia has allowed for easy migration?**
A. low mountains
B. broad plains
C. high mountains
D. coniferous forests

____ **3. In which hemisphere does Central Europe and Northern Eurasia lie?**
A. Western Hemisphere
B. Eastern Hemisphere
C. Southern Hemisphere
D. Northern Hemisphere

____ **4. What city is the coldest place in the world, besides Antarctica?**
A. Irkutsk, Russia
B. Minsk, Belarus
C. Prague, Czech Republic
D. Warsaw, Poland

____ **5. Taiga is**
A. deciduous forest.
B. coniferous forest.
C. grassland.
D. desert scrub.

____ **6. The steppe ecosystem is**
A. a fertile region used for farming.
B. a mountainous region used for herding animals.
C. a frigid region with little wildlife.
D. found only in Russia.

____ **7. The tundra ecosystem can be found in**
A. Serbia and Montenegro.
B. Romania.
C. Russia.
D. Albania.

____ **8. A region that is multiethnic has**
A. many forests.
B. many ethnic groups.
C. an official language.
D. no official language.

____ **9. What religion is important in many Central European countries?**
A. Buddhism
B. Islam
C. Christianity
D. Hinduism

____ **10. Before the 1980s, the national economies of the region were**
A. Marxist.
B. capitalist.
C. communist.
D. democratic.

Name ____________________ Class ____________ Date ____________

Chapter 19

Central and Eastern Europe

Vocabulary

- annex
- collective farm
- diversify
- entrepreneur
- ghetto
- Holocaust
- multiplier effect
- privatization

Vocabulary Development

Directions: *Write a sentence for each pair of terms below that shows you understand the relationship between them. Provide context clues so that a reader who may not know the meaning of the terms could figure them out.*

Holocaust/ghetto

____

____

____

privatization/collective farm

____

____

____

entrepreneur/multiplier effect

____

____

____

annex/diversify

____

____

____

Name ______________________ Class ______________ Date ______________

Section 1: Poland

Guide to the Essentials

Text Summary

Poland has been conquered many times. Yet the Polish people have kept their **national identity,** or sense of what makes them a nation. Their attachment to the land has helped them keep their national identity. So has their religion. Ninety-five percent of the people are Roman Catholic.

THE BIG IDEA

The Polish people kept their culture even when others ruled their country. A love of their land and belief in their religion helped shape the Polish identity.

Poland was a multiethnic country before World War II. Three million Jews lived in Poland. During the war, the Nazis forced Jews to live in **ghettoes,** city areas where minorities must live. Later the Nazis built six major concentration camps, or prison camps, in Poland. People from many countries, especially Jews, were murdered in these camps. By the end of the war, about 6 million Poles had been killed in concentration camps. Half of them were Jews. In all, the Nazis murdered more than 6 million European Jews. This destruction of human life is called the **Holocaust.**

After the war, a Communist government supported by the Soviet Union controlled Poland. It tried to do away with religion, but the Roman Catholic Church remained strong.

During the 1980s, a Polish labor union called Solidarity began to demand economic reforms and more freedom. Poland finally held free elections in 1989.

After communism ended, it was hard to turn state-controlled businesses into private businesses. Prices rose quickly. Many people lost their jobs. By the mid-1990s, the economy started to improve.

Graphic Summary: *Poland*

Poland's coast on the Baltic Sea provides a good opportunity for trade.

Review Questions

1. What helped Poles keep their national identity?

2. **Map Skills** Why do you think Gdańsk is an important city?

Name ______________________ Class ______________ Date ______________

Section 1: Poland

Guided Reading and Review

A. As You Read

Directions: *As you read Section 1, complete the chart below by writing two supporting details under each main idea.*

Main Idea A: Poland has varied natural resources.

1. ____

2. ____

Main Idea B: Since World War II, Poland has become a nation composed of one ethnic group.

3. ____

4. ____

Main Idea C: Communists fell from power in Poland because they lacked popular support.

5. ____

6. ____

B. Reviewing Vocabulary

Directions: *Complete each sentence by writing the correct term in the blank.*

7. Despite centuries of domination by foreign powers, the Polish people maintained their ________________.

8. The Nazi regime of Germany, after occupying Poland, sealed off the Jewish ________________ within Polish cities.

9. Historians refer to the mass killing of millions of Jews and other Europeans during World War II as the ________________, a word for a fire that burns something completely.

Name ______________________ Class ______________ Date ______________

Section 2: The Czech and Slovak Republics, and Hungary

Guide to the Essentials

Text Summary

The Czechs, Slovaks, and Hungarians share historical links with Western Europe. But their countries have major differences.

THE BIG IDEA

The three countries have shifted to free-market economies. Hungary's economy is improving, the Czech Republic has done well, but Slovakia has been struggling.

After World War I, Czechoslovakia became a new nation with two main groups—Czechs and Slovaks. After World War II, the Soviet Union placed a Communist government in Czechoslovakia. In the late 1980s, Czechoslovakia ended Communist rule. In 1993, it divided peacefully into the Czech Republic and Slovak Republic—also called Slovakia.

The Czech Republic began **privatization**, or selling government businesses to private companies. The country has many industries, but many factories are old, and pollution is a serious problem.

Slovakia has a mixed economy of manufacturing and farming. The Communists turned private farms into **collective farms**, where farmers were paid by the government and shared profits. Slovakia is now trying to return farms to private owners. Slovakia has political problems as well as a struggling economy.

About 90 percent of Hungarians are Magyars. Hungary became a nation in the year 1000. It fought off many foreign rulers but could not drive out the Soviet-backed Communist government. In 1990, Hungarians elected their first democratic government in over forty years. It began to return businesses to private companies.

The fertile farm region east of the Danube River in Hungary is called "the breadbasket of Europe."

Graphic Summary: *The Czech Republic, Slovakia, and Hungary*

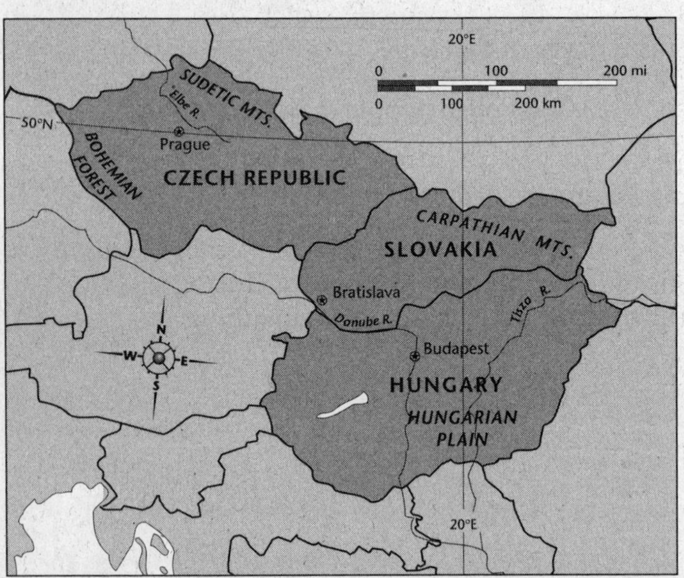

None of these three countries has a seacoast.

Review Questions

1. What united these countries in the years after World War II?

2. **Map Skills** What river forms part of the border between Slovakia and Hungary?

Name ________________________ Class ________________ Date ________________

Section 2: The Czech and Slovak Republics, and Hungary

Guided Reading and Review

A. As You Read

Directions: *As you read Section 2, organize information about the Czech Republic, Slovakia, and Hungary by completing the chart below.*

Country	Details
The Czech Republic	
Size	**1.** ________________
Description of Landscape	**2.** ________________
Description of Regions	**3.** ________________
Slovakia	
Year of Independence	**4.** ________________
Description of Landscape	**5.** ________________
Basis of Economy	**6.** ________________
Hungary	
Dominant Ethnic Group	**7.** ________________
Main Religion	**8.** ________________
Description of Regions	**9.** ________________
Basis of Economy	**10.** ________________

B. Reviewing Vocabulary

Directions: *Read the statements below. If a statement is true, write T in the blank. If it is false, write F.*

_____ **11.** The Czech rebellion against communism came to be called the "velvet revolution" because it was not harsh enough and eventually failed.

_____ **12.** The Czech government has led a vigorous program of selling state-owned businesses called privatization.

_____ **13.** The Communist regimes of Eastern Europe ended private ownership in agriculture by gathering farmland together in collective farms.

Name ______________________ Class ______________ Date ______________

Section 3: The Balkan Peninsula

Guide to the Essentials

Text Summary

The Balkan Peninsula was ruled by the Turks for 500 years. After World War I, the region broke up into small unfriendly countries. This event led to a new word—**balkanize**. Communists controlled the Balkans after 1948. In the late 1980s, these countries began to overthrow their Communist governments.

THE BIG IDEA

The countries of the Balkan Peninsula share a history of conflict and foreign control. Many countries are multiethnic.

Under communism, Romania had serious economic problems. Several leaders promised reform, but the economy grew worse. A United States soft drink maker has helped **entrepreneurs** start shops to sell soft drinks. Entrepreneurs are people who start and build businesses.

Bulgaria has fertile soil and mild weather. It is known as the garden of Eastern Europe. Bulgaria has a democratic government, but Communists still play a large role. By the mid-1990s, Bulgaria had found foreign markets for its goods and was welcoming tourists to its Black Sea resorts.

Albania's Communist leaders kept the country isolated. It became one of the poorest countries in Europe. Since it became democractic in the early 1990s, companies from other countries have opened factories in Albania because wages are low.

After World War I, Yugoslavia became a new country with many ethnic groups that did not get along. After Communist control ended, four of its republics declared independence. Only Serbia and Montenegro stayed in Yugoslavia (however the name was dropped in 2003). Fighting began between the newly independent countries and among their ethnic groups. The worst fighting was in Bosnia and Herzegovina.

Graphic Summary: *The Breakup of Yugoslavia*

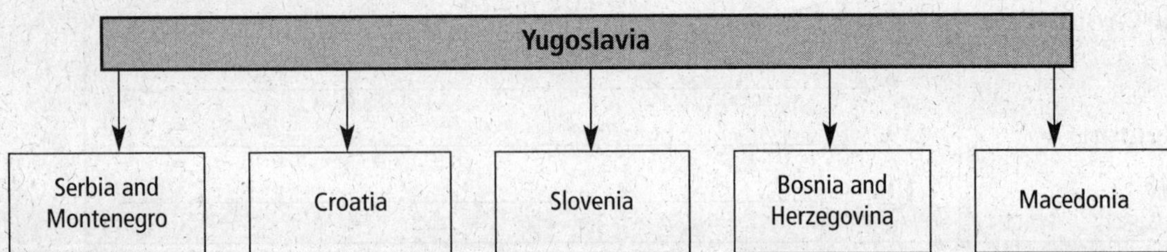

Many countries in the Balkan Peninsula are small, but Yugoslavia broke up into even smaller countries.

Review Questions

1. What does the word *balkanize* mean?

2. **Chart Skills** How many countries were created when Yugoslavia broke up?

Name ______________________ Class ______________ Date ______________

Section 3: The Balkan Peninsula

Guided Reading and Review

A. As You Read

Directions: *As you read Section 3, complete the chart below by answering the questions about the Balkan nations.*

Question	Answer
Which country was ruled by a Communist leader named Nicolae Ceausescu, who led the country to economic chaos?	1. ______________
Which country is known as the garden of Eastern Europe because of its warm summers and mild winters?	2. ______________
Which country, known for decades as "Europe's hermit," is now ending its isolation?	3. ______________
Which republics remained joined in the country of Yugoslavia until the early 2000s?	4. ______________
Which area was the key point of conflict in the late 1990s?	5. ______________
Which part of the former Yugoslavia is expected to recover quickly from the problems brought by war and independence?	6. ______________
Which country was embroiled in war between three different ethnic groups after declaring its independence?	7. ______________
Which country experienced conflict based on its national language policy?	8. ______________

B. Reviewing Vocabulary

Directions: *Define the following terms.*

9. balkanize ______________________________

10. entrepreneur ______________________________

11. multiplier effect ______________________________

Name ______________________ Class ______________ Date ______________

Section 4: Baltic States and Border Nations

Guide to the Essentials

Text Summary

The Baltic states and border nations along Russia's western edge were once republics within the Soviet Union. After 1991, these republics became independent nations.

THE BIG IDEA

The nations of this region were once republics within the Soviet Union. Since independence in 1991, they have struggled to improve their economies.

Lithuania, Latvia, and Estonia are mainly flat with fertile plains. The Baltic Sea has brought both trade and invasion. Soviet forces invaded in 1939 and **annexed**, or formally added, the Baltic states to the Soviet Union.

Since independence, the Baltic states have privatized industries and encouraged foreign investment and trade. They have also begun to **diversify**, or increase the variety of, their industries.

Ukraine was where the first Russian state began over 1,000 years ago. Under Communist Soviet rule, Ukrainians were forced to work on collective farms. Ukrainians protested by burning crops. In response, Soviet forces seized all grain. As a result, 5 to 8 million Ukrainians starved to death. In 1986, an explosion destroyed a nuclear reactor in Chernobyl, causing severe damage to human life and the environment.

Ukraine has large fertile plains and huge coal resources. The export of its many farm products has helped the economy. But outdated machinery, lack of foreign investment, and the need to import oil hold Ukraine back from economic prosperity.

Unlike other former republics, Belarus favors its close ties with Russia. It has strong industrial and service industries, as well as oil, but it must import most of the resources needed for its industries.

Moldova is the most densely populated of the former republics. It was once ruled by Romania, and Romanian is now the language used in schools.

Graphic Summary: *Baltic States and Border Nations*

COUNTRY	AREA (in square miles)	CAPITAL
Belarus	80,154	Minsk
Estonia	17,413	Tallinn
Latvia	24,942	Riga
Lithuania	25,174	Vilnius
Moldova	13,012	Chisinau
Ukraine	233,089	Kiev

Source: *Microsoft Encarta Interactive World Atlas 2000*

All of these nations were once part of the Soviet Union.

Review Questions

1. What have the Baltic states done since independence to improve their economies?

2. **Chart Skills** What is the largest nation in the Baltic states and border nations region? What is the smallest?

Name ______________________ Class ______________ Date ______________

Section 4: Baltic States and Border Nations

Guided Reading and Review

A. As You Read

Directions: *As you read Section 4, complete the chart below by answering the questions about the Baltic states and border nations.*

Question	Answer
Which three nations on the coast of the Baltic Sea were officially republics of the Soviet Union until it broke apart in 1991?	**1.** ______________ **2.** ______________ **3.** ______________
The language of which nation is closely related to Finnish?	**4.** ______________
Which nation is known as a "breadbasket" of Eastern Europe because of its productive farmland?	**5.** ______________
Which nation had more than one fifth of its farmland contaminated by radiation blown across it after the accident at Chernobyl?	**6.** ______________
What nation has a population mostly of Romanian descent and continues to have strong ties to Romania?	**7.** ______________

B. Reviewing Vocabulary

Directions: *Define the following terms.*

8. annex ______________________________

9. diversify ______________________________

Name ______________________ Class ______________ Date ______________

Chapter 19 Test

Identifying Main Ideas

Directions: Write the letter of the correct answer in the blank provided. (10 points each)

____ **1. What is a ghetto?**
- A. an agricultural area
- B. an industrial region
- C. an area where a minority group has to live
- D. an area where people go to build farms

____ **2. The murder of Jews, Poles, and other people by the Nazis during World War II is called**
- A. a ghetto.
- B. a concentration camp.
- C. the Holocaust.
- D. Communist.

____ **3. In Poland, Solidarity is**
- A. the name of the communist government.
- B. the Soviet government which ruled Poland.
- C. a labor union that fought for reform.
- D. the nickname of the president.

____ **4. Czechoslovakia split into two countries**
- A. in a war.
- B. after Communists ordered the split.
- C. because of privatization.
- D. peacefully.

____ **5. When a country starts privatization, it**
- A. sells government-owned businesses to private companies.
- B. sells private companies to the government.
- C. investigates people's private lives.
- D. takes property from private citizens.

____ **6. Hungary is called "the breadbasket of Europe" because**
- A. of its fertile farm region.
- B. it bakes more bread than any other country.
- C. its people eat more bread than those of any other country.
- D. of its special kind of breadbaskets.

____ **7. What is an entrepreneur?**
- A. a person who works on a government farm
- B. a person who works in a government-owned business
- C. a person who starts and builds a business
- D. a political leader

____ **8. Why did Yugoslavia break up?**
- A. It had no central government.
- B. Its people could not earn a living.
- C. Most people wanted to return to communism.
- D. The different ethnic groups did not get along.

____ **9. When the Baltic states were annexed by the Soviet Union they were**
- A. cut off from Soviet support.
- B. formally added to the Soviet Union.
- C. targets for Soviet missiles.
- D. freed from Soviet control.

____ **10. The Chernobyl nuclear explosion occurred in**
- A. Belarus.
- B. Romania.
- C. Ukraine.
- D. Estonia.

Name ________________ Class ________ Date ________

Chapter 20 Russia

Vocabulary

- black market
- chernozem
- command economy
- perestroika
- ruble
- steppe
- taiga
- tundra

Vocabulary Development

Directions: *Divide the vocabulary terms listed into the two categories below, based on each word's significance in the chapter you have just read about Russia.*

Russia's Physical Characteristics	Russia's Economy

Directions: *Write two sentences on each of the following topics using what you have learned in Chapter 20. Use at least three vocabulary terms for each topic.*

Topic: Russia's Physical Characteristics

____

____

____

____

Topic: Russia's Economy

____

____

____

____

Name ______________________ Class ______________ Date ______________

Section 1: Regions of Russia

Guide to the Essentials

Text Summary

THE BIG IDEA

Russia is the largest country on earth. It has rich natural resources, but its size and climate make it hard to develop them.

Russia is the world's largest country. It stretches across ten time zones, encompassing a varied terrain. The land is fairly flat, consisting mainly of plateaus and rolling plains.

The Ural Mountains divide Europe from Asia. These low mountains contain great mineral wealth. Russia has many rivers, including the Ob, Yenisey, and Lena, which flow into the Arctic Ocean. The Volga River, Europe's longest river, drains into the Caspian Sea, the world's largest lake.

The ecosystems are closely related to location and climate. The climate is mainly continental or subarctic. Along the arctic shore is an area of **tundra**, a largely treeless region with only tiny plants and animal life that can survive the polar conditions. Forests cover almost half of Russia and are home to many animals, including the sable and the brown bear. The fertile soil of Russia's grasslands, called **chernozem**, provides nutrients for growing crops.

The Asian part of Russia is known as Siberia. A cool and swampy area, it has a layer of **permafrost**, or permanently frozen soil. It has rich reserves of minerals and oil, but its harsh climate and terrain make mining these resources very difficult.

Graphic Summary: *Russia*

Russia stretches across eastern Europe and northern Asia.

Review Questions

1. What is chernozem?

2. Map Skills What is the capital of Russia?

Name ______________________ Class ______________ Date ______________

Section 1: Regions of Russia

Guided Reading and Review

A. As You Read

Directions: *As you read Section 1, complete the chart below by writing a supporting detail under each main idea.*

Main Idea A: Russia is a large country that contains a variety of physical features.

1. ______________________________

2. ______________________________

Main Idea B: Plant life in Russia is closely related to location and climate.

3. ______________________________

4. ______________________________

Main Idea C: Siberia's geology is complex and presents both problems and wealth.

5. ______________________________

6. ______________________________

B. Reviewing Vocabulary

Directions: *Complete each sentence by writing the correct term in the blank.*

7. Large areas of central Russia are ______________, or broad expanses of rich soil formed by grasslands.

8. Russia's most productive agricultural area has black soil called ______________.

9. Russia's Arctic shore is dominated by a treeless zone, the ______________, containing small plants and animals adapted to polar conditions.

10. The broad forested zone called the ______________ has trees that do not grow to great size because of harsh conditions.

11. In Siberia, a layer of permanently frozen soil called ______________ can extend 5,000 feet below the surface.

Name ______________________ Class ______________ Date ______________

Section 2: Emergence of Russia

Guide to the Essentials

Text Summary

THE BIG IDEA

Russia's history is one of conquest and invasion. The command economy of the Soviet Union led to poverty and dissatisfaction with the government. Since the 1990s, Russia has made many efforts to improve its economy and standard of living.

Modern Russia began in the 800s, when Vikings established a state in what is now Kiev, Ukraine. The Slavic people who lived there accepted the state. Orthodox Christianity became the main religion of the region.

Mongol warriors conquered the area, but Russia regained control and set up a series of monarchs, called **czars**, to rule the land. Under the czars, the nation expanded its borders.

In 1812 Napoleon of France invaded Russia, capturing Moscow. The Russians burned their cities as they fled, and Napoleon began leading his troops back to France. However, the troops were unprepared for Russia's harsh climate and terrain. Almost all of Napoleon's men died on this return trip. By the twentieth century, Russia controlled nearly all of northern Eurasia.

The Russian Revolution in 1917 caused the czar to **abdicate**, or give up his crown. The revolutionaries established a Communist dictatorship called the Union of Soviet Socialist Republics, or the Soviet Union.

The Soviet Union had a **command economy**, which meant the government decided what goods would be produced. The government also controlled people's lives. Those who complained were sent to prison and labor camps or killed.

In the late 1980s, a new leader, Mikhail Gorbachev, introduced a policy of ***glasnost***, or openness, that allowed people to speak freely. The government also offered a plan for **perestroika**, or economic restructuring. This called for a gradual change from a command economy to private ownership.

Since the end of 1991, Russia's government has become democratic, but Communist beliefs are still held by a large number of the population.

Graphic Summary: *Events in Russia up to the Russian Revolution*

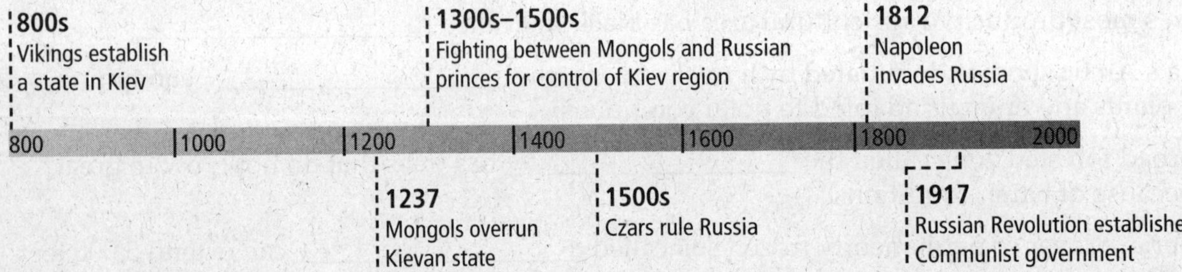

Russia has experienced many invasions and conquests.

Review Questions

1. What policies did the Russian government establish during the late 1980s?

2. **Time Line Skills** What happened in 1237 in Russia?

Name ______________________ Class ______________ Date ______________

Section 2: Emergence of Russia

Guided Reading and Review

A. As You Read

Directions: As you read Section 2, answer the following questions.

1. What two groups established the first Russian state in the 800s?

   ____

2. Which Russian czar expanded Russian rule east to the Pacific?

   ____

3. What French ruler invaded Russia in 1812, and why was he forced to retreat?

   ____

4. What 1917 event put an end to rule by czars and established a Communist government?

   ____

5. How did communism affect Russia's economy?

   ____

6. What Soviet leader began radical reforms in the late 1980s?

   ____

B. Reviewing Vocabulary

Directions: Complete each sentence by writing the correct term in the blank.

7. In the past, Russian monarchs were called ______________.
8. A monarch who gives up his or her crown is said to ______________.
9. A(n) ______________ was a governing council of the U.S.S.R.
10. An economy in which a central authority decides what goods will be produced is a(n) ______________.
11. A policy of ______________, or openness, was instituted in the U.S.S.R. in the late 1980s.
12. In putting ______________ into effect, the Soviets committed to gradual change to an economic system of private ownership.

Name ____________________ Class ____________ Date ____________

Section 3: Geographic Issues in Russia

Guide to the Essentials

Text Summary

THE BIG IDEA

Russia faces many challenges. Ethnic conflict, insufficient transportation, and pollution have left many in the nation struggling.

More than 80 percent of Russia's inhabitants consider themselves Russian, the descendants of the Slavic peoples. Almost three fourths of Russia's people live in urban areas. However, traditional ways of life continue in villages and rural areas.

About 25 million residents of Russia belong to non-Russian ethnic groups. Intense ethnic conflict has occurred in the republics within the Caucasus region. The worst fighting has taken place in Chechnya. Desiring independence, Chechens fought a guerrilla war against Russian control during the 1990s. After a three-year cease-fire, fighting between the two countries resumed.

Transportation within Russia has been a challenge. Travel by road is slow and almost impossible during winter months. Air travel is costly and unsuitable for the transport of resources. The many rivers in Russia provide a good method of transport, but they too cannot be used in the winter when they are frozen. Railroads are the most important means of transportation. Several major railroad systems run through the nation, including the great Trans-Siberian Railroad.

Changing from a command economy to a market economy has been difficult for Russia. Consumer goods are scarce and unemployment is high. Financial instability led to the growth of a **black market**, through which goods and services move unofficially without formal record keeping.

Russia faces many other challenges. The health of the population has declined since the 1990s. Intense industrialization depleted natural resources and contaminated many urban areas and bodies of water. Lack of money hinders Russia's ability to solve these problems.

Graphic Summary: *Comparing Russia and the United States*

Country	Population	Life Expectancy (years)	Per Capita GDP (in U.S. $)
Russia	143,782,338	66.4	8,900
United States	293,027,571	77.4	37,800

Source: *The World Factbook 2004*

Russia's demographic data differs greatly from that of the United States.

Review Questions

1. How many people living in Russia consider themselves Russian?

2. **Chart Skills** Which nation has a stronger economy—Russia or the United States? Why?

Name ______________________ Class ______________ Date ______________

Section 3: Geographic Issues in Russia

Guided Reading and Review

A. As You Read

Directions: *As you read Section 3, complete the chart below by filling in the correct answers to each question.*

Question	Answer
What are three leisure activities Russians may enjoy?	**1.** ______________ **2.** ______________ **3.** ______________
Identify the republic in the Caucasus region where intense fighting recently occurred when it tried to gain independence from Russia.	**4.** ______________
What is Russia's major means of transportation?	**5.** ______________
What are three problems that the transition from a command economy to a market economy has caused Russia?	**6.** ______________ **7.** ______________ **8.** ______________
Identify two bodies of water in or around Russia with major pollution problems.	**9.** ______________ **10.** ______________

B. Reviewing Vocabulary

Directions: *Complete each sentence by writing the correct term in the blank.*

11. The official Russian currency, the ______________, had an official value of U.S. $1.75, but lost value after the fall of communism.

12. The ______________, or an informal transfer of goods and services without official record keeping, has grown in Russian in response to economic instability.

Name ______________________ Class ______________ Date ______________

Chapter 20 Test

Identifying Main Ideas

Directions: *Write the letter of the correct answer in the blank provided. (10 points each)*

____ **1. Europe's longest river is the**
A. Volga.
B. Lena.
C. Ob.
D. Yenisey.

____ **2. The climate of Russia is mainly**
A. continental and Mediterranean.
B. subarctic and continental.
C. arid and subarctic.
D. semiarid and continental.

____ **3. What is chernozem?**
A. Russia's national flower
B. a type of spice found in Siberia
C. a small town in northern Russia
D. the fertile soil of Russia's grasslands

____ **4. Permafrost can be found**
A. in Siberia.
B. in the Caucasus Mountains.
C. around the Caspian Sea.
D. along the Ob River.

____ **5. Where was the first Russian state established?**
A. Kiev, Ukraine
B. Bucharest, Romania
C. Minsk, Belarus
D. Moscow, Russia

____ **6. What is a czar?**
A. a communist leader
B. a Russian monarch
C. a Siberian king
D. a modern president

____ **7. What is the name of the Communist dictatorship that ruled much of Northern Eurasia?**
A. the Russia Empire
B. the Ural Republic
C. Siberia
D. the Soviet Union

____ **8. Perestroika is**
A. a plan for economic restructuring.
B. a policy of openness.
C. the type of economy adopted by the Soviet Union.
D. a type of Russian dance.

____ **9. The most important method of transportation in Russia is the**
A. airplane.
B. boat.
C. train.
D. car.

____ **10. Russia**
A. lacks industrialization.
B. has a command economy.
C. has little unemployment.
D. has severe pollution problems.

Name ______________________ Class ______________ Date ______________

Chapter 21

Regional Atlas: Introduction to Central and Southwest Asia

Vocabulary
agricultural revolution
civilization
monotheism
protectorate
mosque
muezzin

Vocabulary Development

Directions: *Write a brief definition for each of the listed terms. Then, using all the terms, write a paragraph about the history and cultures of Central and Southwest Asia. In your writing, be sure to show that you understand how the concepts work together.*

agricultural revolution

____

civilization

____

monotheism

____

protectorate

____

mosque

____

muezzin

____

Paragraph:

____

____

____

____

____

Name ______________________ Class ______________ Date ______________

Regional Atlas: Central and Southwest Asia

Guide to the Essentials

Text Summary

The Fertile Crescent in Southwest Asia was the birthplace of civilization and agriculture. Around 8000 B.C., people began to plant crops and raise livestock in a process called the **agricultural revolution**.

Central and Southwest Asia's location made it a target for invasion. After World War I, European powers divided the region. Once all countries gained independence, conflict remained as nations fought for land control.

THE BIG IDEA

For hundreds of years, cultures have exchanged goods and ideas and often clashed in this region. Judaism, Christianity, and Islam developed there.

The region, covered mainly with mountains and plains, is mostly arid or semiarid. Seaside areas have steady temperatures, while inland areas have cold winters and hot summers.

Most of the region has a desert ecosystem. The **chaparral** ecosystem, with drought-resistant herbs and bushes, is found near the Black and Mediterranean seas. Pollution and **poaching**, or illegal hunting, threaten the wildlife of the Caspian Sea.

Three major religions began in the region: Judaism, Christianity, and Islam. All are based on **monotheism**, a belief in one God. Most people in the region are Muslims. Religious differences have led to many conflicts. Such conflict is severe in Jerusalem, a sacred city to all three religions.

Most of the population lives in urban areas, where the main economic activities are services and industry. The region contains large reserves of oil and natural gas.

Water shortages are a challenge for the region. Some nations have built **desalination plants**, where seawater is evaporated to obtain fresh water.

The countries in this region rely on trade. Most countries in this region export large amounts of oil to get the goods and foods they need.

Graphic Summary: *Central and Southwest Asia*

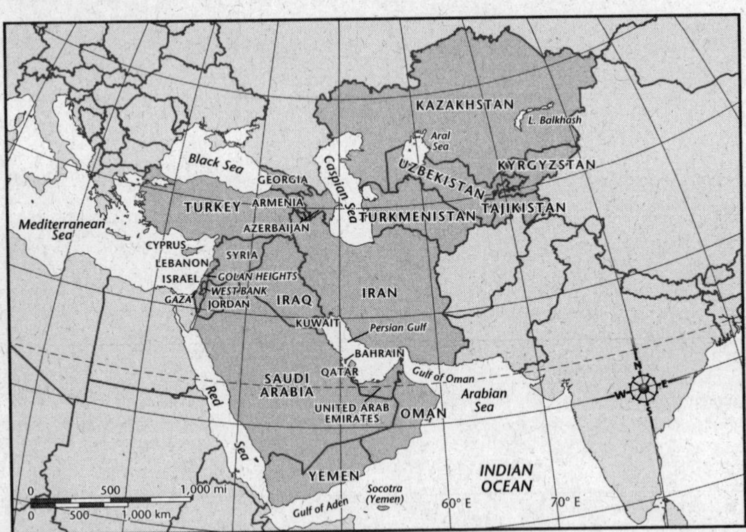

Central and Southwest Asia is a region surrounded by three continents.

Review Questions

1. What three monotheistic religions began in Southwest Asia?

2. **Map Skills** Which four Central and Southwest Asian countries border the Caspian Sea?

Name ______________________ Class ______________ Date ______________

Regional Atlas: Central and Southwest Asia

Guided Reading and Review

A. As You Read

Directions: *As you work through the Regional Atlas, complete the chart below. Under each main idea, write two or three supporting details.*

Main Idea A: Central and Southwest Asia is the birthplace of three of the world's major religions.

1. ______________________

2. ______________________

3. ______________________

Main Idea B: Much of the land in Central and Southwest Asia is dry.

4. ______________________

5. ______________________

Main Idea C: The countries in this region have found ways to compensate for a short supply of fresh water.

6. ______________________

7. ______________________

B. Reviewing Vocabulary

Directions: *Define the following terms.*

8. agricultural revolution ______________________

9. civilization ______________________

10. monotheism ______________________

11. protectorate ______________________

12. chaparral ______________________

13. poaching ______________________

14. mosque ______________________

15. muezzin ______________________

16. minaret ______________________

17. desalination plant ______________________

18. nomad ______________________

19. trade deficit ______________________

20. trade surplus ______________________

Name ____________________ Class ____________ Date ____________

Chapter 21 **Test**

Identifying Main Ideas

Directions: *Write the letter of the correct answer in the blank provided. (10 points each)*

____ **1. The agricultural revolution can be described as**
A. a great migration from urban to rural areas.
B. replacing old ways of farming with modern machinery.
C. the time when people began planting crops and raising livestock.
D. the trade of crops with foreign nations.

____ **2. The climate of the region is mostly**
A. Mediterranean and subtropical.
B. arid and semiarid.
C. semiarid and subtropical.
D. arid and subarctic.

____ **3. Where are steady temperatures most likely to be found?**
A. seaside
B. inland
C. in Tajikistan
D. in central Iran

____ **4. What is chaparral?**
A. a type of coniferous forest
B. an area of drought-resistant bushes
C. another name for a desert
D. a wet, marshy area

____ **5. In which body of water has poaching become a threat to the wildlife?**
A. Black Sea
B. Mediterranean Sea
C. Caspian Sea
D. Red Sea

____ **6. Monotheism is**
A. a belief in several gods.
B. a belief in one god.
C. a belief that God does not exist.
D. a combination of several religions.

____ **7. Most people in Central and Southwest Asia are**
A. Christian.
B. Jewish.
C. Buddhist.
D. Muslim.

____ **8. Where does most of the region's population live?**
A. in urban areas
B. in rural areas
C. in central Saudi Arabia
D. near the Aral Sea

____ **9. The region contains large reserves of what natural resource?**
A. coal
B. gold
C. phosphates
D. oil

____ **10. Desalination plants are used to**
A. pump oil out of the ground.
B. convert saltwater to fresh water.
C. clean urban areas.
D. produce consumer goods.

Name ______________________ Class ______________ Date ______________

Chapter 22

The Caucasus and Central Asia

Vocabulary
autonomy
desertification
fundamentalism
genocide

Vocabulary Development

Directions: *One way to learn more about words is to study their parts. Each of the vocabulary words in the chart below contains either a prefix, a suffix, or both. For each word listed, review its prefixes and suffixes. Then, fill in the definition of the word in the last column based on the information in the chart and what you learned in the chapter.*

Word	Parts	Part meaning	Definition of Word
autonomy	auto-	Prefix meaning *self*	
	-y	Suffix meaning *full of*	
desertification	-fication	Suffix meaning *to make or create*	
fundamentalism	-al	Suffix meaning *of, like, or suitable for*	
	-ism	Suffix meaning *state of*	
genocide	geno-	Prefix meaning *race or kind*	
	-cide	Suffix meaning *killing*	

Directions: *Use each of the words listed above in a sentence of your own.*

autonomy ____

____

desertification ____

____

fundamentalism ____

____

genocide ____

____

Name ____________ Class ____________ Date ____________

Section 1: The Caucasus Nations

Guide to the Essentials

Text Summary

The former Soviet republics of Georgia, Armenia, and Azerbaijan lie in the Caucasus Mountains. Many ethnic groups live here, and their differences have often led to violence.

THE BIG IDEA

After gaining independence in 1991, the Caucasus nations have had to cope with many ethnic and political issues. The nations of the region are still working to resolve conflict.

Georgia is mountainous, with fertile river valleys. Tourists are attracted to the subtropical climate near the Black Sea. A continental climate is found inland.

After the fall of communism, the economy declined. Agriculture and machine manufacturing helped improve the economy after the mid-1990s. Georgia has increased the extraction of its manganese, coal, and oil reserves.

About 70 percent of Georgia's population are descendants of ethnic Georgians. Ethnic groups in the northern region seek **autonomy**, or independence, from Georgia.

Armenia is landlocked and has a rocky terrain. Farmers grow crops in southern valleys. Rug making is a traditional craft. The people are primarily Christian.

Armenia has had bitter relations with its neighbor Turkey. During World War I, Turks attempted to deport the people of Armenia. One third of all Armenians died en route or were killed in this act of **genocide**, the systematic killing or intentional destruction of a people.

Armenia has more recently fought with the Azeri people of Azerbaijan, a mainly Islamic nation. Both Azeris and Armenians have feelings of **nationalism**, the desire of a cultural group to rule themselves as a separate nation. This has led to violent conflicts.

Azerbaijan is on the western coast of the Caspian Sea. Rich deposits of oil are the nation's main source of wealth. Half the population are rural herders. Ninety percent of the population are ethnic Azeris. Most other ethnic groups fled as tensions intensified.

Azerbaijan's conflict with Armenia has caused severe economic problems. With no access to the Mediterranean and Black seas, Azerbaijan has trouble reaching world markets. Oil and chemical industries have caused great environmental damage.

Graphic Summary: *The Caucasus Nations*

Country	Land Area (sq. mi.)	Population	Projected Population 2025
Armenia	11,506	2,991,360	3,433,747
Azerbaijan	33,436	7,868,385	9,429,191
Georgia	26,911	4,693,892	4,718,035

Sources: *Microsoft Encarta World Almanac 2000*, Population Reference Bureau, and *The World Factbook 2004*

The Caucasus nations may be small in size, but the diversity of their populations is large.

Review Questions

1. What is genocide?

2. **Chart Skills** Which nation's population will increase the least by 2025?

Name ______________________ Class ______________ Date ______________

Section 1: The Caucasus Nations

Guided Reading and Review

A. As You Read

Directions: *As you read Section 1, complete the chart below about the Caucasus nations by supplying the missing question or answer.*

Question	Answer(s)
What are the names of the Caucasus nations?	1. ______________ 2. ______________ 3. ______________
4. ______________	Black Sea and Caspian Sea
Which two nations have had recent conflicts due to religious tensions?	5. ______________ 6. ______________
Which two Caucasus nations are not landlocked?	7. ______________ 8. ______________
9. ______________	They are predominantly Islamic.
Which nation's major source of wealth is oil?	10. ______________
Which country's subtropical climate allows growth of wine grapes, citrus fruit, and tea?	11. ______________

B. Reviewing Vocabulary

Directions: *Complete each sentence by writing the correct term in the blank.*

12. Several ethnic groups in Georgia have pressed for more ______________, or independence.

13. ______________ is the systematical killing or intentional destruction of a people.

14. The desire of the Azeri and Armenian cultural groups to rule themselves in separate nations is called ______________.

Name ______________________ Class ______________ Date ______________

Section 2: The Central Asian Nations

Guide to the Essentials

Text Summary

Stretching from the Caspian Sea to mountain ranges along China's western border are the Central Asian nations of Kazakhstan, Kyrgyzstan, Tajikistan, Turkmenistan, and Uzbekistan.

THE BIG IDEA

Kazakhstan, Kyrgyzstan, Tajikistan, Turkmenistan, and Uzbekistan make up Central Asia. Under Soviet rule, these nations withstood dramatic cultural changes. Since independence, they have been developing their economies.

Mountains are found in the southeast. In the east are two of Asia's largest deserts, the Kara Kum and the Kyzyl Kum. Central Asia's climate is mostly arid or semiarid.

Northern Kazakhstan has steppes and grassland with a rich topsoil called **chernozem**. This soil makes the region good for farming. Parts of Central Asia also have large reserves of oil and natural gas.

The Central Asian nations have diverse ethnic, religious, and language groups. Most people in the region are Islamic. Since independence, some leaders have supported Islamic fundamentalism. **Fundamentalism** is a set of religious beliefs based on a strict reading of a sacred text.

Traditionally, most Central Asians were nomadic herders. Under Soviet rule, people were forced to work on government farms. Industrialization was encouraged, spurring the growth of cities. Since independence, industry has grown and tourism has become important.

Rapid industrialization has led to environmental problems. Soviets diverted Central Asian rivers from the Aral Sea for irrigation. The amount of water reaching the Aral Sea decreased, causing the sea to shrink and become more salty. This has also lead to **desertification**, the extension of the desert landscape due to environmental changes caused by humans.

Graphic Summary: *Central Asia*

The terrain of Central Asia is very diverse.

Review Questions

1. What is the most practiced religion in Central Asia?

2. **Map Skills** What Central Asian country is the largest?

Name ____________________ Class ______________ Date ______________

Section 2: The Central Asian Nations

Guided Reading and Review

A. As You Read

Directions: As you read Section 2, fill in the chart on Central Asia below with details for each category listed.

Central Asia	
Nations	**Largest Deserts**
1. ________ **4.** ________ **2.** ________ **5.** ________ **3.** ________	**6.** ________ **7.** ________
Rural Economic Activities	**Major Environmental Problems**
8. ________ **9.** ________	**10.** ________ **11.** ________

B. Reviewing Vocabulary

Directions: Complete each sentence by writing the correct term in the blank.

12. ______________ is a rich topsoil that is good for agriculture.

13. ______________, a set of religious beliefs based on a strict interpretation of a sacred text, is common in many parts of Central Asia.

14. Traditional herders in Central Asia often lived in ______________, large, portable, round tents made of wooden frames covered with felt or skins.

15. The diversion of water from the Aral Sea has caused ______________, the extension of the desert landscape due to changes caused by humans.

Name ______________________ Class ______________ Date ______________

Chapter 22

Test

Identifying Main Ideas

Directions: Write the letter of the correct answer in the blank provided. (10 points each)

____ **1. Between which two seas are the Caucasus nations?**
A. Aral and Black seas
B. Caspian and Aral seas
C. Mediterranean and Black seas
D. Caspian and Black seas

____ **2. If a nation wants autonomy, what is it seeking?**
A. automatic dictatorship
B. economic success
C. independence
D. free trade agreements

____ **3. Which country has trouble reaching world markets because of its location?**
A. Azerbaijan
B. Armenia
C. Georgia
D. Russia

____ **4. Which nation lost one third of its population to genocide?**
A. Armenia
B. Georgia
C. Azerbaijan
D. Turkey

____ **5. The desire of a cultural group to rule itself as a separate nation is called**
A. communism.
B. fundamentalism.
C. capitalism.
D. nationalism.

____ **6. Minority ethnic groups have fled Azerbaijan**
A. in search of jobs.
B. to find new land to farm.
C. to escape religious and ethnic conflict.
D. because the nation is overpopulated.

____ **7. Chernozem is rich soil found on the steppes of which nation?**
A. Kazakhstan
B. Uzbekistan
C. Turkmenistan
D. Tajikistan

____ **8. Most people in Central Asia are**
A. Christian.
B. Buddhist.
C. Jewish.
D. Muslim.

____ **9. When the Soviet Union controlled Central Asia**
A. people were forced to work on government farms.
B. industrialization was discouraged.
C. urban areas declined.
D. most people became nomadic herders.

____ **10. What is desertification?**
A. the name for military troops who leave their posts unattended
B. the irrigation of desert lands
C. the lack of precipitation in an area that usually receives abundant rainfall
D. the extension of the desert landscape due to environmental changes caused by humans

Name ______________________ Class ______________ Date ______________

Chapter 23

The Countries of Southwest Asia

Vocabulary
- anarchy
- ayatollah
- desalination
- embargo
- infrastructure
- mandate
- secular
- Zionist

Vocabulary Development

Directions: *Imagine that you are a journalist reporting on the countries of Southwest Asia. Write a brief article describing the political, economic, or environmental issues that these countries face. Use at least five of the listed vocabulary words. Be specific in your article to help readers appreciate the conflicts and challenges this region endures.*

Name ______________________ Class ______________ Date ______________

Section 1: Creating The Modern Middle East

Guide to the Essentials

Text Summary

THE BIG IDEA

After the Ottoman Empire fell at the end of World War I, it was divided into many countries. The 1948 war between Israel and the Arab countries left Palestinians without a homeland.

The Middle East, located on trade routes between Europe, Africa, and Asia, has been important for thousands of years. In the 600s, Muslims conquered the region. Most of the conquered people began to practice Islam and speak the Arabic language.

In the 900s, Seljuk Turks conquered most of the region. They became Muslims and ruled for more than 400 years. They lost control to the Ottoman Turks. By the late 1700s, the Ottoman Empire was weak and its many ethnic and religious groups wanted independence. The Ottoman Empire was defeated during World War I. The winning countries divided up the region.

Great Britain took Palestine as a **mandate**, or land governed for the League of Nations until it was ready for independence. Two groups—Arabs and Jews—claimed Palestine. In the late 1800s, many Jews had started moving to Palestine. Many were Zionists who wanted to make Palestine an independent Jewish country. Arabs in Palestine wanted **self-determination**, the right to decide their own future.

After World War II, the United Nations split Palestine into two states—one Jewish and one Arab. Jews accepted the plan, but Arabs did not. In 1948, Jews announced the independence of the new country of Israel. Hours later, neighboring Arab countries attacked. Israel won and controlled most of Palestine. Jordan and Egypt divided the rest. The Palestinians were left without a country.

Graphic Summary: *Breakup of the Ottoman Empire*

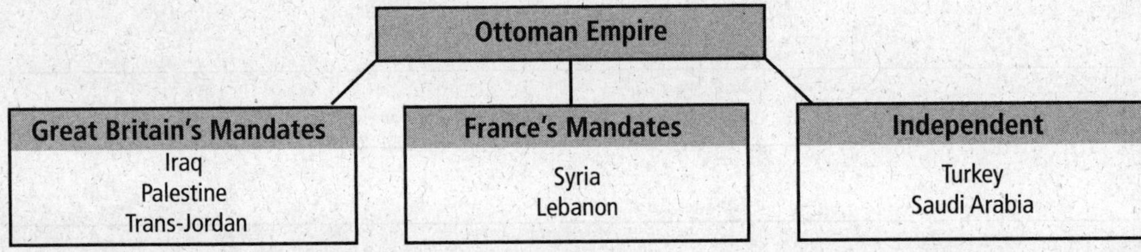

Many new countries were created out of the Ottoman Empire.

Review Questions

1. What two groups claimed Palestine?

2. **Chart Skills** What countries became British mandates?

Name ______________________ Class ______________ Date ______________

Section 1: Creating The Modern Middle East

Guided Reading and Review

A. As You Read

Directions: *As you read Section 1, complete the chart below by writing two supporting details under each main idea.*

Main Idea A: World War I had a great impact on the Middle East.

1. ____

____

2. ____

____

Main Idea B: Both Arabs and Jews had historical ties to Palestine.

3. ____

____

4. ____

____

Main Idea C: In 1947, the British government turned over the problem of Palestine to the United Nations.

5. ____

____

6. ____

____

B. Reviewing Vocabulary

Directions: *Complete each sentence by writing the correct term in the blank.*

7. A(n) ________________ was land to be governed on behalf of the League of Nations until it was ready for independence.

8. A(n) ________________ is a member of a movement founded to promote the establishment of an independent Jewish state in Palestine.

9. Arabs in Palestine were angered when they thought the British took away their right of ________________.

Name ______________________ Class ______________ Date ______________

Section 2: *Israel*

Guide to the Essentials

Text Summary

When the first Zionists arrived in Palestine in the 1880s, they began to irrigate the desert and drain the swamps. Today the Negev Desert, which covers half of Israel, has been turned into fertile farmland. A process called **drip irrigation** is used to preserve water resources by letting precise amounts of water drip onto plants from pipes. Scientists made Israel a leader in high technology. The country also has many service industries. Minerals are mined from the Dead Sea, a huge saltwater lake.

THE BIG IDEA

Israel has turned swamps and desert into good farmland and is a leader in technology. The country has a diverse population and is trying to achieve peace with its Arab neighbors.

About 80 percent of Israelis are Jewish. Before 1948, most came from Europe. Later, many Jews came from other countries in Southwest Asia and from North Africa. Many were poorer and less educated than European Jews. In recent years, many Jews have come from the former Soviet Union. Almost 20 percent of Israel's population is Arab.

During the 1948 war, many Palestinians lost their homes and fled to Arab countries. Even more Jews had to leave Arab countries. After another war in 1967, Israel took control of the West Bank in Jordan and the Gaza Strip. Many Palestinians fled from the West Bank and became refugees. Many of the refugee camps became bases for the Palestine Liberation Organization (PLO). It demanded that Palestine be freed and the refugees be allowed to return to their homes. The PLO refused to recognize Israel as a country. Some members were terrorists.

Tensions remain high and violent outbreaks continue despite several peace agreements between Israel and the Palestinians. Late in 2004, Palestinian leader Yasir Arafat died. With the election of PLO leader Mahmoud Abbas has come hope and renewed interest in reaching a peace agreement.

Graphic Summary: *Israel and Its Neighbors*

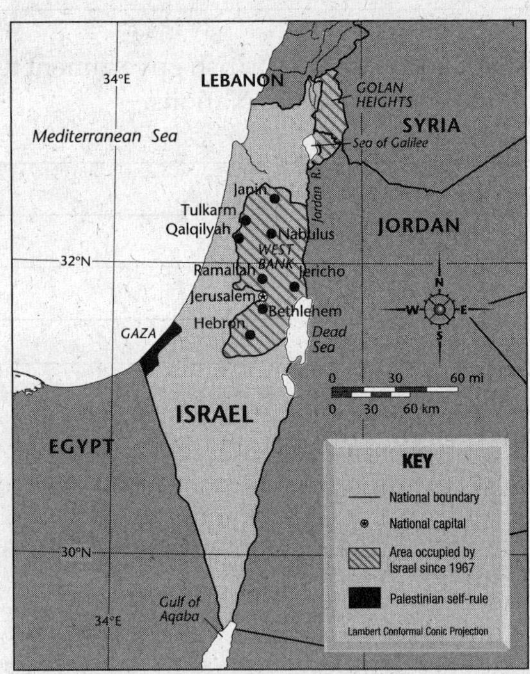

Israel is a small country surrounded by Arab neighbors.

Review Questions

1. How has the land of Israel been changed?

2. Map Skills What four countries border Israel?

Name ________________ Class ____________ Date ____________

Section 2: Israel

Guided Reading and Review

A. As You Read

Directions: *As you read Section 2, complete the chart below to summarize the development of Israel.*

Technology Transforms the Desert	Mining the Dead Sea
1. ________________	3. ________________
2. ________________	4. ________________
Economic Activities	**Diverse Cultures**
5. ________________	7. ________________
6. ________________	8. ________________
Palestinian Refugees	**The Struggle for a Solution**
9. ________________	11. ________________
10. ________________	12. ________________

B. Reviewing Vocabulary

Directions: *Define the following terms.*

13. drip irrigation

____

____

14. potash

____

____

Name ______________________ Class ______________ Date ______________

Section 3: Jordan, Lebanon, Syria, and Iraq

Guide to the Essentials

Text Summary

THE BIG IDEA

Jordan and Lebanon have been greatly affected by conflicts in Southwest Asia. Syria has rich farmland, and oil is important to Iraq.

The countries of Iraq, Jordan, Lebanon, and Syria are at the center of the problems that affect all of Southwest Asia.

After the 1967 Arab-Israeli war, Jordan lost its fertile farmland on the West Bank to Israel. The effect on Jordan's economy was terrible. In addition, many Palestinian refugees fled to Jordan after the 1948 and 1967 wars.

For many years Lebanon had a strong economy. But civil wars among the country's Christian and Muslim groups left Lebanon in a state of **anarchy**, or lawlessness. Most of the fighting ended in the early 1990s, and Syria finally withdrew troops from southern Lebanon in 2005.

Throughout its history, Syria's people have grown cotton, wheat, and other crops on its rich farmland. Today, however, Syria's farming methods are out-of-date. The government has launched reforms to improve Syria's economy.

In recent years, Iraq's people and its economy have been racked by war. In 1990, Iraq attacked Kuwait. In 1991, armed forces led by the United States and supported by the United Nations freed Kuwait. Iraq refused to accept UN terms for a cease-fire. The UN therefore placed an **embargo**, or strict limits on trade, on Iraq. In 2003, the U.S. and Great Britain invaded Iraq. They removed Saddam Hussein from power and oversaw free elections for a new Iraqi government.

Graphic Summary: *Conflicts in Southwest Asia*

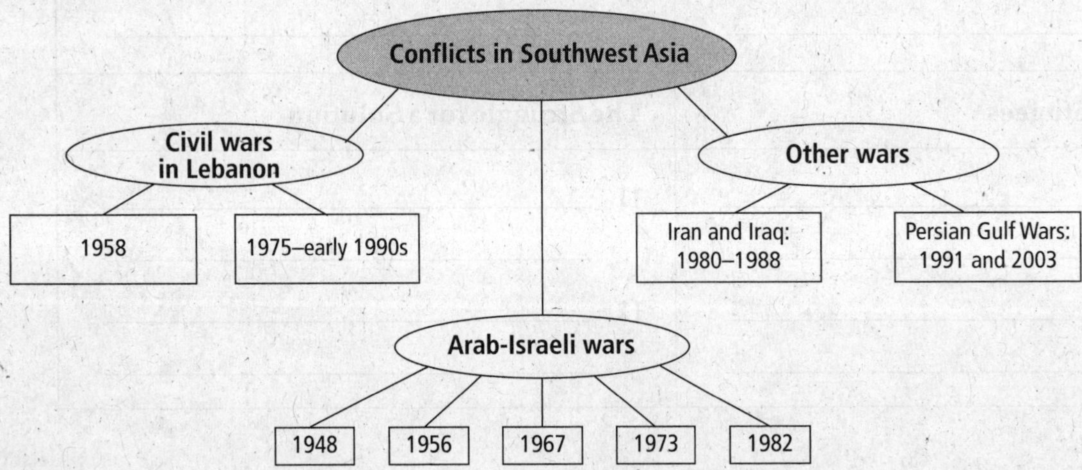

There have been many conflicts among the countries of Southwest Asia.

Review Questions

1. How did war hurt agriculture in Jordan?

2. **Diagram Skills** In what years were there Arab-Israeli wars?

Name ______________________ Class ______________ Date ______________

Section 3: Jordan, Lebanon, Syria, and Iraq

Guided Reading and Review

A. As You Read

Directions: *As you read Section 3, answer the following questions.*

1. What was the impact of the 1967 Arab-Israeli War on Jordan's economy?

   ____

2. What kind of government does Jordan have? ______________________________
3. When did Lebanon become independent from France? ______________________________
4. According to the 1932 census, which religious group held the most power in Lebanon?

   ____

5. What was the major reason behind Lebanon's civil wars?

   ____

6. Why did Israel invade Lebanon in 1982?

   ____

7. What activity has been carried on for centuries in the Syrian cities of Damascus and Aleppo?

   ____

8. What measures has the Syrian government taken to enhance farm production in Syria?

   ____

9. What is Iraq's most important economic activity?

   ____

10. In what ways has Iraq used its oil profits?

    ____

11. From 1980 to 1988, Iraq was engaged in a war with which other Southwest Asian country?

    ____

12. What was the outcome of the American and British invasion of Iraq?

    ____

B. Reviewing Vocabulary

Directions: *Read the following definitions. Then write the correct term on each blank.*

______________ **13.** an arc of rich land in the Middle East where farming and the first civilizations developed

______________ **14.** a private army of a particular fighting faction

______________ **15.** a state of lawlessness, political disorder, and violence

______________ **16.** a restriction on trade with other countries

Name ______________ Class ______________ Date ______________

Section 4: Arabian Peninsula

Guide to the Essentials

Text Summary

The Arabian Peninsula has the world's largest sand desert, the Rub' al-Khali, or the Empty Quarter. The peninsula has no body of fresh water. But it has the world's largest known oil reserves.

THE BIG IDEA

Oil made most countries on the Arabian Peninsula rich and helped them modernize. Oman and Yemen are the least developed countries in the region.

Until oil was discovered in the 1930s, most people lived by fishing, trading, herding, and growing crops in the oases. Oil paid for modernization. Oil money built plants to remove the salt from seawater so it could be used for drinking and irrigation. This process is called **desalination**.

In 1960, Iran, Iraq, Kuwait, and Saudi Arabia joined with Venezuela to form the Organization of Petroleum Exporting Countries (OPEC). OPEC decides how much oil to produce and at what price to sell it. The countries of this region know that they will one day run out of oil and have invested money to develop other industries.

Saudi Arabia has spent billions of dollars to build its **infrastructure**. An infrastructure is a country's basic support facilities, such as schools, roads, airports, and communication systems.

Saudi Arabia has Islam's most sacred cities—Mecca and Medina. Each year two million Muslims from all over the world visit Saudi Arabia for the hajj, or religious journey to Mecca.

Oman and Yemen have changed little. They only recently began to develop oil resources. Yemen is the poorest country on the peninsula.

Graphic Summary: *Countries of the Arabian Peninsula*

COUNTRY	AREA (in square miles)	CAPITAL
Bahrain	266	Manama
Kuwait	6,880	Kuwait City
Oman	82,031	Muscat
Qatar	4,247	Doha
Saudi Arabia	829,996	Riyadh
United Arab Emirates	32,278	Abu Dhabi
Yemen	203,849	Sanaa

Source: Microsoft Encarta Interactive World Atlas 2000

The countries of the Arabian Peninsula vary greatly in size.

Review Questions

1. Why are countries on the Arabian Peninsula investing money in other industries besides oil?

2. Chart Skills Which is the largest country in the Arabian Peninsula?

Name ____________________ Class ____________ Date ____________

Section 4: Arabian Peninsula

Guided Reading and Review

A. As You Read

Directions: *As you read Section 4, complete the chart below by writing two supporting details under each main idea.*

Main Idea A: Discovery of oil in the 1930s greatly changed traditional ways of life in the Arabian Peninsula.

1. ____________________

2. ____________________

Main Idea B: Many changes have occurred in Saudi Arabia since the mid-1960s.

3. ____________________

4. ____________________

Main Idea C: Oman and Yemen are different from other countries on the Arabian Peninsula.

5. ____________________

6. ____________________

B. Reviewing Vocabulary

Directions: *Match the definitions in Column I with the terms in Column II. Write the correct letter in each blank.*

Column I

_____ **7.** process of removing salt from seawater so that it can be used for drinking and irrigation

_____ **8.** a country's basic support facilities, such as roads, schools, and communication systems

_____ **9.** an ancient system of underground and surface canals in Oman

Column II

a. *falaj* system

b. desalination

c. infrastructure

Name ______ Class ______ Date ______

Section 5: Turkey, Iran, and Cyprus

Guide to the Essentials

Text Summary

THE BIG IDEA

Turkey is a modern nation. An Islamic revolution in Iran hurt its economy. Cyprus is split by ethnic conflict.

Although the majority of people in Turkey and Iran are Muslims, they are not Arabs.

Present-day Turkey consists of just a small part of the former Ottoman Empire. In 1923, Mustafa Kemal overthrew the sultan and made Turkey a republic. His goal was to make Turkey a modern country. He separated the Islamic religion and the government. The Turks gave him the name Atatürk, meaning "father of the Turks." Conflicts remain in Turkey about how much influence Islam should have.

Persians are the main cultural group in Iran. In 1925, army officer Reza Khan declared himself **shah,** or ruler. His son, Mohammad Reza Pahlavi, used profits from the oil industry to try to make Iran into a modern, Westernized nation. Religious leaders called **ayatollahs** wanted Iran to be ruled by strict Islamic law. They led a revolution in 1979 that forced the shah to flee. They declared Iran an Islamic republic and got rid of Western influences. Revolution and an eight-year war with Iraq hurt Iran's economy. Recently, Iran's economy has improved, but the 2005 election of President Mahmoud Ahmadinejad, an Islamic conservative, may limit some liberal reforms. Iran is under international scrutiny because of allegations that it is developing nuclear weapons.

The population of Cyprus is four-fifths Greek and one-fifth Turkish. Civil war divided the island in the 1960s when some Greek Cypriots wanted to unite with Greece. Turkey sent troops to Cyprus and took control of the northeast, which has a majority Turkish population. Efforts to reunite the two parts of the nation failed when Greek Cypriots rejected a United Nations proposal in 2004.

Graphic Summary: *The Countries of Southwest Asia*

Country	Population	Life Expectancy (years)	Per Capita GDP (in U.S. $)
Cyprus	775,927	77.5	16,000
Iran	69,018,924	69.7	7,000
Iraq	25,374,691	68.2	1,600
Israel	6,199,008	79.1	19,700
Jordan	5,611,202	78.1	4,300
Kuwait	2,257,549	76.8	18,100
Lebanon	3,777,218	72.3	4,800
Oman	2,903,165	72.8	13,400
Saudi Arabia	25,795,938	75.2	11,800
Syria	18,016,874	69.7	3,300
Turkey	68,893,918	72.1	6,700
Yemen	20,024,867	61.3	800

Source: *The World Factbook 2004*

The countries of Southwest Asia have great differences in life expectancy and per capita income.

Review Questions

1. How did Atatürk change Turkey?

2. Chart Skills Which country—Turkey, Iran, or Cyprus—has the largest population?

Name ______________________ Class ______________ Date ______________

Section 5: Turkey, Iran, and Cyprus

Guided Reading and Review

A. As You Read

Directions: *As you read Section 5, answer the following questions.*

1. What kind of language and culture did the Turks have?

   ____

2. What are three changes that Mustafa Kemal brought to Turkey?

   ____

   ____

   ____

3. What are two challenges that face Turkey today?

   ____

   ____

4. What are two major changes that Shah Mohammad Reza Pahlavi brought to Iran?

   ____

   ____

5. What are two major social changes that the Khomeini government brought to Iranian society?

   ____

   ____

6. To what branch of Islam do the majority of Iranians belong?

   ____

7. What is the chief language spoken in Cyprus?

   ____

8. Which two groups were involved in the civil war in Cyprus?

   ____

   ____

B. Reviewing Vocabulary

Directions: *Define the following terms.*

9. secular ____
10. shah ____
11. ayatollah ____

Name ______________________ Class ______________ Date ______________

Chapter 23 Test

Identifying Main Ideas

Directions: Write the letter of the correct answer in the blank provided. (10 points each)

____ **1. What happened to the Ottoman Empire after World War I?**
A. It was divided into many different countries.
B. It grew into the world's largest empire.
C. It spread across all of Southwest Asia.
D. It became one large Arab country.

____ **2. How did Arab countries react to Israel's independence?**
A. They welcomed Israel as a neighbor.
B. They offered Israel a peace plan.
C. They attacked Israel.
D. They planned a conference.

____ **3. How did the Israelis change the Negev Desert?**
A. They drained its swamps to create highways.
B. They used irrigation to turn it into swamps.
C. They used irrigation to turn it into fertile farmland.
D. They turned it into a sea.

____ **4. What did the Palestine Liberation Organization demand?**
A. that Palestine become the capital of Israel
B. that Palestinians be allowed to live in any country
C. that Palestinians be allowed to join the Israeli army
D. that Palestine be freed

____ **5. Lebanon's strong economy was destroyed by**
A. war with Iran.
B. civil war between Greeks and Turks.
C. civil wars among Muslim and Christian groups.
D. an Islamic revolution.

____ **6. What is an embargo?**
A. a large supply of oil
B. strict limits on trade
C. free trade
D. a fertile farm

____ **7. What has helped the Arabian Peninsula to modernize rapidly?**
A. money from oil
B. money from the United States
C. money from other Arab countries
D. new factories

____ **8. Mecca and Medina are Islam's most sacred cities. In which country are they located?**
A. Yemen
B. Oman
C. Kuwait
D. Saudi Arabia

____ **9. Who was Kemal Atatürk?**
A. the last sultan of Turkey
B. the leader who made Turkey a modern republic
C. the first shah of Turkey
D. the Turkish leader who set up an Islamic republic

____ **10. What happened as a result of Iran's revolution of 1979?**
A. Iran became an Islamic republic and its economy became weaker.
B. Iran became an Islamic republic and its economy grew better.
C. Iran became a democratic republic and ended Islamic law.
D. Iran modernized and adopted European laws instead of Islamic laws.

Name ______________________ Class ______________ Date ______________

Chapter 24

Regional Atlas: Introduction to Africa

Vocabulary
chaparral
colonialism
escarpment
leaching
nomadic herding
plateau
Sahel
savanna

Vocabulary Development

Directions: *Write a sentence for each pair of terms below that shows you understand the relationship between them. Provide context clues so that a reader who may not know the meaning of the terms could figure them out.*

Sahel/colonialism

____

____

____

plateau/escarpment

____

____

____

chaparral/savanna

____

____

____

nomadic herding/leaching

____

____

____

Name ______________________ Class ______________ Date ______________

Regional Atlas: Africa

Guide to the Essentials

Text Summary

THE BIG IDEA

Africa lies between the Atlantic Ocean on the west and the Indian Ocean on the east. The continent's location and varied landforms and climates play a role in shaping the lives of the many people of the region.

The first modern humans emerged from Africa over 100,000 years ago. African kingdoms arose and trade with Europe and Asia became common. The **Sahel,** the area just south of the Sahara, became an important trade region.

European countries colonized Africa, dividing the land without regard to existing divisions. By the 1960s, most African nations had achieved independence, but they have had difficulty uniting because they have maintained the borders imposed by Europeans.

Most of Africa consists of **plateaus,** or elevated blocks of land with flat or gently rolling surfaces. Mountains and **escarpments,** or steep cliffs, are found near coasts. The desert known as the Sahara is the primary geographic feature in the north. Waterfalls and cataracts along rivers make navigation from inland to the coasts difficult.

Rain falls in broad zones on either side of the Equator in Africa. Moving north and south, the land becomes drier as it turns to desert. The northern and southern edges of Africa have a Mediterranean climate. Africa's ecosystems have diverse wildlife.

South of the Sahara, more than 800 languages are spoken. Africa's most common economic activities are subsistence farming and **nomadic herding,** in which herders move their animals to different pastures throughout the year.

In many parts of Africa, the population is growing very rapidly and urbanization is increasing. Other parts have high death rates from disease that cancel out high birthrates.

Graphic Summary: *Regions of Africa*

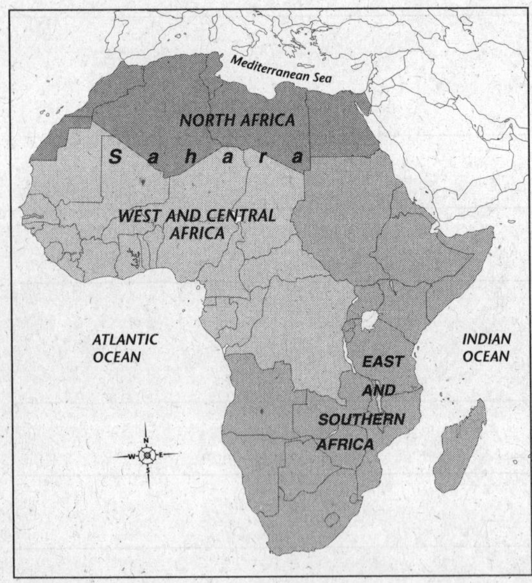

Africa is often divided into three distinct regions—North Africa, West and Central Africa, and East and Southern Africa.

Review Questions

1. What is the Sahara?

2. Map Skills Which region has a coast on the Indian Ocean?

Name ______________________ Class ______________ Date ______________

Regional Atlas: Africa

Guided Reading and Review

A. As You Read

Directions: *As you work through the Regional Atlas, complete the chart below by supplying an effect for each cause listed.*

Cause-and-Effect Relationships	
Cause	**Effect**
European countries divided Africa without regard to existing political and cultural divisions.	**1.** ______________
Many of Africa's rivers have waterfalls.	**2.** ______________
People in Africa clear rain forest areas for farming, grazing, and lumbering.	**3.** ______________
Poverty is widespread in many rural areas of Africa.	**4.** ______________

B. Reviewing Vocabulary

Directions: *Complete each sentence by writing the correct term in the blank.*

5. The region just south of the Sahara is the ______________.
6. ______________ is a system in which a foreign power controls a nation and exploits its resources and markets.
7. A(n) ______________ is an elevated block of land with a flat or gently rolling surface.
8. A(n) ______________ is a steep slope or cliff.
9. Drought-resistant brush is called ______________.
10. A(n) ______________ is a grassland with scattered trees.
11. Africa has a tradition of ______________, or history passed down by word of mouth.
12. In ______________, herders move flocks to different pastures throughout the year.
13. The dissolving and washing away of nutrients in soil is ______________.
14. The reduction in the productive potential of land is ______________.
15. The ______________ of a country is the average number of people in a given unit of area.

Name ______________________ Class ______________ Date ______________

Chapter
24 Test

Identifying Main Ideas

Directions: *Write the letter of the correct answer in the blank provided. (10 points each)*

____ **1. Africa's history can be traced back to**
A. the development of the slave trade.
B. the origins of modern humans.
C. the establishment of ancient kingdoms.
D. the colonialism by Europeans.

____ **2. What is the Sahel?**
A. the area north of the Sahara
B. the area south of the Sahara
C. poor farmland of the rain forest
D. rich farmland of the rain forest

____ **3. When Europeans colonized Africa in the 1800s, colonial borders were creaed based on**
A. agreements made by European nations.
B. agreements made by African leaders.
C. existing divisions.
D. the physical features of the land.

____ **4. What is a plateau?**
A. desert land with few plants
B. land below sea level
C. a steep mountain
D. elevated land with a flat or gently rolling surface

____ **5. Escarpments can be found**
A. in the desert.
B. near the coast.
C. in the Sahara.
D. in fertile plains.

____ **6. Navigation on Africa's rivers is made difficult by**
A. narrow straits.
B. shallow water.
C. many waterfalls.
D. rocky sandbars.

____ **7. In Africa**
A. several hundred languages are spoken.
B. very few languages are spoken.
C. there is complete ethnic unity.
D. the land lacks mineral wealth.

____ **8. Africa's population lives mainly**
A. in urban areas.
B. near bodies of water.
C. along the Equator.
D. in the Sahel.

____ **9. Africa's Mediterranean climate can be found**
A. near the east coast.
B. around the Equator.
C. in Madagascar.
D. along the northern and southern tips.

____ **10. Nomadic herding is**
A. the hunting of wild animal herds.
B. uncommon in Africa.
C. traveling to different pastures during the year.
D. often done in rain forests.

Name ______________________ Class ______________ Date ______________

Chapter 25

North Africa

Vocabulary
basin irrigation
bazaar
caravan
delta
reservoir
souk

Vocabulary Development

Directions: *Using what you learned in Chapter 28, decide whether the underlined term in each sentence below is used correctly. Indicate your answer by circling either "Correct" or "Incorrect." If the sentence is incorrect, write a sentence of your own that uses the term correctly.*

1. A delta is land formed by soil in the water that is dropped as a river slows and enters the sea.
Correct Incorrect
____

2. In Egypt, there are many modern-day shopping malls called bazaars.
Correct Incorrect
____

3. Basin irrigation by the Nile River controls heavy flooding and works all year.
Correct Incorrect
____

4. In the 1960s, Egyptian President Nasser built a dam to store Nile floodwaters in a huge reservoir, or lake.
Correct Incorrect
____

5. Caravans are large groups of merchants who used camels to travel across the desert.
Correct Incorrect
____

6. In North Africa, souks cook large meals for the kings and queens.
Correct Incorrect
____

Name ______________________ Class ______________ Date ______________

Section 1: Egypt

Guide to the Essentials

Text Summary

Egypt's location in northeast Africa and its large size and population make it an important country. It is a land of deserts, except near the Nile River. The Nile is the longest river in the world.

THE BIG IDEA

Most Egyptians live near the Nile River. Rapid growth of its population and cities has created challenges for Egypt.

About 99 percent of Egypt's people live near the Nile, where land is fertile. In rural villages, the way of life has changed slowly. Life in the fast-growing cities has changed quickly. Many people who move to the cities cannot find jobs or housing.

Egypt is more than 5,000 years old. Ancient Egyptians were among the first people in the world to set up an organized government and religion and to invent a written language. The famous pyramids of ancient Egypt were built as tombs for its pharaohs, or rulers. Arabs conquered Egypt in A.D. 642, bringing Islam and the Arabic language.

The Suez Canal, linking the Mediterranean and Red seas, was built in 1869. Britain controlled Egypt for many years until 1952 when the Egyptian army overthrew the government.

Egypt joined other Arab countries in wars against Israel. In 1979 Egypt became the first Arab country to make peace with Israel.

Until recently, the Nile flooded every year, providing Egyptians with water and fertile soil. Egypt built the Aswan High Dam to store water in a **reservoir**, or artificial lake. The dam and reservoir ended the flooding and now provide water and hydroelectric power throughout the year.

Graphic Summary: *Egypt's Major Imports*

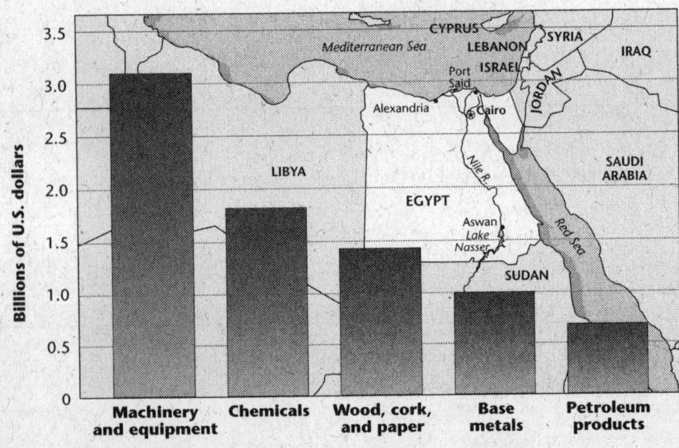

Source: Egypt State Information Service

Lacking investments to start new industries, Egypt must import most industrial products.

Review Questions

1. Why do most Egyptians live near the Nile River?

2. **Graph Skills** What is Egypt's major import?

Name ______________________ Class ______________ Date ______________

Section 1: Egypt

Guided Reading and Review

A. As You Read

Directions: *As you read Section 1, complete each sentence in the boxes below to provide details about Egypt.*

Egypt and Its People

1. Most of the population lives ______________________.
2. Desert regions lie ______________________
______________________.
3. Many rural people migrate to the cities for ______________________
______________________.
4. Today, Egyptian farmers are both helped and hindered by ______________________
______________________.

The Economy

5. Egypt's economy is strained by its ______________________.
6. Egypt's main exports now are ______________________, but Egypt needs a(n) ______________________ to ensure its economic stability.
7. Industrial development has been limited by a lack of ______________________ and ______________________.

B. Reviewing Vocabulary

Directions: *Complete each sentence by writing the correct term in the blank.*

8. A(n) ______________ is land formed by soil in the water that is dropped as a river slows and enters the sea.
9. Egyptian peasants are called the ______________.
10. The *khamsin* creates ______________ that blow hot air, dust, and grit into the Nile Valley.
11. A(n) ______________ is a traditional Arab open-air market.
12. Trapping floodwaters by building walls around fields is called ______________.
13. A(n) ______________ is an artificial lake behind a dam.
14. A system for providing additional water to crops year-round is ______________.
15. ______________ is money invested in building and supporting new industry.

Name ______________________ Class ______________ Date ______________

Section 2: Libya and the Maghreb

Guide to the Essentials

Text Summary

Libya and the Maghreb countries—Tunisia, Algeria, and Morocco—are west of Egypt. The word *Maghreb* comes from the Arabic term meaning "land farthest west." Most people in this region are Muslims who speak Arabic. They live mainly along the Mediterranean coast. Inland from this narrow coast is the Sahara.

THE BIG IDEA

North Africa has been influenced by African, Arab, and European cultures. There are big differences between cities and rural areas.

The Romans brought camels from central Asia. These animals, which can travel for days without water, allowed North Africans to trade with people south of the Sahara. Traders crossed the desert in **caravans**, large groups of merchants that traveled together for safety.

Arab armies invaded during the mid-600s. The region soon became a center of trade between Europe, Africa, and Asia. In the 1800s and early 1900s, France ruled Algeria, Tunisia, and Morocco and Italy conquered Libya.

Most farmers live in rural villages and have kept traditional ways of life. The cities are growing rapidly. People migrating from rural villages have trouble finding jobs and houses.

Oil was found in Libya in 1961 and soon became its main export. Oil money was used to modernize the country. Algeria's main export is also oil. But the government wants rural Algerians to continue farming to reduce the need to buy food from other countries.

Tunisia and Morocco do not have much oil. Both countries spend a lot on schools and on developing their manufacturing.

Graphic Summary: *The Countries of North Africa*

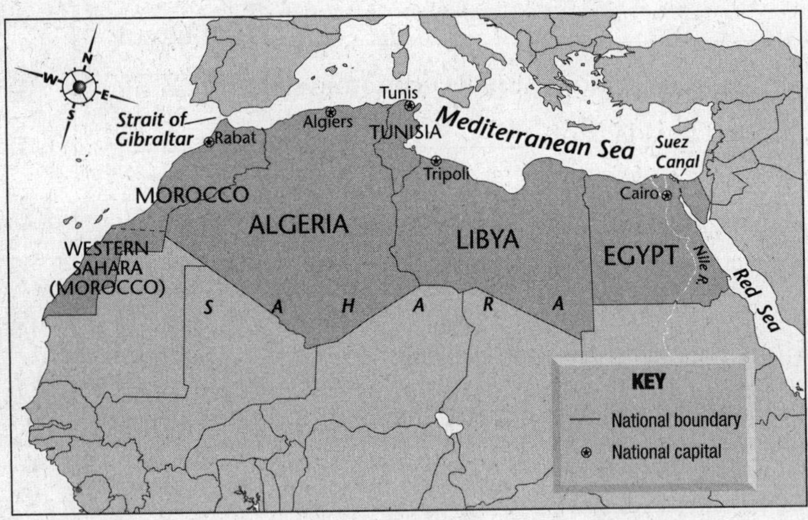

The countries of North Africa border the Mediterranean Sea.

Review Questions

1. In which two countries is oil the major export?

2. Map Skills Which countries border Tunisia?

Name ______________________ Class ______________ Date ______________

Section 2: Libya and the Maghreb

Guided Reading and Review

A. As You Read

Directions: As you read Section 2, complete the charts below to summarize the way of life in North African nations.

The People of North Africa
Effect of Location on Culture
1. ______________________
Population of North Africa
2. ______________________
Rural Life
3. ______________________
Nomadic Life
4. ______________________
Urban Life
5. ______________________

North Africa Today
Libyan Economy and Government
6. ______________________
7. ______________________
Algerian Economy and Government
8. ______________________
9. ______________________
Tunisian and Moroccan Economy
10. ______________________

B. Reviewing Vocabulary

Directions: Complete each sentence by writing the correct term in the blank.

11. Dry riverbeds and sharp gullies, or ______________, cut across the North African desert.
12. Merchants joined together in ______________ to cross the desert in safety.
13. The older Arab sections of North African cities, called ______________, are usually centered around mosques.
14. North African markets are called ______________.

Name ______________________ Class ______________ Date ______________

Chapter 25

Test

Identifying Main Ideas

Directions: *Write the letter of the correct answer in the blank provided. (10 points each)*

____ **1. Where do most Egyptians live?**
A. on the Mediterranean coast
B. near the Nile
C. in the desert
D. in the mountains

____ **2. What problem do Egypt's fast-growing cities have?**
A. They cannot find enough people to work in their factories.
B. Not enough people are moving to cities from farms.
C. Nobody wants to live in the cities.
D. They are growing too fast to provide enough houses and jobs.

____ **3. Ancient Egyptians were among the first people to**
A. speak Arabic.
B. develop a written language.
C. become Muslims.
D. use camels to cross the desert.

____ **4. What two bodies of water are connected by the Suez Canal?**
A. the Mediterranean Sea and the Red Sea
B. the Red Sea and the Indian Ocean
C. the Indian Ocean and the Mediterranean Sea
D. the Mediterranean Sea and the Atlantic Ocean

____ **5. The Aswan High Dam**
A. provided Egypt with hydroelectric power.
B. made farming possible in Egypt.
C. created the desert.
D. made Egypt's soil fertile.

____ **6. Which countries are included in the Maghreb?**
A. Libya and Egypt
B. Egypt, Morocco, and Libya
C. Tunisia, Algeria, and Morocco
D. Libya, the Sudan, and Ethiopia

____ **7. What is a caravan?**
A. a large group that travels together for safety
B. a family of camels in the desert
C. a show of riding skills on camels
D. any large group of Arabs

____ **8. Which country ruled Libya?**
A. Maghreb
B. France
C. Egypt
D. Italy

____ **9. Where have most people kept traditional ways of life?**
A. in rural villages
B. in cities
C. on the coasts
D. in none of these countries

____ **10. Which two countries of the Maghreb do not have much oil?**
A. Libya and Algeria
B. Morocco and Tunisia
C. Tunisia and Algeria
D. Morocco and Libya

Name ______________________ Class ______________ Date ______________

Chapter 26

West and Central Africa

Vocabulary
- animism
- barter
- deforestation
- forage
- mercenary
- refugee

Vocabulary Development

Directions: *Write a brief definition for each of the listed terms. Then, using all the terms, write a paragraph about the nations of West and Central Africa. In your writing, be sure to show that you understand how the concepts work together.*

animism

____

barter

____

deforestation

____

forage

____

mercenary

____

refugee

____

Paragraph:

____

____

____

____

____

____

____

Name ______________________ Class ______________ Date ______________

Section 1: The Sahel

Guide to the Essentials

Text Summary

THE BIG IDEA

Ancient empires ruled the Sahel, an area between the Sahara and the tropical rain forest. Interaction between people and the environment in the Sahel has created serious problems.

The Sahara was not always desert. As its climate grew drier, people moved north or south. Traders linked them, selling salt from the north for ivory, slaves, and gold from the south. Sahel rulers grew rich by taxing the traders. The region had three great empires—Ghana, Mali, and Songhai. (See chart below.)

Today, the northern Sahel has five countries—Mauritania, Mali (named for the ancient kingdom), Burkina Faso, Niger, and Chad. Many people are farmers. Because the soil is poor, they use **shifting agriculture**. They clear a part of the forest to grow crops. Then after the soil is no longer useful, farmers move on and clear another part of the forest. They grow millet and sorghum to eat and peanuts to sell. Others in the Sahel herd camels, cattle, and sheep.

Herding, shifting agriculture, and chopping firewood hurt the environment. Land stripped of trees suffers from **deforestation**. When there is a drought, huge areas of the Sahel may lose all vegetation, which is called **desertification**. The savanna turns to desert.

As desertification increases, people leave for the cities. They join camps of **refugees**, people who flee to escape danger.

Aid from other countries has helped Sahel countries survive in their harsh environment. But these countries are also working to develop their natural resources—rivers and minerals—and people's skills.

Graphic Summary: *Ancient Empires of the Sahel*

GHANA	MALI	SONGHAI
Ghana becomes a great kingdom in 400. By 800 Koumbi Saleh, the capital, has a very large population.	Mali is one of the largest empires in the world in the 1300s. Its most famous emperor, Mansa Musa, makes a journey to Mecca. Tombouctou, the capital, is an important trading city and a center for Islamic arts and learning.	The Songhai Empire takes over as Mali declines. Under Mohammad Askia, Tombouctou reaches the height of its influence and learning.

Three great empires once ruled lands in the Sahel.

Review Questions

1. What is desertification?

2. **Chart Skills** Which empire ruled in the Sahel most recently?

Name ______________________ Class ______________ Date ______________

Section 1: The Sahel

Guided Reading and Review

A. As You Read

Directions: *As you read Section 1, complete the chart below with information about the rich and varied history of the Sahel.*

Dates	History of the Sahel
5000 B.C.	**1.** ______________________
A.D. 400 to 1076	**2.** ______________________
1300 to 1600	**3.** ______________________
The present	**4.** ______________________
The future: three goals	**5.** ______________________ **6.** ______________________ **7.** ______________________

B. Reviewing Vocabulary

Directions: *Complete each sentence by writing the correct term in the blank.*

8. Moving crops to new soil every couple of years is called ______________.

9. Food for grazing animals is called ______________.

10. ______________ strips land of its trees.

11. The land's loss of all vegetation is called ______________.

12. A person fleeing home to live elsewhere and escape danger or unfair treatment is a(n) ______________.

13. A country is ______________ when it has no seaport.

14. A(n) ______________ is an area of lakes, creeks, and swamps away from the ocean.

Name ______________________ Class ______________ Date ______________

Section 2: *The Coastal Countries*

Guide to the Essentials

Text Summary

The countries of this region, along the coast of West Africa, have advantages over the Sahel. They have a wetter climate and are located on the sea. They trade more with Europe than across the Sahara.

THE BIG IDEA

A good location has allowed the region to trade with Europe since the 1400s. Many countries have had shifts of power. Some are turning to democracy.

Most coastal countries export raw materials to other nations. Peanuts and cocoa beans are also exported.

The economies of the coastal countries suffer because they import more than they export. They have large debts because they borrowed money and now pay billions of dollars in interest.

When African countries gained independence, their economies were weak. Few countries have been able to recover from these economic problems. Most had weak governments, and the army seized power in **coups**, sudden political takeovers. One-man rule was common. Civil strife and warfare have often erupted in many West African nations, including Liberia and Sierra Leone.

Many West Africans have begun grass-roots efforts to improve the economy. People have taken it upon themselves to improve the economy instead of relying on the government for change. Women in particular have played an important role in these efforts. In many countries, women grow crops and work together to improve the economic conditions of their villages. They also organize food markets and have begun running small businesses. These efforts help to boost the depressed economy.

Graphic Summary: *The Coastal Countries*

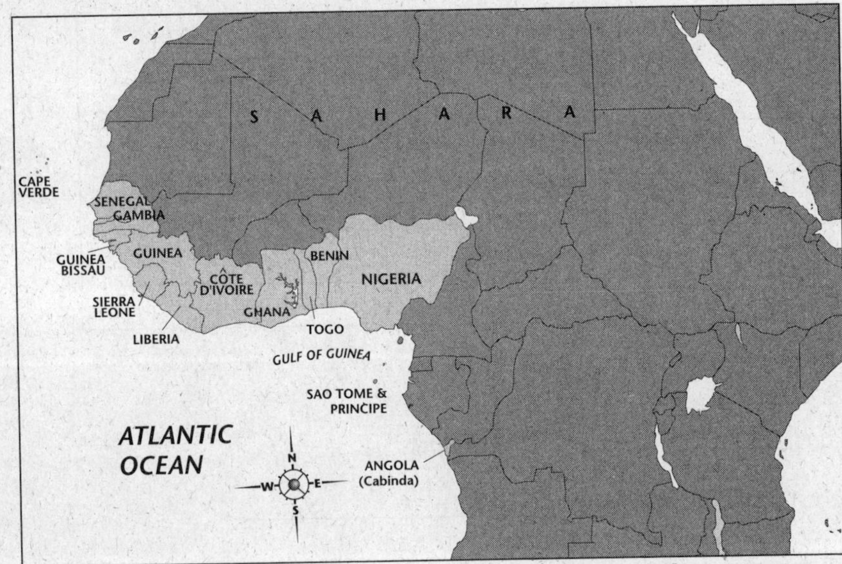

The coastal nations lie to the south of the countries of the Sahel.

Review Questions

1. What is a coup?

2. **Map Skills** On what ocean are the coastal countries located?

Name ______________________ Class ______________ Date ______________

Section 2: The Coastal Countries

Guided Reading and Review

A. As You Read

Directions: *As you read Section 2, complete the chart below by writing two supporting details under each main idea.*

Main Idea A: Because of their location near the sea, the coastal countries of West Africa have a long history of trade with foreign nations.

1. ____

____

____

2. ____

____

____

Main Idea B: Since gaining independence, both the government and the people of West Africa are struggling to improve economic conditions.

3. ____

____

4. ____

____

Main Idea C: The cultures of West Africa still reflect many traditional roles and beliefs.

5. ____

____

6. ____

____

B. Reviewing Vocabulary

Directions: *Complete each sentence by writing the correct term in the blank.*

7. A(n) ________________ is a sudden political takeover.
8. The idea that the spirits of the dead will live on if the people still living continue to honor and respect them is the basis of ________________.
9. The belief that gods or spirits can be found in ordinary things such as the sky and trees is called ________________.

Name ____________________ Class ____________ Date ____________

Section 3: Nigeria

Guide to the Essentials

Text Summary

Nigeria was once seen as Africa's hope. Instead, poor leadership and lack of unity have caused problems. Nigeria is not united because it has many regions and ethnic groups. Vegetation includes coastal swamps, rain forests, savanna, and desert scrub. Climate varies from heavy rainfall to little rain.

THE BIG IDEA

Nigeria could be an economic leader in Africa, but it is not united. A harsh military government brought hard times.

Different groups control each area. The south has the best land. Yoruba took the southwest, and Ibo the southeast. Hausa and Fulani control the most fertile northern lands. Nigeria's middle region has the poorest soil and weakest groups. Nigeria's people often face problems because of religious or political differences.

Nigeria's main export is oil. The economy was good until oil prices fell in the early 1980s. Then military leaders overthrew the government in a coup. The new leaders asked the **World Bank** and the **International Monetary Fund** for help. Both are United Nations agencies that lend money to countries. Nigeria agreed to make the economic changes suggested by these agencies. Nigeria sold government-owned businesses to private companies, fired some government workers, and kept wages and prices down. People protested and called for free elections.

In 1993, the military held an election but threw out the results. The military remained in control, and political opponents were jailed or killed. Free elections were finally held in 1999, but Nigeria faces many challenges as it attempts to deal with its cultural and political disunity.

Graphic Summary: *The Coastal Countries*

Country	Population	Life Expectancy (years)	Per Capita GDP (in U.S. $)
Benin	7,250,033	50.8	1,100
Cape Verde	415,294	70.1	1,400
Côte d'Ivoire	17,327,724	42.5	1,400
Gambia	1,546,848	54.8	1,700
Ghana	20,757,032	56.2	2,200
Guinea	9,246,462	49.7	2,100
Guinea-Bissau	1,388,363	46.9	900
Liberia	3,390,635	47.9	1,000
Nigeria	137,253,133	50.5	800
Senegal	10,852,147	56.7	1,600
Sierra Leone	5,883,889	42.7	500
Togo	5,556,812	53.0	1,500

Source: *The World Factbook 2004*

Nigeria has the largest population in Africa.

Review Questions

1. Why did Nigeria have to turn to the World Bank and the International Monetary Fund for help?

2. **Chart Skills** What is the population of Nigeria?

Name ______________________ Class ______________ Date ______________

Section 3: Nigeria

Guided Reading and Review

A. As You Read

Directions: *As you read Section 3, complete the chart below to organize information about influences on Nigerian history.*

Cause	Effect
Nigeria is a land of both good and poor soil.	**1.** ______________
Nigeria's people come from many different groups.	**2.** ______________
In Nigeria in the early 1980s, the sale of oil provided most of the country's income.	**3.** ______________
The World Bank imposed a structural adjustment program.	**4.** ______________
The military declared Moshood Abiola's election void and seized power.	**5.** ______________

B. Reviewing Vocabulary

Directions: *Define the following terms.*

6. World Bank

____

____

7. International Monetary Fund

____

____

8. structural adjustment program

____

____

Name ______________________ Class ______________ Date ______________

Section 4: Central Africa

Guide to the Essentials

Text Summary

The countries of Central Africa range from the tiny island nation of São Tomé and Príncipe to the Democratic Republic of the Congo, the largest country south of the Sahara.

THE BIG IDEA

Rivers, forests, and grasslands affect movement in Central Africa. Misuse of rivers and forests hurts the environment.

The largest river of the region is the Congo. This river system is a highway providing food, water, and transportation. A thick rain forest in the Congo Basin limits movement. Its valuable wood can be cut and exported only near rivers or railroads. Both the savanna and rain forest have poor soil. Large numbers of people have moved to Kinshasa, the capital.

Across the Congo River from Kinshasa is Brazzaville, capital of the Congo Republic. Its railroad serves the inland countries of Chad and the Central African Republic.

Many countries of West and Central Africa belong to an economic community known as the CFA. They use a form of money called the CFA franc.

Central African countries have many mineral resources. The Democratic Republic of the Congo has copper, cobalt, and diamonds. But the country's problems have kept them from being mined.

After independence in 1960, the Democratic Republic of the Congo was torn apart by Belgian troops, United Nations forces, rebel armies, and hired soldiers called **mercenaries**. A general by the name of Mobutu Sese Seko became dictator. The nation fell deeply into debt, and in 1997 Mobutu's rule was overthrown.

Graphic Summary: *The Countries of Central Africa*

The countries of Central Africa extend inland from the Atlantic Ocean.

Review Questions

1. Why is the Congo River important to the region?

2. **Map Skills** Which Central African country does not have a seacoast?

Name ______________________ Class ______________ Date ______________

Section 4: Central Africa

Guided Reading and Review

A. As You Read

Directions: *As you read Section 4, complete the chart below with examples of the movement of people in Central Africa.*

	Movement in Central Africa
Methods of moving people and goods	**1.** ______________________ ______________________ **2.** ______________________ ______________________
Barriers to movement	**3.** ______________________ ______________________ **4.** ______________________ ______________________
Direction of movement	**5.** ______________________ ______________________
Effect of movement	**6.** ______________________ ______________________

Directions: *As you read Section 4, fill in two examples of the interaction between the people of Central Africa and their environment.*

7. ____
____

8. ____
____

B. Reviewing Vocabulary

Directions: *Complete each sentence by writing the correct term in the blank.*

9. A(n) ________________ is a central ridge dividing two river basins.
10. Fighting that involved foreign troops, rebel armies, and ________________ plagued the Democratic Republic of Congo for many years.
11. When people don't use money, they may exchange goods through ________________.

Name ______________________ Class ______________ Date ______________

Chapter 26

Test

Identifying Main Ideas

Directions: Write the letter of the correct answer in the blank provided. (10 points each)

____ **1. Farmers who use shifting agriculture have to**
A. move often because the soil is no longer useful.
B. remain in one place because the soil gets more fertile.
C. pay high rent to the landowners.
D. use modern tools to grow crops.

____ **2. Ghana, Mali, and Songhai were**
A. countries in the Sahel.
B. countries with large debts.
C. empires in Central Africa.
D. empires in the Sahel.

____ **3. What advantage do coastal countries have over the Sahel?**
A. easier trade across the Sahara
B. a wetter climate and a seacoast
C. no large debts
D. stronger governments

____ **4. What is a coup?**
A. a sudden political takeover
B. a democratic election
C. a weak economy
D. an important mineral export

____ **5. Why are women an important part of the economy in West Africa?**
A. They run most of the banks.
B. They own the factories and mines.
C. They grow crops and run food markets.
D. They are the political leaders.

____ **6. Nigeria has had problems because of poor leadership and**
A. high oil prices.
B. too few people.
C. no national unity.
D. no international loans.

____ **7. Nigeria's main export is**
A. peanuts.
B. manufactured goods.
C. oil.
D. cocoa beans.

____ **8. What happened after the 1993 election in Nigeria?**
A. A democratic government took over.
B. All political prisoners were let out of jail.
C. Nigeria paid off all its debts.
D. The military threw out the results.

____ **9. What is the largest African country south of the Sahara?**
A. Democratic Republic of the Congo
B. Algeria
C. São Tomé and Príncipe
D. Nigeria

____ **10. What is the CFA franc?**
A. a favorite food in Africa
B. the postage stamp used by the Central African Republic
C. the money used by several countries in West and Central Africa
D. a railroad that carries goods to the coast

Name ______________________ Class ______________ Date ______________

Chapter

27 East and Southern Africa

Vocabulary
apartheid
ethnocracy
land redistribution
harambee
malnutrition
sanction
segregation
white flight

Vocabulary Development

Directions: *Match each term in Column A with the correct definition in Column B.*

Column A

1. *harambee*
2. malnutrition
3. ethnocracy
4. apartheid
5. land redistribution
6. segregation
7. sanction
8. white flight

Column B

a. the departure of white people from a region

b. an action taken by the international community to punish a country for unacceptable behaviors

c. a policy by which land is taken from those who own large amounts and given to those who have little or none

d. a system of government in which one ethnic group rules over others

e. a policy of cooperation adopted in Kenya after independence to encourage economic growth

f. disease caused by a lack of food or an unbalanced diet

g. a policy of strict racial segregation formerly used in the Republic of South Africa

h. the separation of races

Directions: *Write two sentences on each of the following topics using what you have learned in Chapter 27. Use at least three vocabulary terms for each topic.*

Topic: Race Relations in South Africa

____

____

____

____

Topic: Economic Programs and Policies in Other Countries of East and Southern Africa

____

____

____

____

Name ______________________ Class ______________ Date ______________

Section 1: Kenya

Guide to the Essentials

Text Summary

THE BIG IDEA

After independence, Kenyans worked together to build a strong economy. But today Kenya is struggling to keep its economy strong and its people united.

Kenya is known for its national parks where wild animals roam freely and are protected. It is located on the east coast of Africa. The Equator runs through Kenya, and some places are very hot. The Great Rift Valley crosses the highlands, where elevation makes the climate cooler.

Most people live in the fertile highlands of the southwest, which have forests, grasslands, and enough rain to grow crops. When the British took control of Kenya in the early 1890s, they built a railroad west from the coast. They encouraged whites to settle in the highlands. Africans, especially Masai and Kikuyu, lost their land.

In the 1950s, the Kikuyu fought the British settlers. The British crushed the uprising. But a Kikuyu leader, Jomo Kenyatta, became president when Kenya gained independence. He returned some land to the Kikuyu.

Kenyatta encouraged ***harambee***, which means "pulling together." He wanted the government, private companies, and individuals to work to create a strong economy. The government encouraged farmers to grow cash crops—coffee and tea. That left little farmland for food, forcing Kenya to import food. Many people suffer from **malnutrition**, a disease caused by an unhealthy diet.

Kenya began to face hard times in the 1980s. It could not provide its fast-growing population with enough food or jobs. Ethnic conflict replaced *harambee.* After many years of one-party rule, Kenyans hope for fair elections and national unity.

Graphic Summary: *Countries of East Africa*

Country	Population	Life Expectancy (years)	Per Capita GDP (in U.S. $)
Burundi	6,231,221	43.3	600
Djibouti	466,900	43.1	1,300
Eritrea	4,447,307	52.7	700
Ethiopia	67,851,281	40.9	700
Kenya	32,021,856	44.9	1,000
Rwanda	7,954,013	39.2	1,300
Somalia	8,304,601	47.7	500
Sudan	39,148,162	58.1	1,900
Tanzania	36,588,225	44.4	600
Uganda	26,404,543	45.3	1,400

Source: *The World Factbook 2004*

Most of the people of the region have a short life expectancy.

Review Questions

1. What is *harambee* and how did it help Kenya?

2. Chart Skills In which one of these countries do people have the longest life expectancy?

Name ______________________ Class ______________ Date ______________

Section 1: Kenya

Guided Reading and Review

A. As You Read

Directions: *As you read Section 1, answer the following questions.*

1. Where is Kenya located?

____

2. Where do most Kenyans live?

____

3. Describe the land and climate of the highlands.

____

____

4. What two groups occupied the central highlands in the 1890s?

____

5. How did the British affect the development of Kenya?

____

____

6. What group of people fought against the British in the Mau Mau Rebellion?

____

____

7. How did *harambee* affect Kenya after independence?

____

____

____

8. Why do many Kenyans suffer from malnutrition?

____

____

B. Reviewing Vocabulary

Directions: *Define the following terms.*

9. *harambee* ____

10. pyrethrum ____

11. malnutrition____

Name ______________________ Class ______________ Date ______________

Section 2: Other Countries of East Africa

Guide to the Essentials

Text Summary

THE BIG IDEA

Several countries in the region have important locations. Conflicts have badly hurt some countries in East Africa.

Ethiopia, Eritrea, Djibouti, and Somalia are located on a landform known as the Horn of Africa. They are near the oil supplies of the Middle East and the shipping lanes of the Red Sea and the Gulf of Aden.

Several countries have been torn by civil wars, wars with each other, and the effects of severe droughts. Ethiopia had to allow the province of Eritrea to become independent in 1993. Civil war and drought caused a terrible famine in Somalia. The people of the Sudan are divided. Arab Muslims live in the north. People in the south belong to several African ethnic groups and practice African religions or Christianity. North and south have fought since independence in 1956.

Uganda, Rwanda, and Burundi are landlocked, or entirely surrounded by land. Uganda is recovering from a civil war and a ruthless dictator. It is becoming more democratic.

Rwanda and Burundi are each ruled by an **ethnocracy**—a government controlled by one ethnic group. In Rwanda, the Hutu majority murdered great numbers of Tutsi in 1994. About 2 million Rwandans became refugees. Burundi is controlled by the Tutsi, although they are a minority. Many thousands of Hutu have been killed by Tutsi.

Tanzania has fertile land and mineral wealth but remains very poor. Tanzania's economy failed when people were subjected to **villagization**—forced to work on collective farms. After Tanzania abandoned this policy, the economy began to improve.

Graphic Summary: *The Countries of East Africa*

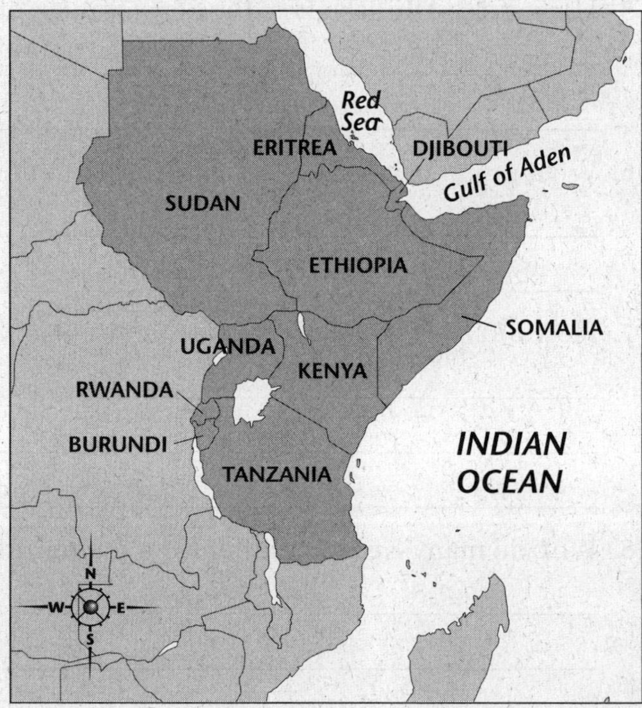

Several countries in the region have strategic locations on water routes. Others are landlocked.

Review Questions

1. Which country was once a province of Ethiopia?

2. **Map Skills** What bodies of water are east and north of the Horn of Africa?

Name ______________________ Class ______________ Date ____________

Section 2: Other Countries of East Africa

Guided Reading and Review

A. As You Read

Directions: *As you read Section 2, complete the chart by identifying the correct East African nations.*

Other Countries of East Africa	
Which four countries have strategic value because of their location on the Horn of Africa?	**1.** ____________ **2.** ____________ **3.** ____________ **4.** ____________
Which country is the largest in area in all of Africa?	**5.** ____________
Which four countries of East Africa are landlocked?	**6.** ____________ **7.** ____________ **8.** ____________ **9.** ____________
Which two countries of East Africa are ethnocracies?	**10.** ____________ **11.** ____________
In which East African country did the economy turn around after socialism ended?	**12.** ____________

B. Reviewing Vocabulary

Directions: *Complete each sentence by writing the correct term in the blank.*

13. The value of a country's location for nations planning large-scale military action is called its ____________.

14. A form of government in which one ethnic group rules over others is a(n) ____________.

15. Forcing rural people to move into towns and work on collective farms is called ____________.

Name ______________________ Class ______________ Date ______________

Section 3: South Africa

Guide to the Essentials

Text Summary

The Republic of South Africa is the wealthiest country in Africa. Although three quarters of the population is black, a white minority ruled for most of the 1900s. Whites also controlled the land, jobs, and gold and diamond mines.

THE BIG IDEA

For most of the 1900s, a white minority controlled South Africa. In the 1990s, the apartheid system was abolished. South Africa now has a new, democratic constitution.

The Dutch were the first Europeans to settle in South Africa. Their descendants, called Boers or Afrikaners, speak Afrikaans. The British followed and defeated the Afrikaners. The Africans were forced into separate lands or made to work for low pay.

South Africa became independent in 1961 and passed laws to keep black Africans from moving to the cities. Each African was assigned to a region called a homeland. Africans needed a pass to live somewhere else. The whites also passed a system of laws called **apartheid**, which means "apartness." Apartheid laws **segregated** black South Africans, or forced them to live separately.

Apartheid and the homelands were so unjust that other countries protested. In 1986, the United States and other countries placed **sanctions** against South Africa. Sanctions punish a country for behaving in a way that other nations do not approve.

In 1989, a new prime minister named F. W. de Klerk promised reform. Black leader Nelson Mandela was released from jail after 27 years. All apartheid laws were ended. In 1994, Mandela was elected the country's first black president. South Africa adopted a new constitution guaranteeing equal rights for all South Africans.

Graphic Summary: *The End of Apartheid*

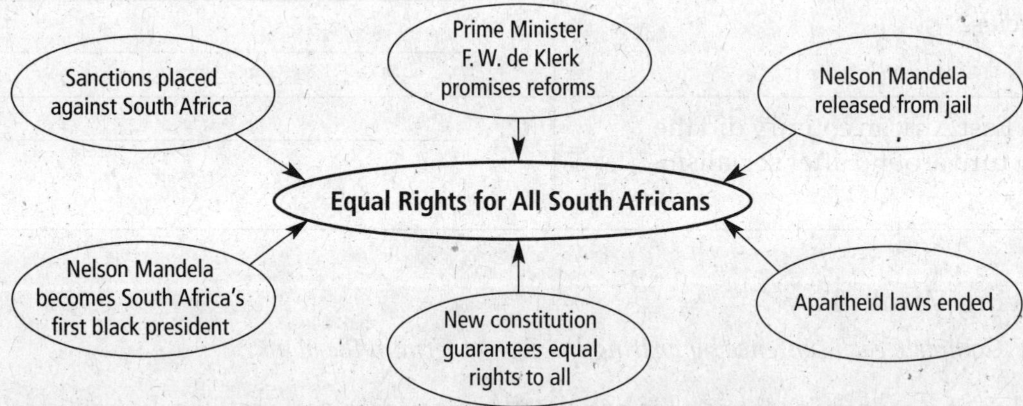

After years of white rule, all South Africans are now guaranteed equal rights.

Review Questions

1. What is apartheid?

2. Diagram Skills Name two actions that led to equal rights for all South Africans.

Name ______________________ Class ______________ Date ______________

Section 3: South Africa

Guided Reading and Review

A. As You Read

Directions: *As you read Section 3, complete the chart below by writing three supporting details under each main idea.*

Main Idea A: A white minority controlled South Africa for many years.

1. ______________________________

2. ______________________________

3. ______________________________

Main Idea B: To control black South Africans, the South African government established homelands and apartheid.

4. ______________________________

5. ______________________________

6. ______________________________

Main Idea C: External and internal pressures forced the South African government to end apartheid and move toward majority rule.

7. ______________________________

8. ______________________________

9. ______________________________

B. Reviewing Vocabulary

Directions: *Complete each sentence by writing the correct term in the blank.*

10. A system of laws instituted in South Africa to keep black Africans and whites apart was called ______________.

11. Forced separation of racial groups is called ______________.

12. ______________ are actions that punish a country for behavior unacceptable to the international community of nations.

Name ______________________ Class ______________ Date ______________

Section 4: Other Countries of Southern Africa

Guide to the Essentials

Text Summary

South Africa is so powerful that it affects all of southern Africa. Lesotho is an **enclave** of South Africa. An enclave is completely surrounded by a larger country. The economies of Lesotho and Swaziland depend on South Africa. Until recently, Namibia was controlled by South Africa. Many people from Malawi are migrant workers in South Africa. Botswana sells diamonds, copper, coal, and beef cattle.

THE BIG IDEA

All the countries of southern Africa are affected by South Africa.

Angola and Mozambique became independent in 1975 after long wars with Portugal. Both countries adopted Communist economic systems. Rebel groups, helped by South Africa, fought these governments for many years. Their economies fell apart and disease and malnutrition became common. Angola held its first free election in 1992, although fighting has continued. War ended in Mozambique, and its economy has improved. However, in 2000 floods devastated much of the land.

Zambia's government counted on money from the export of copper to buy food. When the price of copper dropped, Zambia did not have enough money to feed all its people. Today its economy is still trying to recover.

Before full independence, Zimbabwe's white minority had control of the government, as well as most of the nation's fertile land and wealth. This caused conflict with the black majority. Although full independence came in 1980, racial conflicts ignited once again. White-owned farmland was forcibly taken away and given to black farmers. Violent protest erupted and the government repressed many of the people's democratic freedoms.

Graphic Summary: *The Countries of Southern Africa*

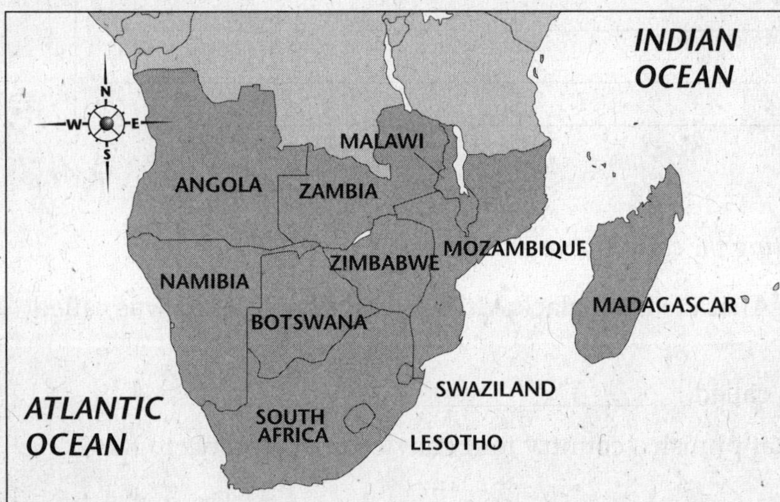

Most countries in the region are dependent on South Africa.

Review Questions

1. How did Zambia's dependence on copper exports create a problem?

2. **Map Skills** Which countries in the region have borders with South Africa?

Name ____________________ Class ______________ Date ______________

Section 4: Other Countries of Southern Africa

Guided Reading and Review

A. As You Read

Directions: *As you read Section 4, complete the chart by identifying the correct southern African nations.*

Question	Answer(s)
Which two countries are completely or almost completely surrounded by and dependent on South Africa?	**1.** ____________ **2.** ____________
Which country until recently was almost a colony of South Africa?	**3.** ____________
Which landlocked country of southern Africa has attracted a large population because of its fertile land and excellent water supply?	**4.** ____________
In which landlocked, arid country does the relatively small population benefit from the sale of diamonds, copper, coal, and beef cattle?	**5.** ____________
Which two countries were once Portuguese colonies, suffered from white flight after achieving independence, and established Communist economic systems?	**6.** ____________ **7.** ____________
Which country became poor after relying on copper as a source of revenue and allowing agriculture to decline?	**8.** ____________
Which country kept agriculture productive by pursuing a gradual land redistribution program after independence?	**9.** ____________

B. Reviewing Vocabulary

Directions: *Define the following terms.*

10. enclave ____________________

11. white flight ____________________

12. land redistribution ____________________

Name ________________ Class ____________ Date ____________

Chapter 27

Test

Identifying Main Ideas

Directions: *Write the letter of the correct answer in the blank provided. (10 points each)*

____ **1. Why does much of Kenya have a cool climate even though it is on the Equator?**
A. The elevation keeps Kenya's low-land area cool.
B. Winds from the south bring cool air to Kenya.
C. The elevation keeps Kenya's high-land area cool.
D. Kenya's river system cools the air.

____ **2. What is *harambee*?**
A. a system of growing cash crops
B. working together
C. a new kind of grain
D. a one-party government

____ **3. What problems do many countries in East Africa face?**
A. too much seacoast
B. too few ethnic groups
C. too much farmland
D. civil wars and famine

____ **4. What is an ethnocracy?**
A. a government controlled by one ethnic group
B. a study of all the ethnic groups in a country
C. a system of getting ethnic groups to work together
D. a fair distribution of government jobs among ethnic groups

____ **5. What helped cause Tanzania's poverty?**
A. It had no fertile land.
B. It had no mineral wealth.
C. People had to work on collective farms.
D. Most of its people fled the country.

____ **6. What percentage of South Africa's population is black?**
A. 25 percent
B. 50 percent
C. 60 percent
D. 75 percent

____ **7. South Africa's apartheid laws**
A. segregated black South Africans.
B. created jobs for everyone.
C. gave black South Africans homes in cities.
D. redistributed land.

____ **8. What are sanctions?**
A. laws that allow free trade
B. free and fair elections
C. discussions between countries
D. acts to punish a country for its behavior

____ **9. Which country is an enclave of South Africa?**
A. Swaziland
B. Angola
C. Malawi
D. Lesotho

____ **10. Why did Zambia have a problem with copper exports?**
A. When the price of copper rose, Zambia could not produce enough copper.
B. When the price of copper fell, Zambia did not have enough money to buy food.
C. Zambia did not have enough money to buy copper.
D. Zambia's mines ran out of copper.

Name ______________________ Class ______________ Date ______________

Chapter 28

Regional Atlas: Introduction to South Asia

Vocabulary
alluvial plain
monsoon
nonaligned nation
subcontinent
sultanate

Vocabulary Development

Directions: *Use the vocabulary terms from the list to complete the crossword puzzle.*

ACROSS

1. state ruled by a sultan
2. nation that adopted neutrality during the Cold War
4. seasonal shift in the prevailing winds that influences large climate regions

DOWN

1. large landmass forming a distinct part of a continent
3. broad expanse of land along riverbanks, consisting of rich, fertile soil left by floods

Name ______________________ Class ______________ Date ______________

Regional Atlas: South Asia

Guide to the Essentials

Text Summary

THE BIG IDEA

The Himalayas formed a barrier that allowed the people of South Asia to develop their own unique cultures. South Asia is one of the most densely populated regions of the world.

The Indus Valley civilization, one of the world's oldest civilizations, began in South Asia. The region was invaded many times throughout history. The invaders introduced new ideas and beliefs to the region, which became influential in the shaping of South Asia's culture.

South Asia is a **subcontinent**, or large landmass forming a distinct part of a continent, in the southern part of Asia. The Himalayas, a mountain system with many of the world's highest mountains, separate South Asia from the rest of Asia.

Climate within the region depends on altitude and distance from the Indian Ocean. Portions of the region are seasonally affected by **monsoons**, winds that bring dry air in winter and rain in summer. Other areas, like the Thar Desert, receive very little precipitation.

South Asia's various ecosystems support its plentiful and diverse wildlife. However, poaching and the loss of habitat threaten several species.

South Asia has one of the most densely settled populations on earth. The population is becoming more urban as more people move to the cities in search of work. Many languages are spoken in South Asia, but about half the population of India speaks Hindi. The dominant religions are Hinduism and Islam, except in Bhutan, where Buddhism is the dominant religion.

Agriculture dominates South Asia's economy. Faced with an ever-increasing population, however, South Asia has had difficulty producing enough food. A large film industry boosts the economy of India. In some areas, women have found economic opportunity in the technological and business fields.

Graphic Summary: *South Asia Monsoons*

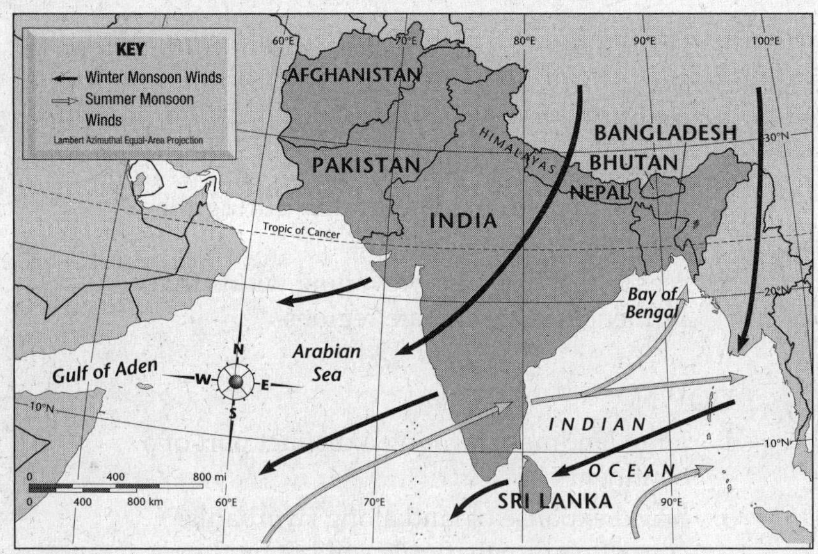

Winter monsoons bring dry air. Summer monsoons bring moisture and rain from the Indian Ocean.

Review Questions

1. What landform separates South Asia from the rest of Asia?

2. **Map Skills** Does the east coast or west coast of India get the summer monsoon rains?

Name ______________________ Class ______________ Date ______________

Regional Atlas: South Asia

Guided Reading and Review

A. As You Read

Directions: *As you work through the Regional Atlas, complete the chart below by identifying each of the South Asian features or characteristics listed.*

Features or Characteristics	Descriptions
Early Civilizations and States of South Asia	**1.** ____________ **3.** ____________ **2.** ____________
Countries of South Asia	**4.** ____________ **8.** ____________ **5.** ____________ **9.** ____________ **6.** ____________ **10.** ____________ **7.** ____________
Major Cities of South Asia	**11.** ____________ **13.** ____________ **12.** ____________
Major Mountain Ranges of South Asia	**14.** ____________ **15.** ____________
Major Religions of South Asia	**16.** ____________ **18.** ____________ **17.** ____________

B. Reviewing Vocabulary

Directions: *Define the following terms.*

19. sultanate

____

20. nonaligned nation

____

21. subcontinent

____

22. alluvial plain

____

23. monsoon

____

Name ______________________ Class ______________ Date ______________

Chapter 28

Test

Identifying Main Ideas

Directions: Write the letter of the correct answer in the blank provided. (10 points each)

____ **1. What is a subcontinent?**
A. an island near a continent
B. any area that is cut off by mountains
C. a large landmass forming a distinct part of a continent
D. a continent surrounded by water

____ **2. South Asia's climate depends on**
A. altitude and distance from the Indian Ocean.
B. the Himalayas, which block all precipitation.
C. the temperature of the Indian Ocean.
D. China's climate.

____ **3. Why are some South Asian species threatened?**
A. New animal species have killed off native species.
B. Poaching and loss of habitat threaten many plants and animals.
C. The monsoon winds have destroyed many plant species.
D. South Asia relies on animal hunting for its economy.

____ **4. Why are so many people in South Asia moving to cities?**
A. to leave the crowded farmland
B. to go to school
C. to find work
D. to escape civil wars

____ **5. About how much of the Indian population speaks Hindi?**
A. one third
B. one half
C. one fifth
D. one fourth

____ **6. The major religions of South Asia are**
A. Hinduism and Islam.
B. Christianity and Judaism.
C. Buddhism and Christianity.
D. Hinduism and Judaism.

____ **7. What are monsoons?**
A. religious leaders of South India
B. seasonal winds that bring rains in summer and dry air in winter
C. animals found only in South Asia
D. any method of preventing floods

____ **8. The Himalayas separate South Asia from**
A. the monsoons.
B. Africa.
C. the rest of Asia.
D. the Indian Ocean.

____ **9. What is the major economic activity of South Asia?**
A. livestock grazing
B. manufacturing and trade
C. fishing
D. agriculture

____ **10. Women in South Asia are offered more economic opportunity in the fields of**
A. technology and business.
B. engineering and manufacturing.
C. fishing and livestock raising.
D. textiles and entertainment.

Name ______________________ Class ______________ Date ______________

Chapter 29

The Countries of South Asia

Vocabulary

boycott
caste system
embankment dam
irrigate
nonviolent resistance
purdah
reincarnation
sari

Vocabulary Development

Directions: *Write a sentence for each pair of terms below that shows you understand the relationship between them. Provide context clues so that a reader who may not know the meaning of the terms could figure them out.*

nonviolent resistance/boycott

____

____

____

caste system/reincarnation

____

____

____

sari/purdah

____

____

____

irrigate/embankment dam

____

____

____

Name ______________________ Class ______________ Date ______________

Section 1: Road to Independence

Guide to the Essentials

Text Summary

THE BIG IDEA

Mohandas Gandhi led a nonviolent struggle to gain independence for India from Britain. When India became independent it was divided into two countries—India and Pakistan.

On August 15, 1947, India became independent from Britain. British rule of India began in the mid-1700s. The colonial rulers ended slavery, improved schools, and built railroads. Other changes, however, hurt India. The British tried to end India's textile industry so they could sell British cloth in India. Indians were not allowed to hold high government and army positions.

In the late 1800s, Indians developed a strong feeling of **nationalism**, or pride in one's nation. Mohandas Gandhi led an independence movement. Gandhi encouraged **nonviolent resistance**—opposing an enemy by any means except violence. One method was to **boycott**—refuse to buy or use—British cloth. The sale of British cloth in India fell sharply.

For a while Hindus and Muslims worked together for independence. But as their goal got closer, conflicts between the two religious groups grew stronger. In 1947, the leaders agreed to **partition**, or divide, the subcontinent into separate Hindu and Muslim countries. The two new countries were the mostly Hindu India and the mostly Muslim Pakistan.

At independence, 12 million people moved on the subcontinent. Hindus moved to India and Muslims moved to Pakistan. About one million people were killed in fighting between Hindus and Muslims.

India and Pakistan have fought three wars. After the third war, in 1971, part of Pakistan became the independent country of Bangladesh.

Graphic Summary: *Religions in South Asia*

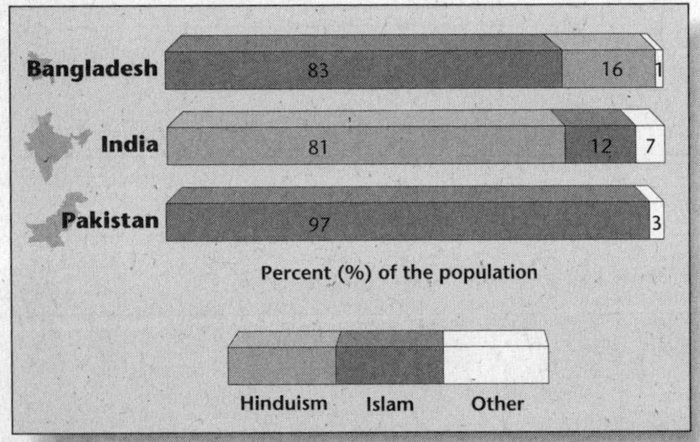

Almost all people of India, Pakistan, and Bangladesh are Hindus or Muslims.

Source: *The World Factbook 2004*

Review Questions

1. What is nonviolent resistance?

2. **Chart Skills** What percentage of Indians are Hindus?

Name ______________________ Class ______________ Date ______________

Section 1: Road to Independence

Guided Reading and Review

A. As You Read

Directions: *As you read Section 1, answer the following questions.*

1. Why was India's textile industry almost completely destroyed?

____

2. What Western ideas were spread among the Indian middle class in the late 1800s?

____

3. What was Gandhi's most powerful weapon against the British?

____

4. In what way did Gandhi use nonviolent resistance to show opposition to the sale of British cloth?

____

5. What happened to the sale of British cloth in India as a result of Gandhi's actions?

____

6. What decision did the British government make in 1935?

____

7. What was the basis of the partition of the Indian subcontinent in 1947?

____

8. What results did the 1947 independence of India and Pakistan have on their inhabitants?

____

____

9. What problems arose between the regions of West Pakistan and East Pakistan, and what was the result?

____

____

B. Reviewing Vocabulary

Directions: *Complete each sentence by writing the correct term in the blank.*

10. A strong sense of ______________, or pride in one's nation, developed in India during the late 1800s.

11. ______________ is the policy of opposing an enemy or oppressor by any means other than violence.

12. To ______________ a product or service is to refuse to purchase, sell, or use it.

13. To ______________ a nation is to divide it into parts.

Name ______________________ Class ______________ Date ______________

Section 2: India's People and Economy

Guide to the Essentials

Text Summary

THE BIG IDEA

Most Indians live in rural villages and follow traditional ways. Cities have a growing middle class. The government is working to improve the country's standard of living.

Most Indians are Hindus. Hindu society is based on the **caste system**. This is a social system in which each person is born into a caste, or group. Each caste has its own duties. Caste determines the work people do. At the top of the caste system are Brahmans—priests, teachers, and judges. (See graph below.) Untouchables have the lowest rank and do work that is thought to be "unclean."

About seven out of ten Indians live in farming villages. Many people own bicycles, but few own cars. Many villages now have electricity. Television, radio, and movies are important for spreading new ideas because many people cannot read. As people have moved to towns and cities, urban areas have become very crowded. People believe they have more opportunity in a city than in a village.

India's government is trying to raise the standard of living for people in both cities and villages. A major goal has been to feed the growing population. Increased irrigation and better farming methods have produced more and better crops. Many farmers have set up **cottage industries** to earn more money. People in cottage industries make goods at home.

India has become one of the world's leading industrial countries. It has made advances in computers and space research. There is a growing middle class. About half the people can read and write, and this percentage is growing. However, many people live on the streets or in slums.

Graphic Summary: *The Caste System*

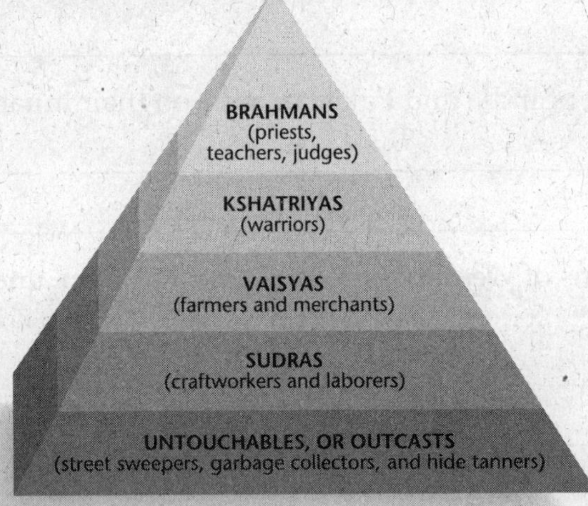

Hindus are born into castes, which help determine how they live.

Review Questions

1. Why are many Indians moving to cities?
2. **Diagram Skills** What are the main jobs of the Vaisyas?

Name ______________________ Class ______________ Date ______________

Section 2: India's People and Economy

Guided Reading and Review

A. As You Read

Directions: *As you read Section 2, complete the chart below by writing three supporting details under each main idea.*

Main Idea A: The caste system involves a social hierarchy.

1. ______________________________

2. ______________________________

3. ______________________________

Main Idea B: People in rural Indian villages follow a traditional way of life.

4. ______________________________

5. ______________________________

6. ______________________________

Main Idea C: India is one of the leading industrial nations in the world.

7. ______________________________

8. ______________________________

9. ______________________________

B. Reviewing Vocabulary

Directions: *Define the following terms.*

10. reincarnation ______________________________

11. caste system ______________________________

12. charpoy ______________________________

13. sari ______________________________

14. purdah ______________________________

15. joint family system ______________________________

16. cottage industry ______________________________

Name ____________________ Class ____________ Date ____________

Section 3: Other Countries of South Asia

Guide to the Essentials

Text Summary

THE BIG IDEA

Water—too little or too much—has a major effect on Pakistan and Bangladesh. Other countries in the region have been shaped by their physical geography.

Each of India's neighbors has its own physical and cultural identity. In Pakistan, the Hindu Kush mountain range towers along its northern and western borders. The Baluchistan Plateau covers much of western Pakistan. To the east is the Thar Desert. Most Pakistanis live in the fertile valley of the Indus River. Most are farmers. The river provides **hydroelectric power**—electricity produced by the movement of the water—and **irrigates** the land, supplying water to dry areas. Islam links Pakistanis together, but ethnic conflicts divide them.

Mountainous Afghanistan has fertile valleys at the foot of the Hindu Kush. Semiarid plains lie to the north. As in Pakistan, Islam is the religion of almost all the people. In 1979, the Soviet Union invaded Afghanistan. About 3 million Afghans fled. In 1989, the Soviets withdrew, but fighting among Afghan groups continued. In recent decades, Afghanistan has undergone great turmoil. A repressive government gained control in the late 1990s, but the United States helped topple it after the September 11 attacks in 2001 and helped establish a democracy in 2004.

Bangladesh has fertile soil, but floods happen regularly. In good times, farmers harvest three crops a year. In bad times, overflowing rivers and tropical storms flood the land. Bangladesh is working to control flooding and overpopulation.

Nepal and Bhutan are in the Himalayas. Each has hot, humid southern lowlands with monsoon rains. Mount Everest, the world's highest mountain, is in Nepal.

Sri Lanka is an island country in the Indian Ocean. The majority of its people are Sinhalese, who control the government. A smaller group, the Tamils, have been fighting for independence. Norway helped negotiate a cease-fire in 2001, but formal peace talks made little progress. Both sides had to cooperate to deal with a devastating tsunami in December 2004 that killed more than 40,000 people in Sri Lanka.

Graphic Summary: *The Countries of South Asia*

Country	Population	Life Expectancy (years)	Per Capita GDP (in U.S. $)
Afghanistan	25,513,677	42.3	700
Bangladesh	141,340,476	61.7	1,900
Bhutan	2,185,569	53.9	1,300
India	1,065,070,607	63.9	2,900
Nepal	27,070,666	59.4	1,400
Pakistan	159,196,336	62.6	2,100
Sri Lanka	19,905,165	72.9	3,700

Source: *The World Factbook 2004*

The countries of South Asia differ greatly in size and income.

Review Questions

1. Why is the Indus River important to Pakistan?

2. Graph Skills Which South Asian country has the highest per capita GDP?

Name ______________________ Class ______________ Date ______________

Section 3: Other Countries of South Asia

Guided Reading and Review

A. As You Read

Directions: *As you read Section 3, organize information about other countries of South Asia by completing the chart below.*

Country	Physical and Other Features
Pakistan	**1.** ______________________
	2. ______________________
Afghanistan	**3.** ______________________
	4. ______________________
Bangladesh	**5.** ______________________
	6. ______________________
Nepal and Bhutan	**7.** ______________________
	8. ______________________
Sri Lanka	**9.** ______________________
	10. ______________________

B. Reviewing Vocabulary

Directions: *Define the following terms.*

11. hydroelectric power ______________________

12. irrigate ______________________

13. embankment dam ______________________

14. buffer state ______________________

15. malnutrition ______________________

16. deforestation ______________________

Name ____________ Class ____________ Date ____________

Chapter 29

Test

Identifying Main Ideas

Directions: Write the letter of the correct answer in the blank provided. (10 points each)

____ **1. Who was Mohandas Gandhi?**
A. the leader of India's independence movement
B. the head of India's textile industry
C. the leader of the group that used violence to gain independence
D. a high official of the British government

____ **2. An example of nonviolent resistance would be**
A. forming an army to fight the enemy.
B. kidnapping and killing one's enemies.
C. giving in to the enemy to avoid violence.
D. refusing to buy or use an enemy's products.

____ **3. What countries were created by the 1947 partition of British India?**
A. India, Pakistan, and Afghanistan
B. Pakistan and Bangladesh
C. India and Pakistan
D. India, Pakistan, Nepal, and Bhutan

____ **4. How is a person's life affected by the caste system in India?**
A. People's lives are no longer affected at all by the caste system.
B. The caste system helps people do whatever they want in life.
C. Caste determines people's work and their rules for living.
D. Caste determines if an Indian has the right to vote.

____ **5. People in India who cannot read get information from**
A. newspapers and magazines.
B. radio and television.
C. messengers on bicycles.
D. the Internet.

____ **6. Why do many people in India move from farm villages to cities?**
A. There is more opportunity in cities.
B. Cities have more space than villages.
C. Hardly any villages have electricity.
D. They do not want to use farm machinery.

____ **7. In what kinds of industry is India making great advances?**
A. hand weaving
B. computers and space research
C. automobiles and trucks
D. televisions and radios

____ **8. Where in Pakistan do most people live?**
A. in the Baluchistan Plateau
B. in the Thar Desert
C. in the Indus River valley
D. in the Hindu Kush

____ **9. What country invaded Afghanistan in 1979?**
A. Great Britain
B. the Soviet Union
C. India
D. Pakistan

____ **10. In what country is Mount Everest located?**
A. India
B. Sri Lanka
C. Bhutan
D. Nepal

Name ______________________ Class ______________ Date ______________

Chapter 30

Regional Atlas: Introduction to East Asia and the Pacific World

Vocabulary
concession
intensive farming
terrace

Vocabulary Development

Directions: *Write a brief definition for each of the listed terms. Then, using all the terms, write a paragraph that describes the history and agriculture of East Asia and the Pacific World. In your writing, be sure to show how related concepts work together.*

concession

____

____

intensive farming

____

____

terrace

____

____

Paragraph:

____

____

____

____

____

____

____

____

Name ______________________ Class ______________ Date ______________

Regional Atlas: East Asia and the Pacific World

Guide to the Essentials

Text Summary

East Asia is located where the Pacific and Indian oceans meet. Its location made it a great trading area for centuries. The geography of Southeast Asia consists mainly of mountains, river valleys, peninsulas, and islands. Australia is flat with broad deserts and low mountains.

Rain falls seasonally across much of the region. Monsoons occur in the tropical climates near the Equator. Australia is mostly arid and semiarid, though southern Australia and New Zealand have Mediterranean and marine west-coast climates.

THE BIG IDEA

This huge region includes countries on the continent of Asia as well as many island nations. The continents of Australia and Antarctica are also included.

Many plants and animals are found in the ecosystems of the region. Tropical rain forests line the coasts of northern Australia and East and Southeast Asia. Parts of East Asia, Australia, and New Zealand are deciduous forests; the interiors of China, Mongolia, and Australia are grasslands.

East Asia is heavily populated, with about 2 billion inhabitants. China's population alone is over 1 billion, with a third of them living in rural areas. Many ethnic, religious, and language groups live in the region. This has led to great cultural diversity.

The economies of the nations within the region contrast sharply with each other. While Japan and Australia are highly industrialized, China and much of Southeast Asia are focused on agriculture, where **intensive farming**—farming that requires much labor to produce food—is done. In hilly areas, farmers create **terraces**, flat ledges of land, like steps, to plant their crops.

Graphic Summary: *East Asia and the Pacific*

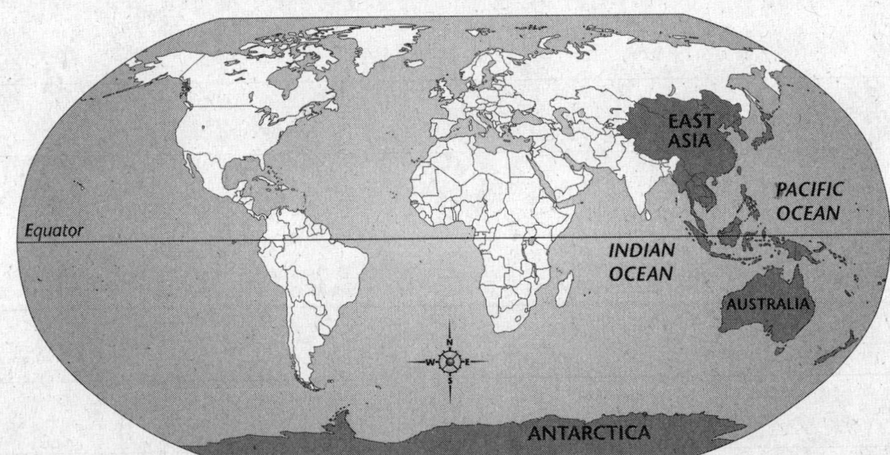

The region extends between the Indian and Pacific oceans.

Review Questions

1. What is intensive farming?

2. Map Skills Where are Australia and Antarctica located in relation to East Asia?

Name ______________________ Class ______________ Date ______________

Regional Atlas: East Asia and the Pacific World

Guided Reading and Review

A. As You Read

Directions: *As you work through the Regional Atlas, complete the chart below by writing at least one supporting detail under each main idea.*

Main Idea A: Some of humanity's earliest technological advances occurred in East and Southeast Asia.

1. ____

Main Idea B: The collision of the Eurasian and Indian tectonic plates has altered the geography of East and Southeast Asia.

2. ____

Main Idea C: Seasonal rainfall affects parts of East Asia, Southeast Asia, Australia, and New Zealand in a variety of ways.

3. ____

Main Idea D: East Asia and the Pacific region have many different ecosystems.

4. ____

Main Idea E: Much of the world's population lives in East and Southeast Asia.

5. ____

Main Idea F: Many factors explain great differences in transportation systems among the countries of China, Japan, Australia, and Thailand.

6. ____

B. Reviewing Vocabulary

Directions: *Define the following terms.*

7. concession ______________________________

8. intensive farming ______________________________

9. terrace ______________________________

10. bullet train ______________________________

Name ______________________ Class ______________ Date ______________

Chapter 30 Test

Identifying Main Ideas

Directions: *Write the letter of the correct answer in the blank provided. (10 points each)*

____ **1. What two oceans are found in East Asia?**
A. Atlantic and Pacific
B. Pacific and Indian
C. Indian and Atlantic
D. Pacific and Arctic

____ **2. Australia's landscape can be described as**
A. mountainous with many snow-covered peaks.
B. flat with deserts and low mountains.
C. river valleys with ample vegetation.
D. a peninsula with many rivers.

____ **3. What type of climate region can be found in the interior of China and Mongolia?**
A. desert scrub
B. rain forests
C. grasslands
D. highlands

____ **4. About how much of China's population is rural?**
A. one half
B. one fourth
C. two thirds
D. one third

____ **5. East Asia and the Pacific world have**
A. very few ethnic groups.
B. only one main religion.
C. diverse language groups.
D. a population of 1 billion.

____ **6. China's climate is**
A. similar to the climate of the United States.
B. not at all like the climate of the United States.
C. the same throughout China.
D. different in every part of China.

____ **7. What kind of climate does most of Southeast Asia have?**
A. arid
B. semiarid
C. continental
D. tropical

____ **8. The economies of China and Southeast Asia are mostly based on**
A. agriculture.
B. manufacturing.
C. commercial fishing.
D. nomadic herding.

____ **9. What is a terrace?**
A. a restaurant where farmers eat lunch
B. an area where farmers burn crops
C. a flat ledge of land farmers make to allow farming in hilly areas
D. a vast plain that is good for farming

____ **10. Australia's climate is mostly**
A. wet and tropical.
B. arid and semiarid.
C. subarctic.
D. tropical wet and dry.

Name ____________________ Class ____________ Date ____________

Chapter 31 China

Vocabulary
- abdicate
- atheism
- autonomous region
- double cropping
- exodus
- provisional government
- sphere of influence
- theocrat

Vocabulary Development

Directions: *Imagine that you are a tourist visiting China and its neighbors. Write a letter to a friend or a family member of one or more paragraphs describing what you have learned about the places and people you have visited. Use at least five of the listed vocabulary words. Be specific in your paragraph(s) to help your readers appreciate the excitement of your travels.*

Dear ______________________________,

Sincerely,

____

Name ____________ Class ____________ Date ____________

Section 1: The Emergence of Modern China

Guide to the Essentials

Text Summary

THE BIG IDEA

Mao Zedong made China a Communist nation. The Four Modernizations changed the economy. The government responded with violence to the call for democratic reforms.

Chinese civilization was born around 3000 B.C. Feeding China's large population has required large amounts of rice and other crops. By 1900, some European countries and the United States had divided China into **spheres of influence**. Countries had political and economic control in these areas but did not govern them directly.

In 1911, Chinese Nationalists forced the emperor to **abdicate**, or give up his throne. China was declared a republic. In the 1920s, the Nationalists attacked supporters of Communist ideas. In 1934, the Communists, led by Mao Zedong, fled to the mountains, beginning the Long March.

Japan invaded China in the 1930s. Nationalists and Communists cooperated to fight Japan but fought again after World War II. By 1949, the Communists won and Mao Zedong established the People's Republic of China.

Mao started the Great Leap Forward. Chinese peasants were forced to work on huge collective farms. Communist officials made all economic decisions. When production fell, Mao called for a Cultural Revolution to destroy the old order. These actions ruined the economy and destroyed many people's lives.

The next leader, Deng Xiaoping, started the Four Modernizations—improving agriculture, industry, science and technology, and defense. Farmers could rent land and sell extra crops for profit. Farm production increased.

Economic improvement led people to want freedom and democracy. In 1989, thousands demonstrated in Tiananmen Square in Beijing. Troops killed more than 1,000 people.

Graphic Summary: *China's Nationalists and Communists*

In the 1900s, there were many attempts to change China.

Review Questions

1. What were the results of the Great Leap Forward and the Cultural Revolution?

2. **Time Line Skills** When did Nationalists and Communists cooperate?

Name ____________________ Class ______________ Date ______________

Section 1: The Emergence of Modern China

Guided Reading and Review

A. As You Read

Directions: *As you read Section 1, complete the chart below to organize information about China, by writing supporting details under each idea.*

Main Idea A: In the 1920s, a split developed in the Nationalist party.

1. ____

____

2. ____

____

Main Idea B: Mao Zedong's economic and political reforms did not succeed.

3. ____

____

4. ____

____

Main Idea C: The Four Modernizations gave a boost to China's economy.

5. ____

____

6. ____

____

B. Reviewing Vocabulary

Directions: *Complete each sentence by writing the correct term in the blank.*

7. An area controlled by a country but not directly governed by it is called a(n) ______________.

8. To ______________ is to give up a throne.

9. In China, a(n) ______________ was a regional leader with an army.

10. The production of small consumer goods is usually referred to as ______________.

11. In May of 1989, the Chinese government imposed ______________ in China.

Name ______________________ Class ______________ Date ______________

Section 2: Regions of China

Guide to the Essentials

Text Summary

THE BIG IDEA

Each of China's four main regions has its own character and is defined largely by geography.

For centuries, China's core was in the Northeast region. It contains Beijing, the country's capital, and the greatest concentrations of China's population.

Considered one of China's major industrial areas, the Northeast is also a farm region, made fertile by loess, a yellow soil carried by the Huang He. This river is a transportation route. It was called "China's Sorrow" because of destructive floods. Now people use so much of its water that it dries up for months.

The Southeast is warmer, wetter, and more mountainous than the Northeast. The Southeast, once China's main agricultural region, has become its economic center. The Yangzi River is a major east-west route. Shanghai, at its mouth, is China's major port and largest city. Four Special Economic Zones, set up to attract foreign money and technology, have made this region economically strong.

China's Northwest region is rugged and barren, with a small population. The Gobi Desert forms China's northern boundary. Herding is the main economic activity. The Silk Road, an ancient trade route, crossed this region. Stopping places at oases became towns.

The Plateau of Tibet dominates the Southwest and is the world's highest region. Tibet's farmers and herders are Buddhists led by a **theocrat**—a person who claims to rule by religious or divine authority—called the Dalai Lama. China invaded Tibet in 1950, destroying Buddhist monasteries and driving the Dalai Lama into exile. It tried to destroy Tibet's culture and designated the area as an **autonomous** region, a political unit with limited self-government. However, most Tibetans maintained their traditions and beliefs.

Graphic Summary: *The Four Regions of China*

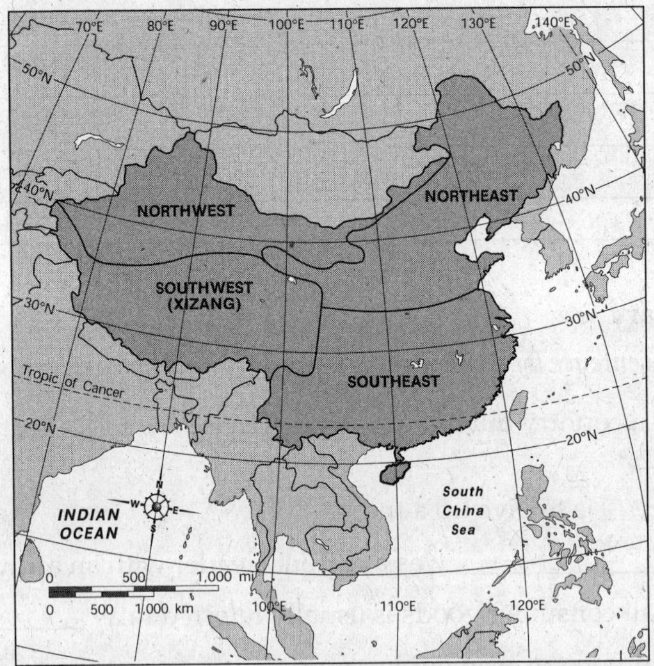

Most of China's people live in the two eastern regions.

Review Questions

1. Which region was considered China's core for centuries?

2. **Map Skills** Name the regions of China.

Name ____________________ Class ____________________ Date ____________________

Section 2: Regions of China

Guided Reading and Review

A. As You Read

Directions: *As you read Section 2, answer the following questions.*

1. In the past few decades, what region of China has become the center of its booming economy?
____

2. What color is the loess soil? ____________________

3. Why is the Huang He also called China's Sorrow? ____________________
____

4. What is the purpose of terrace farming along the slopes of hills?
____
____

5. What river serves as China's east-west highway?
____

6. Three of the four Special Economic Zones are located in which province of China?
____

7. What is the chief economic activity in Northwest China?
____

8. What physical feature dominates the Southwest region?
____

9. What religion is the Tibetan society based on?
____

10. What was the result of the Tibetan uprising of 1959?
____

B. Reviewing Vocabulary

Directions: *Complete each sentence by writing the correct term in the blank.*

11. Growing more than one crop a year on the same land is called ____________________.

12. A(n) ____________________ is someone who claims to rule by religious or divine authority.

13. A political unit with limited self-government is known as a(n) ____________________.

Name ____________ Class ____________ Date ____________

Section 3: China's People and Culture

Guide to the Essentials

Text Summary

With 1.3 billion people, China has the world's largest population. Most Chinese share a common culture and written language.

THE BIG IDEA

China has more people than any other country. Most share a common culture.

Mao Zedong thought that China needed a large population. He urged people to have more children. By the mid-1960s, China had more people than it could feed or house.

When Deng Xiaoping took over, he said China had to reduce its population growth. He wanted each couple to have just one child. China rewarded families who had only one child with better housing, jobs, and pay. Couples who had more children faced fines, pay cuts, and loss of jobs. City dwellers usually followed this policy, but rural dwellers, who needed larger families to help in the fields, did not.

China has about 56 ethnic minorities, who live mostly in the west. But more than 1 billion people—92 percent—belong to the Han ethnic group. The Chinese speak different dialects, but all use the same written language. Chinese writing is not based on a phonetic alphabet. It is based on **ideograms**, pictures or characters that represent a thing or idea. To make the spoken language the same, most children are now taught the Mandarin dialect in school.

Chinese people follow several religions, especially Buddhism, Daoism, and Confucianism. Communist China discourages religion and encourages **atheism**, a denial that God exists.

Graphic Summary: *Population of China*

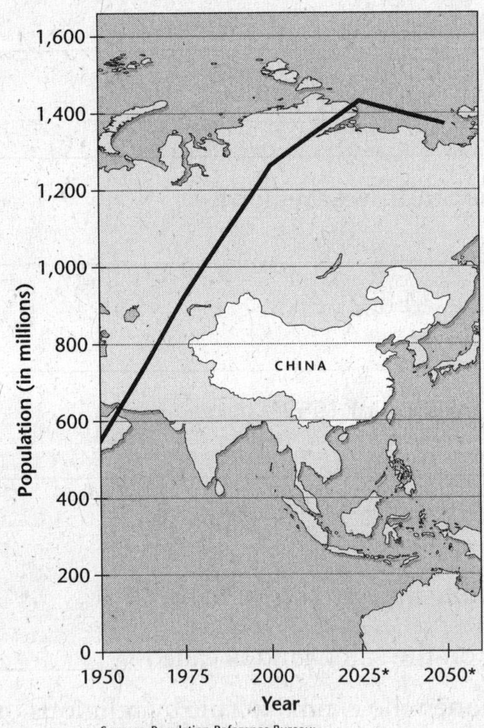

Sources: Population Reference Bureau; China Population Information and Research Center
*Projected population.

China's population has more than doubled since 1950.

Review Questions

1. How did Deng's Communist government control population growth?

2. **Graph Skills** Around what year did China's population reach 1 billion?

Name ______________________ Class ______________ Date ______________

Section 3: China's People and Culture

Guided Reading and Review

A. As You Read

Directions: As you read Section 3, complete the chart below to organize information about China by writing two supporting details under each main idea.

Main Idea A: China's "one-couple, one-child" population policy has had differing effects in different parts of China.

1. ____

2. ____

Main Idea B: China is a land of great ethnic diversity.

3. ____

4. ____

Main Idea C: Written Chinese is different from many other written languages.

5. ____

6. ____

Main Idea D: Officially, China is an atheist country, but religious belief is not absent.

7. ____

8. ____

B. Reviewing Vocabulary

Directions: Complete each sentence by writing the correct term in the blank.

9. Pictures or characters that represent a thing or an idea are called ______________.

10. ______________ is the denial of the existence of God.

11. The Chinese use ______________, which is the practice of inserting needles into the body to cure diseases or ease pain.

Name ______________________ Class ______________ Date ______________

Section 4: China's Neighbors

Guide to the Essentials

Text Summary

Taiwan is an island off China's southeast coast. When the Chinese Nationalists were defeated in 1949, they fled to Taiwan, setting up a temporary **provisional government** there.

THE BIG IDEA

Taiwan is a leading economic power in Asia. Mongolia is gradually becoming more modern and democratic. The British returned Hong Kong to China in 1997.

The Nationalists claimed to represent all of China. So did the mainland Communists. For many years, Western countries supported Taiwan. But in 1971, the United Nations recognized mainland China and removed Taiwan.

Most countries do not officially recognize Taiwan, but they trade with it. It has become one of Asia's leading economic powers.

The Nationalists improved Taiwan's farming and industry. The standard of living is high, and the people have maintained their culture. Until 1987, people in Taiwan had no official contact with China. Now they are investing money in China's Special Economic Zones.

Hong Kong is located on China's southern coast. Beginning in 1898, the British had a 99-year lease on Hong Kong. During that time Hong Kong became a leader in world trade. In 1997, Britain returned it to China. China agreed to allow economic and political freedom.

Mongolia is a vast, dry land. The Gobi Desert occupies the south. The rest has mostly steppe vegetation. In the 1200s, Genghiz Khan ruled a huge Mongol empire. Later Mongolia came under Chinese rule.

In 1911, Mongolia declared its independence. Ten years later, Mongolia became a communist country. Mongolia held democratic elections after Russia ended its communist system in the early 1990s.

Graphic Summary: *China and its Neighbors*

Country	Population	Life Expectancy (years)	Per Capita GDP (in U.S. $)
China	1,298,847,624	72.0	5,000
Mongolia	2,751,314	64.2	1,800
Taiwan	22,749,838	77.1	23,400

Source: *The World Factbook 2004*

The countries in East Asia differ from one another in many ways.

Review Questions

1. Which country represented China in the United Nations in the 1950s?

2. **Chart Skills** Which country has the longest life expectancy?

Name ______________________ Class ______________ Date ______________

Section 4: China's Neighbors

Guided Reading and Review

A. As You Read

Directions: *As you read Section 4, complete the chart below by writing a brief description of each topic listed.*

Topic	Description
China's neighbors	**1.** ______________________
Nationalist migration	**2.** ______________________
Taiwanese industries	**3.** ______________________
Hong Kong	**4.** ______________________
Mongols	**5.** ______________________

Directions: *Use the chart above and your textbook to answer questions 6–10.*

6. Which of China's neighboring countries is also an island? ______________
7. Who was the leader of the Nationalists? ______________
8. On what kind of industries has Taiwan concentrated recently? ______________
9. When did Hong Kong become part of China again? ______________
10. Politically, has Mongolia been influenced more by China or Russia? ______________

B. Reviewing Vocabulary

Directions: *Define the following terms.*

11. buffer ______________
12. provisional government ______________
13. exodus ______________

Name ______________________ Class ______________ Date ______________

Chapter 31 **Test**

Identifying Main Ideas

Directions: *Write the letter of the correct answer in the blank provided. (10 points each)*

____ **1. What was the Long March?**
A. the Communists' journey to the mountains of China
B. the Nationalists' escape to Taiwan
C. the emperor's escape after he abdicated
D. another name for the Great Leap Forward

____ **2. Why did Nationalists and Communists cooperate during World War II?**
A. They thought a democratic election would end their fighting.
B. They both wanted farmers to move to collective farms.
C. They both wanted to drive out the Japanese who invaded China.
D. The emperor forced them to cooperate.

____ **3. What do the Special Economic Zones do?**
A. improve farm production
B. attract foreign money in China
C. destroy old ideas
D. bring industry to the Gobi Desert

____ **4. Which is NOT true about the Huang He?**
A. It is a transportation route.
B. Floods caused many people to die.
C. People caused Huang He's floods.
D. People caused the Huang He to run dry.

____ **5. The Plateau of Tibet is located in China's**
A. Northeast
B. Southeast
C. Northwest
D. Southwest

____ **6. After Chinese invaded Tibet, they**
A. rebuilt many Buddhist monasteries.
B. destroyed many Buddhist monasteries.
C. invited the Dalai Lama to return.
D. brought in many other religions.

____ **7. Deng Xiaoping tried to reduce China's population growth by telling each family to have**
A. no children.
B. no more than one child.
C. no more than two children.
D. no more than three children.

____ **8. One thing that the people of China share is**
A. a system of writing.
B. a spoken language.
C. a belief in Christianity.
D. a belief in atheism.

____ **9. How do most other countries today treat Taiwan?**
A. They do not recognize Taiwan, but they trade with it.
B. They recognize Taiwan, but they do not trade with it.
C. They neither recognize nor trade with Taiwan.
D. They recognize Taiwan as the true government of China.

____ **10. Why is Hong Kong now part of China?**
A. The people of Hong Kong voted to be part of China.
B. The people of China voted for Hong Kong to be part of China.
C. Britain returned Hong Kong to China at the end of a 99-year lease.
D. Hong Kong's economy was failing, and Britain no longer wanted it.

Name ______________________ Class ______________ Date ______________

Chapter 32 Japan and the Koreas

Vocabulary
demilitarized zone
downsize
homogenous
militarism
proliferation
quota
seismograph
tariff
typhoon

Vocabulary Development

Directions: *Match each term in Column A with the correct definition in Column B.*

Column A

1. seismograph
2. typhoon
3. homogenous
4. militarism
5. downsize
6. tariff
7. quota
8. demilitarized zone
9. proliferation

Column B

a. having a similar nature; uniform in structure or quality
b. an instrument that measures and records movement in the earth's crust
c. a strip of land on which troops or weapons are not allowed
d. a destructive tropical storm that forms over the Pacific Ocean
e. the glorification of the military and a readiness for war
f. a tax imposed by a government on imported goods
g. to fire employees in order to reduce costs
h. an increase in the number of something
i. a fixed quantity

Directions: *Write one or two sentences on each of the following topics using what you have learned in Chapter 32. Include at least two vocabulary terms for each topic.*

Topic: Japan: The Land of the Rising Sun

____

____

____

Topic: Japan's Economic Development

____

____

____

Topic: The Koreas: A Divided Peninsula

____

____

____

Name ______________________ Class ______________ Date ______________

Section 1: Japan: The Land of the Rising Sun

Guide to the Essentials

Text Summary

THE BIG IDEA

Japan is made up of islands. The people belong to the same ethnic group and share a common culture.

Japan calls itself the Land of the Rising Sun because ancient Japanese thought it was the first land to see the rising sun.

Japan is a chain of islands off the coast of East Asia. Most people live on four large islands, especially Honshu, the largest island. Only some land is good for farming. To create more farmland, people built terraces into hillsides and drained swamps.

Japan is part of the Ring of Fire, an area with many earthquakes and active volcanoes. **Seismographs**, machines that register movements in the earth's crust, are used to record the thousands of earthquakes that strike Japan each year. The climate varies with latitude. The northern island of Hokkaido has long winters and cool summers. Southern Honshu has hot summers and mild winters. Monsoons affect Japan and vary by season. **Typhoons** occur from late summer to early fall. They are tropical hurricanes that cause floods and landslides.

Japan is one of the most densely populated countries. Although Japan is about the same size as California, it has nearly four times that state's population. In crowded cities, prices for land and housing are high. To solve problems of pollution and waste disposal, Japan recycles 50 percent of its solid waste.

More than 99 percent of Japan's people share a common heritage and language. They also share a religion, Shinto. Shintoists worship forces of nature and their ancestors' spirits. Most Japanese also practice Buddhism. As Japan grew more modern, its middle class grew. Today, most Japanese are middle class.

Graphic Summary: *Japan and the Koreas*

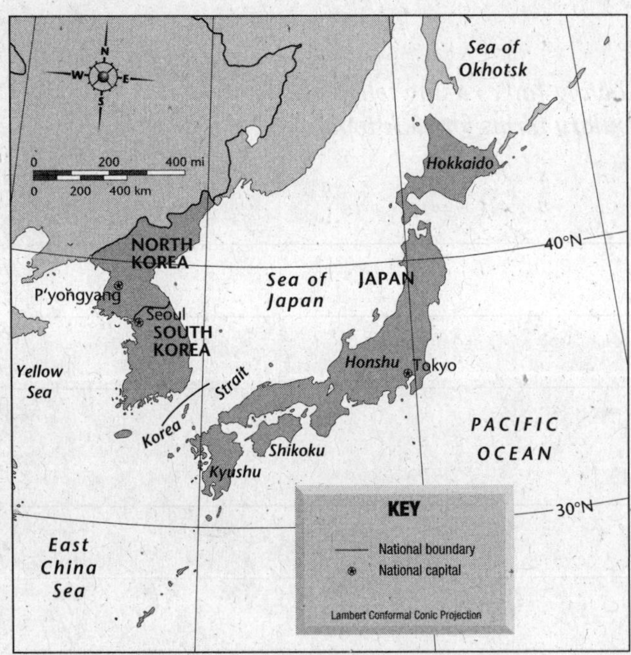

Japan and the Koreas have coasts on the Sea of Japan.

Review Questions

1. What do Japanese people share that gives them unity?

2. **Map Skills** List Japan's four big islands from south to north.

Name ______________________ Class ______________ Date ______________

Section 1: Japan: The Land of the Rising Sun

Guided Reading and Review

A. As You Read

Directions: *As you read Section 1, complete the chart below by writing a brief description of each feature of Japan.*

Feature	Description
Landform	1. ______________________
Landscape	2. ______________________
Tectonic activity	3. ______________________
Influences on climate	4. ______________________ 5. ______________________ 6. ______________________
Population density	7. ______________________
Ethnic makeup	8. ______________________
Religious influences	9. ______________________

B. Reviewing Vocabulary

Directions: *Complete each sentence by writing the correct term in the blank.*

10. A(n) ______________________ is a device that detects movements in the earth's crust.

11. Tropical hurricanes that bring heavy rains to Japan in late summer and early fall are called ______________________.

12. Japan's population is considered to be ______________________, because 99 percent of the people share the same cultural background.

Name ______________________ Class ______________ Date ______________

Section 2: Japan's Economic Development

Guide to the Essentials

Text Summary

> **THE BIG IDEA**
>
> **Japan developed from an isolated agricultural country to a modern industrial power. Despite its lack of natural resources, its economy grew quickly.**

When Japan had its first contact with the West, it was a wealthy and highly developed civilization. It welcomed Portuguese visitors in 1543. Later, Japan worried that European nations would try to conquer it. In 1639, it ordered Europeans to leave and closed its doors to the West.

Beginning in 1853, Western nations forced Japan to sign unequal treaties. In 1868, the new Meiji government began to make Japan more modern and industrial. By 1900, it ended the unequal treaties with the West.

Japan has few natural resources. It fought to take control of weaker nations that had resources. In the early 1900s, Japan won wars against China and Russia. In 1910, it made Korea part of Japan.

The worldwide depression that began in 1929 ruined Japanese businesses. Military leaders wanted an overseas empire to gain markets and raw materials. Japan became a military dictatorship. The new leaders promoted **militarism**, the glorification of the military and a readiness for war.

Japan sided with Nazi Germany during World War II. It attacked the United States naval base at Pearl Harbor, Hawaii, in 1941. In August 1945, Japan surrendered, after the United States dropped atomic bombs on two Japanese cities.

United States troops occupied Japan until 1952. They began democratic reforms. Japan was not allowed to rebuild its military.

After World War II, Japan had the world's fastest-growing economy. It imported raw materials and exported finished goods. One reason for Japan's success is its educated work force.

Graphic Summary: *Japan's Economic Success*

REASONS FOR JAPAN'S ECONOMIC SUCCESS
• People are very highly educated.
• Companies encourage loyalty and team spirit.
• Japan is located at the center of trade routes.
• The government takes an active role in business.

There are a variety of reasons why Japan has been economically successful.

Review Questions

1. Since World War II, how has Japan dealt with a lack of natural resources?

2. **Chart Skills** Why has Japan been economically successful?

Name ______________________ Class ______________ Date ______________

Section 2: Japan's Economic Development

Guided Reading and Review

A. As You Read

Directions: *As you read Section 2, complete the chart below by supplying an effect for each cause listed.*

Cause	Effect
Japan's government feared that early European traders might take over their country. (1639)	**1.** ______________________
Commodore Perry used a show of force to negotiate a trade agreement between the United States and Japan. (1853)	**2.** ______________________
The new Meiji government decided to strengthen Japan so it would no longer be at the mercy of foreign powers. (1868–1912)	**3.** ______________________
Japan's lack of natural resources was an obstacle to industrialization. (1900–1937)	**4.** ______________________
In World War II, Japan fought on the side of Nazi Germany and was defeated. (1939–1945)	**5.** ______________________
The Japanese obtained raw materials through trade and worked to improve efficiency and quality in manufacturing. (1945–1960s)	**6.** ______________________

B. Reviewing Vocabulary

Directions: *Define the following terms.*

7. militarism ______________________

8. downsizing ______________________

9. tariffs ______________________

10. quotas ______________________

Name ______________________ Class ______________ Date ______________

Section 3: *The Koreas: A Divided Peninsula*

Guide to the Essentials

Text Summary

North Korea is a Communist country. South Korea is not. But both countries' people share a common history and culture.

After World War II, the Soviet Union took charge of North Korea and set up a Communist government. The United States supervised southern Korea. Elections were held in South Korea, and United States troops left in 1949.

In 1950, North Korea attacked South Korea to unite the country under communism. United Nations forces, including United States troops, helped South Korea. In 1953, a cease-fire ended the war. A **demilitarized zone**—an area with no troops or weapons allowed—separates the two Koreas.

North Korea has rich natural resources and its rivers have been harnessed for electric power.

South Korea has more than twice as many people and is densely populated. Almost a quarter of its people live in Seoul, the capital. Its flatter land and warmer climate make it more suitable for agriculture than North Korea.

Communist countries traded with North Korea. South Korea traded with the United States and Japan. South Korea built industries and nuclear power plants. As its economy grew, so did the middle class. South Korea's economy and standard of living are stronger than that of its neighbor.

Many Koreans want the two parts to unite, but North Korea wants communism while South Korea does not. In the late 1990s, North Korea suffered flooding, famine, and economic disaster.

THE BIG IDEA

The Korean Peninsula has been divided since 1945 into two countries: North Korea and South Korea. South Korea's capitalist system has boomed, but North Korea's Communist economy has suffered.

Graphic Summary: *Facts about Japan and the Two Koreas*

Country	Population	Life Expectancy (years)	Per Capita GDP (in U.S. $)
Japan	127,333,002	81.0	28,000
North Korea	22,697,553	71.2	1,000
South Korea	48,598,175	75.6	17,700

Source: *The World Factbook 2004*

South Korea is slightly smaller in area than North Korea, but their populations are very different in size.

Review Questions

1. What caused Korea to separate into two countries?

2. **Chart Skills** Which of the Koreas has a larger population?

Name ______________________ Class ______________ Date ______________

Section 3: The Koreas: A Divided Peninsula

Guided Reading and Review

A. As You Read

Directions: *As you read Section 3, complete the charts below to summarize the similarities and differences between North and South Korea.*

Similarity	North and South Korea
Culture	**1.** ______________________
Religion	**2.** ______________________

Difference	North Korea	South Korea
Government	**3.** ______________	**4.** ______________
Climate	**5.** ______________	**6.** ______________
Land and resources	**7.** ______________	**8.** ______________
Economy today	**9.** ______________	**10.** ______________

B. Reviewing Vocabulary

Directions: *Define the following terms.*

11. demilitarized zone ______________________

12. proliferation ______________________

Name ______________________ Class ______________ Date ______________

Chapter 32 Test

Identifying Main Ideas

Directions: *Write the letter of the correct answer in the blank provided. (10 points each)*

____ **1. On which island do most Japanese live?**
A. Hokkaido
B. Kyushu
C. Shikoku
D. Honshu

____ **2. What are typhoons?**
A. year-round weather patterns
B. tropical hurricanes
C. the Japanese word for monsoons
D. the Japanese word for population

____ **3. What is Shinto?**
A. a religion shared by most Japanese
B. a religion the Japanese outlawed
C. a densely populated area in Japan
D. a Japanese political party

____ **4. What has happened to Japan's middle class since World War II?**
A. It nearly disappeared.
B. It remained about the same size.
C. It grew a little.
D. It grew to include the majority of Japanese.

____ **5. Why did Japan order foreigners to leave in 1639?**
A. Foreigners were backward in industry.
B. Japan worried that foreigners wanted its rich natural resources.
C. Japan feared foreigners would try to conquer it.
D. Foreigners were taking all the good farmland.

____ **6. What changes did the Meiji government make?**
A. It made Japan more modern.
B. It brought Buddhism to Japan.
C. It became very warlike.
D. It gave women the right to vote.

____ **7. What happened to Japan's military after World War II?**
A. The military began rebuilding its weapons.
B. The military started a new war.
C. The military was not allowed to rebuild.
D. All the military leaders were executed.

____ **8. When did Korea become two separate countries?**
A. after Japan invaded in 1910
B. after World War I
C. after World War II
D. in the 1980s

____ **9. What is a demilitarized zone?**
A. a strip of land where troops and weapons are not allowed
B. an area where military leaders aim guns at one another
C. a country that is at peace with its neighbors
D. a war zone

____ **10. What prevents North Korea and South Korea from reuniting?**
A. Their people do not speak the same language.
B. The Korean people do not want them to reunite.
C. The United Nations will not let them reunite.
D. They cannot agree on the form of government a united Korea would have.

Name ____________ Class ____________ Date ____________

Chapter 33

Southeast Asia

Vocabulary
barbarian
heterogeneity
indigenous
insurgent
paddy

Vocabulary Development

Directions: *Use the vocabulary terms from the list to complete the crossword puzzle.*

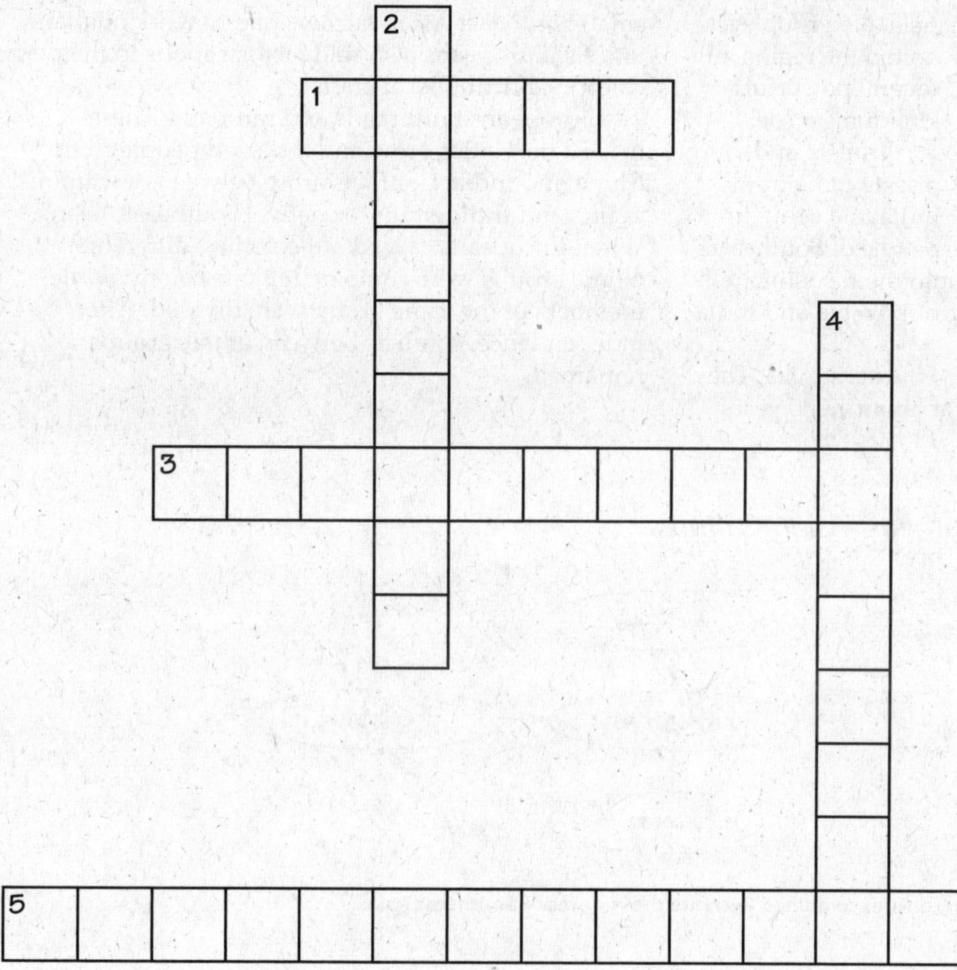

ACROSS

1. irrigated or flooded land on which rice is grown
3. native to or living naturally in an area or environment
5. a lack of similarity

DOWN

2. a person without manners or civilized customs
4. a person who rebels against his or her government

Name ____________________ Class ____________ Date ____________

Section 1: Historical Influences on Southeast Asia

Guide to the Essentials

Text Summary

THE BIG IDEA

Over time, many different ethnic groups settled in Southeast Asia, influencing its culture and religion. European control affected its geography.

Southeast Asia's location makes it one of the world's great geographic crossroads. Many came to trade, leaving behind many cultures. The earliest settlers of the mainland probably came from China and South Asia. Later, people came from central Asia. No group ever united the region, but several powerful kingdoms arose.

Traders and priests came from India and brought Hinduism and Buddhism. The people of Southeast Asia absorbed these religions into their existing religious beliefs. Muslim traders from Arabia and India brought Islam.

Many Chinese migrated to Southeast Asia. They controlled northern Vietnam for about 1,000 years, starting in 100 B.C. Chinese culture affected Vietnam's language, religion, art, government, and farming. But the Vietnamese never lost their identity.

Europeans came for silks, spices, and precious metals. By the late 1800s, the Europeans had colonized all of Southeast Asia except Thailand. Europeans greatly changed the region's physical and human geography. They cleared forests for plantations to grow coffee, tea, tobacco, and other cash crops. Many small Southeast Asian farmers had to work on plantations. Europeans also sold factory goods to their colonies, hurting local crafts.

Europeans built roads and railroads. These helped port cities grow and attracted people from China and India. Conflicts arose between new immigrants and **indigenous**, or native, Southeast Asians. When Europeans carved out colonies, different ethnic groups were combined in one colony, while members of the same group were divided. After independence, conflicts between ethnic groups remained.

Graphic Summary: *Southeast Asian Cultures*

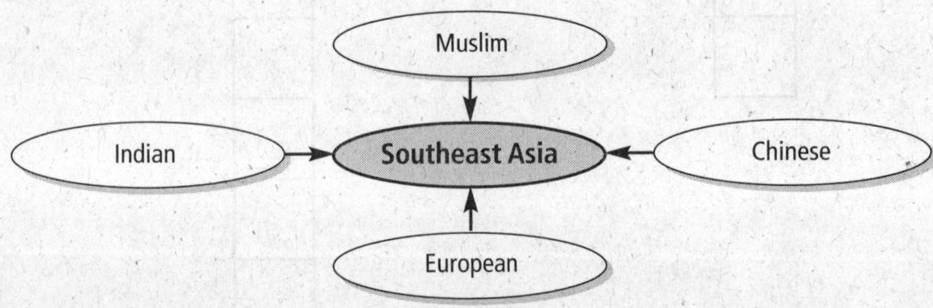

Many different cultures combined to create the cultures of Southeast Asia.

Review Questions

1. What major religions are found in Southeast Asia?

2. **Diagram Skills** What were the four main influences on Southeast Asia's cultures?

Name ______________________ Class ______________ Date ______________

Section 1: Historical Influences on Southeast Asia

Guided Reading and Review

A. As You Read

Directions: *As you read Section 1, organize information about the different cultural influences on Southeast Asia by completing the chart below. For each culture, list the appropriate historical events and the impact of that culture's interaction with Southeast Asia.*

Culture	History and Impact
Indian	**1.** History ______________________ ______________________ **2.** Impact ______________________ ______________________
Muslim	**3.** History ______________________ ______________________ **4.** Impact ______________________ ______________________
Chinese	**5.** History ______________________ ______________________ **6.** Impact ______________________ ______________________
European	**7.** History ______________________ ______________________ **8.** Impact ______________________ ______________________

B. Reviewing Vocabulary

Directions: *Define the following terms.*

9. barbarians ______________________

10. paddy ______________________

11. indigenous ______________________

Name ______________________ Class ______________ Date ______________

Section 2: The Countries of Southeast Asia

Guide to the Essentials

Text Summary

THE BIG IDEA

National unity is difficult for many of these countries because of ethnic differences. Although most of these nations had an economic boom, some have political dictatorships.

Most countries in the region belong to the Association of Southeast Asian Nations (ASEAN). ASEAN promotes economic cooperation and peace among its members.

Unity within each country of Southeast Asia has been difficult to achieve. Myanmar, formerly called Burma, was a British colony until 1948. Since independence, several ethnic groups have fought against military dictatorship. Warfare and **insurgents**, people who rebel against their government, have slowed Myanmar's economic growth. Thailand, the only country in Southeast Asia that did not become a European colony, has a strong national identity and a successful economy.

Vietnam was a French colony. After World War II, France wanted it back. Ho Chi Minh declared Vietnam's independence and defeated the French in 1954. Vietnam was divided into Communist North Vietnam and non-Communist South Vietnam. War broke out when the Communists in the North and South tried to reunite the two countries. The United States entered the war to help South Vietnam.

South Vietnam fell to the Communists in 1975. Vietnam reunited one year later. In the 1990s, Vietnam attracted foreign investors, and its economy boomed.

Indonesia is made up of more than 13,000 islands. The people speak more than 250 languages and dialects. The Philippines were ruled by the Spanish, and then by the United States. It became independent in 1946. The Roman Catholic religion and Spanish culture unify ethnic groups. The tiny island of Singapore is an economic power.

Graphic Summary: *Similarities and Differences among Vietnam, Laos, and Cambodia*

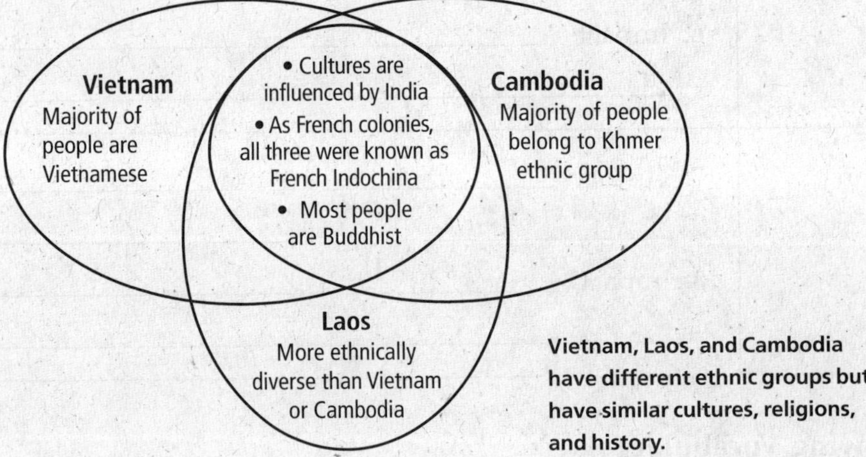

Review Questions

1. How has Vietnam changed recently?

2. **Diagram Skills** What do Vietnam, Laos, and Cambodia have in common?

Name ____________________ Class ____________ Date ____________

Section 2: The Countries of Southeast Asia

Guided Reading and Review

A. As You Read

Directions: *As you read Section 2, complete the chart about the countries of Southeast Asia by writing supporting details under each main idea.*

Main Idea A: Several factors have contributed to Myanmar's weak economy.

1. ____________________

2. ____________________

Main Idea B: Although Thailand's economy was once dependent on agriculture, it is now diversified.

3. ____________________

4. ____________________

5. ____________________

Main Idea C: Although Vietnam, Laos, and Cambodia are ethnically different, they have much in common.

6. ____________________

7. ____________________

8. ____________________

Main Idea D: Singapore's success has much to do with its physical features and location.

9. ____________________

10. ____________________

B. Reviewing Vocabulary

Directions: *Define the following terms.*

11. insurgent ____________________

____

12. *doi moi* ____________________

____

13. heterogeneity ____________________

____

Name ______________________ Class ______________ Date ______________

Chapter 33

Test

Identifying Main Ideas

Directions: *Write the letter of the correct answer in the blank provided. (10 points each)*

____ **1. What are two major religions of Southeast Asia?**
A. Shinto and Hinduism
B. Christianity and Hinduism
C. Buddhism and Islam
D. Daoism and Confucianism

____ **2. What country controlled northern Vietnam for about 1,000 years?**
A. India
B. China
C. Indonesia
D. Malaysia

____ **3. What first drew European countries to Southeast Asia?**
A. oil and natural gas
B. invitations from countries in the region
C. a need for more railroads
D. silks, spices, and precious metals

____ **4. What changes did Europeans make in Southeast Asia?**
A. They created plantations and built railroads.
B. They changed the religion of most people in the region.
C. They encouraged local crafts.
D. They helped small farmers work their farms.

____ **5. What problems remained in Southeast Asia after countries became independent?**
A. They did not have enough plantations.
B. The countries in the region had no leaders.
C. They had no port cities.
D. Ethnic groups fought with each other.

____ **6. What is ASEAN?**
A. a group of European countries that rule Southeast Asia
B. an association that works for cooperation among countries in Southeast Asia
C. a Communist government in Southeast Asia
D. a form of money in Southeast Asia

____ **7. Which Southeast Asian country was independent during colonial times?**
A. Burma
B. Vietnam
C. Thailand
D. Indonesia

____ **8. What led to the war in Vietnam?**
A. South Vietnam wanted a communist government and invaded North Vietnam.
B. The French insisted that Vietnam be an independent country.
C. The Communists in North and South Vietnam wanted to reunite the countries under communism.
D. North Vietnam wanted more investments from the United States.

____ **9. Which country ruled the Philippines until 1946?**
A. Thailand
B. the United States
C. Britain
D. France

____ **10. What tiny country is an important economic power?**
A. Singapore
B. Indonesia
C. Myanmar
D. the Philippines

Name ______________________ Class ______________ Date ______________

Chapter 34

The Pacific World and Antarctica

Vocabulary
- Aborigine
- convergence zone
- crevasse
- cyclone
- ice shelf
- lagoon
- outback
- pack ice

Vocabulary Development

Directions: *Write a sentence for each pair of terms below that shows you understand the relationship between them. Provide context clues so that a reader who may not know the meaning of the terms could figure them out.*

Aborigine/outback

____

____

____

cyclone/lagoon

____

____

____

crevasse/ice shelf

____

____

____

convergence zone/pack ice

____

____

____

Name ______________________ Class ______________ Date ______________

Section 1: Australia

Guide to the Essentials

Text Summary

Australia is both a country and a continent. It is the world's sixth largest country and the smallest continent. Scientists think that Australia's first people, called **Aborigines**, arrived more than 50,000 years ago, probably from Southeast Asia. They lived by hunting and gathering plants.

In 1770, Britain claimed the land. European settlement in Australia began in 1787 when British prisoners were sent from overcrowded British prisons. After their release, many prisoners stayed. Other British settlers came for land on which to raise sheep and grow wheat. Many Aborigines died from European diseases or weapons. Their number declined from 300,000 in the 1700s to only about 50,000 today. After World War II, immigrants came from Greece, Italy, and other parts of Europe. Today, many come from Southeast Asia, drawn by Australia's high standard of living.

THE BIG IDEA

Australia has a small population because of its location and climate. Its major cities are near the coast. Ranching and mining are important activities in Australia.

Australia's harsh climate has greatly affected where people live. The interior is very hot and dry. Most people live along the eastern and southeastern coasts, where the climate is moist.

Most of Australia west of the Great Dividing Range is arid plain or dry plateau. This harsh wilderness region is known as the **outback**. The Aborigines were the first to live there. European settlers found gold and other minerals. Some built farms and huge ranches for sheep and cattle. Australian sheep supply meat and merino wool.

Graphic Summary: *Australia and New Zealand*

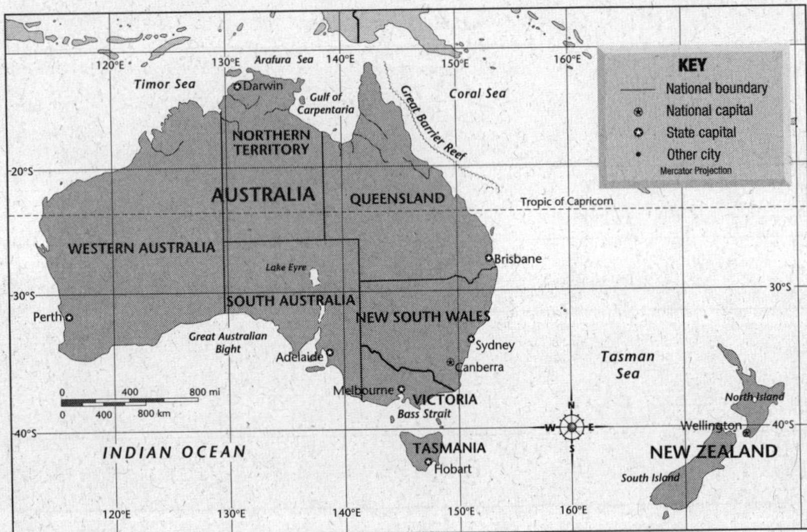

Australia is divided into seven states.

Review Questions

1. According to scientists, who were the first Australians?

2. **Map Skills** What are Australia's seven state capitals?

Name ______________________ Class ______________ Date ______________

Section 1: Australia

Guided Reading and Review

A. As You Read

Directions: *As you read Section 1, complete the chart below with the names of Australia's major cities and one feature that makes each one unique.*

Australia's Major Cities	
City	**Unique Feature**
1. ______________	**2.** ______________
3. ______________	**4.** ______________
5. ______________	**6.** ______________
7. ______________	**8.** ______________
9. ______________	**10.** ______________
11. ______________	**12.** ______________
13. ______________	**14.** ______________
15. ______________	**16.** ______________

Directions: *In the space provided, write the correct answer to each question.*

17. What obligation did the Aborigines pass down in their myths about the Dreamtime?

____

____

18. What are three major economic activities in Australia today?

____

B. Reviewing Vocabulary

Directions: *Complete each sentence by writing the correct term in the blank.*

19. The first Australians, the ______________, probably crossed a land bridge from Southeast Asia to Australia about 50,000 years ago.

20. A(n) ______________ is a shallow body of water with an outlet to the ocean.

21. Darwin, Australia, has twice been leveled by ______________.

22. The harsh wilderness region of the central and western plains and plateaus in Australia is called the ______________.

23. Ranchers provide their sheep and cattle herds with water from ______________ bored deep in the earth.

Name ______________________ Class ______________ Date ______________

Section 2: New Zealand and the Pacific Islands

Guide to the Essentials

Text Summary

THE BIG IDEA

Most New Zealanders are of European descent. The Maori are a minority. The two kinds of Pacific islands are high islands and low islands.

Many tiny islands dot the vast Pacific Ocean. Two of the larger islands, called North Island and South Island, make up the country of New Zealand. North Island is narrow and hilly, with a central plateau and active volcanoes. There are many **geysers**, hot springs that shoot out jets of steam and hot water into the air. South Island has New Zealand's highest mountains.

The Maori were the first people to live in New Zealand. Europeans arrived in 1769. In 1840, the Maori accepted British rule in exchange for land rights. Today, the Maori number less than 10 percent of the population.

New Zealand is an agricultural country with dairy cows and sheep. Yet a majority of people live in large cities along the coast.

Many Pacific islands, called high islands, are the tops of underwater mountains. Low islands, called **atolls**, can also be found in the Pacific. An atoll is a ring-shaped coral island surrounding a lagoon.

The Pacific Islands are divided into three groups: Melanesia, Micronesia, and Polynesia. Farming, fishing, and tourism are the islands' main economic activities. After World War II, the Pacific Islands were divided into **trust territories**, or territories supervised by other nations. Most Pacific islands became independent in the 1960s and 1970s.

Graphic Summary: *Comparing Australia, New Zealand, and the Pacific Islands*

Country	Population	Life Expectancy (years)	Per Capita GDP (in U.S. $)
Australia	19,913,144	80.3	28,900
Fiji	880,874	69.2	5,800
Marshall Islands	57,738	69.7	1,600
New Zealand	3,993,817	78.5	21,600
Palau	20,016	69.8	9,000
Samoa	177,714	70.4	5,600
Solomon Islands	523,617	72.4	1,700
Vanuatu	202,609	62.1	2,900

Source: *The World Factbook 2004*

The countries of this region vary greatly in size and GDP.

Review Questions

1. Who are the Maori?

2. **Chart Skills** What Pacific country has the largest population after Australia and New Zealand?

Name ______________________ Class ______________ Date ______________

Section 2: New Zealand and the Pacific Islands

Guided Reading and Review

A. As You Read

Directions: *As you read about New Zealand in Section 2, complete the chart below with a brief description of each feature listed.*

Topography	Original People	Land
1. ______	2. ______	3. ______
Climate	**Economy**	**Major Cities**
4. ______	5. ______	6. ______

Directions: *As you read about the Pacific Islands in Section 2, fill in the blanks in the following sentences.*

7. The two main types of Pacific Islands are ______________________________.
8. The three groups of the Pacific Islands are ______________________________.
9. Tourism is an important activity in the Pacific Islands because it ______________________________.
10. Two examples of economic activity in the Pacific Islands that are not related to tourism are ______________________________.
11. Most islands achieved independence in the ______________________________.

B. Reviewing Vocabulary

Directions: *Define the following terms.*

12. geyser ______________________________
13. atoll ______________________________
14. trust territory ______________________________

Name ______________________ Class ______________ Date ______________

Section 3: Antarctica

Guide to the Essentials

Text Summary

Antarctica is a frozen continent, with no permanent human settlers. Few plants and animals can survive in its icy conditions. Antarctica has many different kinds of ice. Scientists from many countries spend time doing research in Antarctica.

THE BIG IDEA

Antarctica is covered and surrounded by ice. Early exploration of this region was difficult. Now, forty countries share scientific research in Antarctica.

Antarctica was the last of the world's continents to be explored. It was first seen by sailors from Russia, Great Britain, and the United States. Humans did not set foot on the continent until 1895.

Some nations tried to claim parts of Antarctica, but claims were not recognized because no country had permanent settlers there. Antarctica's greatest resource is its wealth of scientific information. Scientists worked to convince the world that the continent should remain open to all countries that wanted to conduct research there. In 1961, twelve nations signed the Antarctic Treaty for peaceful use of the continent and sharing of scientific research. These nations and twenty-eight others renewed the treaty in 1989.

Graphic Summary: *The Antarctic Treaty*

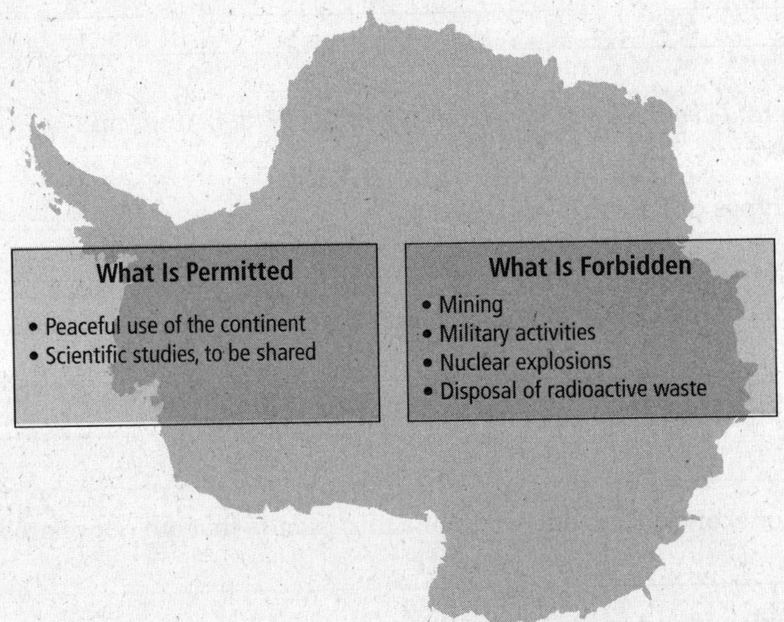

Forty countries have agreed to honor the Antarctic Treaty.

Review Questions

1. Why did countries refuse to recognize claims to Antarctica?
2. **Chart Skills** What activities are forbidden under the Antarctic Treaty?

Name ______________________ Class ______________ Date ______________

Section 3: Antarctica

Guided Reading and Review

A. As You Read

Directions: *As you read Section 3, organize information about Antarctica's ice by filling in the charts below.*

The Effect of Antarctic Ice	
On the continent's elevation	**1.** ______________________
On the land surface	**2.** ______________________
On the Antarctic climate	**3.** ______________________

Types of Ice Formations		
	Location	**Characteristics**
Ice Sheets	**4.** ______________________	**5.** ______________________
Glaciers	**6.** ______________________	**7.** ______________________
Ice Shelves	**8.** ______________________	**9.** ______________________
Pack Ice	**10.** ______________________	**11.** ______________________

B. Reviewing Vocabulary

Directions: *Complete each sentence by writing the correct term in the blank.*

12. A large crack in a glacier is a(n) ______________________.

13. Ice that extends out over the ocean is a(n) ______________________.

14. ______________________ is a mix of icebergs and other floating ice.

15. A(n) ______________________ is a spot where Antarctic waters meet warmer waters.

16. ______________________ are shrimplike creatures in Antarctic waters.

Name ______________________ Class ______________ Date ______________

Chapter 34 Test

Identifying Main Ideas

Directions: *Write the letter of the correct answer in the blank provided. (10 points each)*

____ **1. The Aborigines were the first people to settle in**
A. Malaysia.
B. Indonesia.
C. New Zealand.
D. Australia.

____ **2. The first large group of British settlers in Australia came as**
A. explorers.
B. sheep herders.
C. prisoners.
D. explorers.

____ **3. What is Australia's outback?**
A. the arid area that covers much of Australia's interior
B. Australia's coastal areas with many cities
C. the prisons where British convicts were sent
D. the highest mountains on the continent

____ **4. What is a geyser?**
A. a fruit grown in New Zealand
B. a mountain ridge
C. a volcanic mountain
D. a hot spring that shoots out steam and hot water

____ **5. Who were the first settlers in New Zealand?**
A. the British
B. the Dutch
C. the Maori
D. the Aborigines

____ **6. Atolls are**
A. tops of underwater mountains.
B. ring-shaped islands.
C. islands that people created by bringing in soil.
D. colonies of other countries.

____ **7. What is a trust territory?**
A. a country that is supervised by another country
B. a country that supervises another country
C. a country that wants to become a state of a larger country
D. a permanent colony

____ **8. What countries own Antarctica?**
A. Russia and the United States
B. Great Britain and France
C. the United States and Great Britain
D. None; it is a research center for many countries.

____ **9. Antarctica's greatest resource is**
A. its variety of plants and flowers.
B. its many kinds of ice.
C. its diverse ethnic background.
D. its wealth of scientific information.

____ **10. The Antarctic Treaty**
A. grants ownership of the continent to several countries.
B. allows all countries to make peaceful use of the continent.
C. allows military activity and nuclear explosions.
D. is limited to only a few countries.

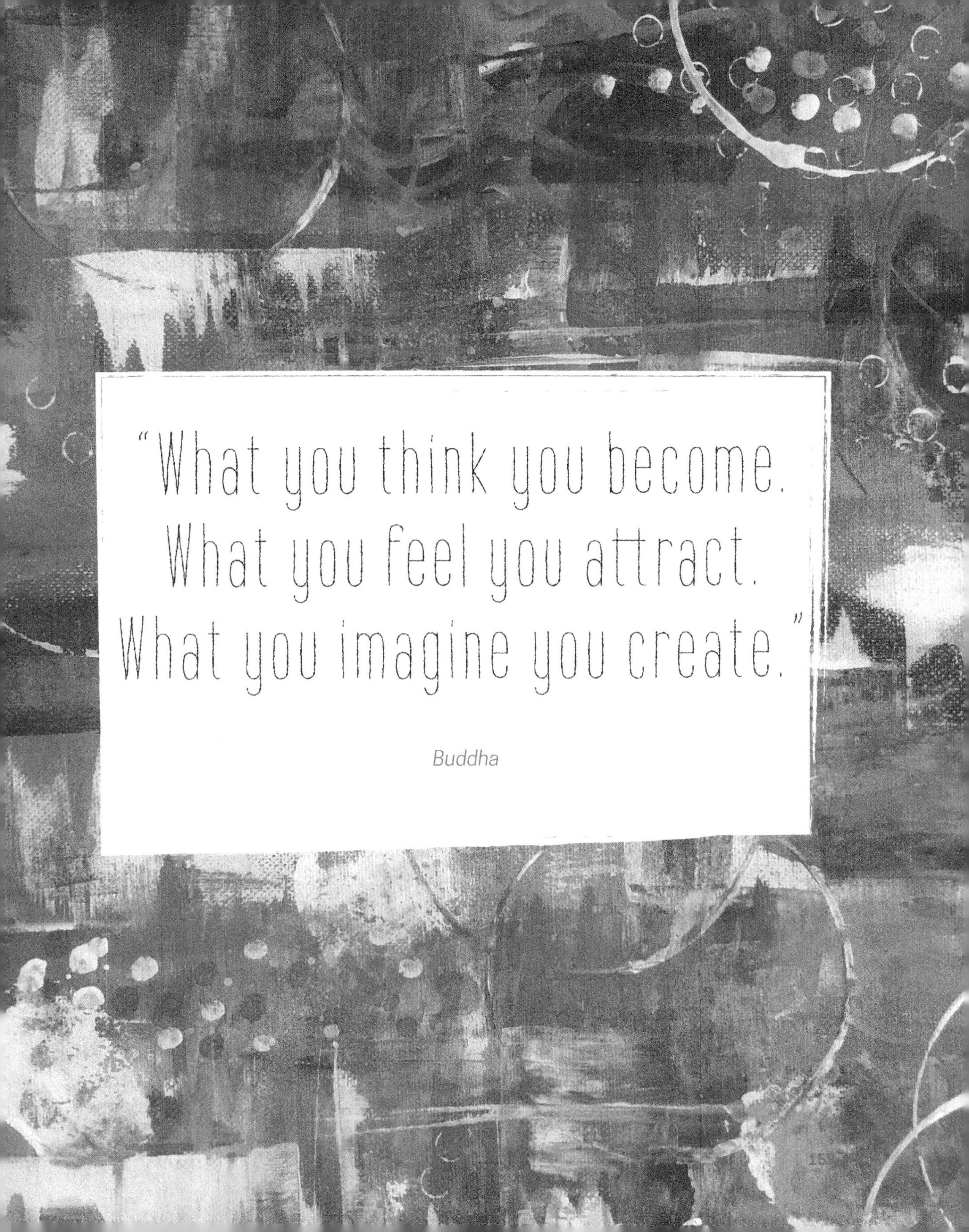
"What you think you become.
What you feel you attract.
What you imagine you create."
Buddha